David Robinson,

Thank you for your keen eye + interest in my story. You have seen what is the soul of my survival. May joy, good health, & success be with you.

Cheers, Jim B

PATRIOT, PRISONER, SURVIVOR

———— ★ ————

An American Family At War

GBU n GUH

Henry James Bedinger

Written by Henry James Bedinger

MONTEZUMA PUBLISHING

San Diego, California

Published by
Montezuma Publishing
Aztec Shops Ltd.
San Diego State University
San Diego, California 92182-1701
619-594-7552
www.montezumapublishing.com

ISBN: 978-0-7442-7785-2

Publishing Manager: Kim Mazyck
Cover Design: Angelica Lopez
Design and Layout: Lia Dearborn and Angelica Lopez
Formatting: Angelica Lopez
Editing: Sandra Parsons

CONTENTS

ACCOLADES

"Jim Bedinger's family has a long tradition of service and sacrifice to this nation; his is a family that has been forged in steel. Jim's remarkable journey is one that makes all of us proud of his service and sacrifice. He has been a leader in war and peace and this is his story."

Vice Admiral J. Cutler Dawson, U.S. Navy (Ret.)

Former CEO of Navy Federal Credit Union

"All of us, the Navy pilots from Air Wing 14 aboard the *USS Constellation*, knew the dangers of being shot down over Laos—it was a hellhole from which few returned. Jim Bedinger was one of the few who survived captivity in Laos. He brought us his personal story when he finally joined 467 crewmen captured in North Vietnam. The survival stories of the LULUs both shocked and dismayed all of us. Jim is one of our true heroes."

Captain J. Mike McGrath, U.S. Navy retired

Author of "POW—Six Years in the Hanoi Hilton"

"Jim was a member of a very special group of Vietnam War POWs called the LULUs—Legendary Union of Laotian Unfortunates—men shot down in Laos; few of whom survived to be captured. His story is an important one to tell and makes wonderful reading with keen insights. As an archivist for all Vietnam War POWs for the last 46 years and Director/Curator of the Maine Military Museum, I am proud to have Jim call me his friend and thank him for adding to the POW history with this account."

Master Sergeant Lee Humiston, U.S. Air Force (Ret.)

Director/ Curator of the Maine Military Museum

"This is a little-known, historical, All-American story. Jim Bedinger comes from a long line of American patriots dating back to the Revolutionary War, with one of his direct ancestors being a POW in that war. Ironically, 232 years later, Jim, too, would become a POW in the Vietnam War. After surviving over three years of inhumane treatment, he returned with honor to complete a highly successful Navy career. As a fellow POW, I am fortunate to have served with Jim and to call him a friend and shipmate."

Captain Jack Ensch, U.S. Navy (Ret.)

Former Director of Military Affairs, San Diego Padres

"Jim Bedinger flew with me in Vietnam and then again in 1976 when he joined the VF-114 Aardvarks. As a junior officer, Jim was always the quiet, well-read, studious one. When he told a story, about half-way through it he would get a twinkle in his eye and a big smile that told us he was enjoying the story as much as we were. And his stories always have a lesson within them. This new book is an important niche within the history of this period and Jim shares the values he accrued from his family and from the Navy's training that all helped him to survive over three years in the hands of our nation's adversary."

Vice Admiral Walter J. Davis, U.S. Navy (Ret.)

Co-founder EvoNexus Incubator

"Here, for the first time, is the story of the Bedinger family's history and the ten men who fell captive in Laos and were held in Hanoi until the general release of all POWs in late March 1973. They were called the LULUs, Legendary Union of Laotian Unfortunates. We are fortunate to now have their complete story."

Colonel Frederick J. Kiley, U.S. Air Force (Ret.)

Coauthor of "Honor Bound: The History of American POWs in Southeast Asia, 1961-1973"

FOREWORD

One of a small band of individuals captured in Laos during the Vietnam War, Commander (Ret.) Henry James "Jim" Bedinger offers a unique and straight forward perspective on the POW experience that anyone with interest in that conflict should read. From his family's long military history; through his own military service, capture, and subsequent confinement; and culminating with his homecoming and eventual reintegration into American society, Jim synthesizes his experiences in an honest and cohesive manner providing key elements rarely discussed in narratives of this type before. As the nation comes to terms with its most recent conflicts, it must continue to look back at the trials and tribulations endured by a previous generation who answered the call to service as a way to maintain the collective historical narrative of American service members. This is not just Jim's story. It is a story of a too-often forgotten group of warriors who make up a compelling chapter of our nation's military history.

— Todd Kennedy

Higher education professional and U.S. Marine Corps veteran

PATRIOT, PRISONER, SURVIVOR

DEDICATION

This book is dedicated to the many people who have shared my life's experiences. First, of course to my wife, Laura, who was with me at the beginning and who is still by my side—loving, patient, and always encouraging. The joy of returning home to her after my imprisonment was surpassed only by the joy of freedom.

To my sons, Daniel M. and William J. Bedinger, and family members who have listened repeatedly to tales of our ancestors and to my stories.

To my fellow LULU members and the other Vietnam POWs whom I love as brothers and am proud to have served with. And especially Ernie Brace, who probably saved my life several times. He was a hero to us all.

ACKNOWLEDGMENTS

After waiting over sixty years to write her book, my Great Aunt Margery once told me: "Good reads come from hard writing and then a lot of rewriting." I found this very true with this work. And I am grateful to the many people who encouraged, supported, and helped me to make this story come to life in the written word.

First, I am very grateful by the many active duty military people who heard me speak and then told me to write this in a book. Their sincerity and hope to have some of what I had spoken to them was something they wanted to share with others. In addition, there were several family members who insisted I had to write our family history and how it helped me survive. They are too numerous to name individually; but I love and want you to know they were a constant voice in my head when I was discouraged or told by some that there were already enough POW stories on the market. Thanks for never losing faith in me and what I had to say.

When several publishers turned my work in the rough draft form down, I was fortunate to discuss some of my lack of progress with Todd Kennedy, a retired marine working as a student veteran advisor at San Diego State University. He introduced me to Montezuma Publishing and the manager in 2018, Kim Mazyck. I was so fortunate to make that connection. In less than one month, I had copyright, ISB number, and a senior editor. We were on our way to rewriting the book to delete the typos, inaccurate information and mistakes that I had continually read over for over two years. And then Kim was promoted and Lia Dearborn took her position without missing a thing. They made a great team to work with.

In six months, I was impressed with and most grateful to have Sandra Parsons lead the editing effort. There was no detail too small or too minor to not get improved. Her keen eye for where more fact checking was needed has helped to make this work more accurate and her sensitive ear and eye for clarifying awkward phrases or sentences has made this much more readable. I especially enjoyed her questions that were about military or aviation points, because I like many retired military folks had used acronyms and jargon that the average reader would not understand. My heartfelt thanks and respect go to Sandra Parsons and the great team at Montezuma Publishing. As a San Diego State alumnus and proud Aztec, I have many more reasons to be proud of how well they work. At this point, I must add that any errors that remain in the text are my mistakes alone.

And finally, I want to thank my wife, Laura, who has stood by my side figuratively and literally for over half a century. She is my "North Star" so many ways.

Laura pins on NFO wings in February 1968 at
NAS Glynco GA

INTRODUCTION

After my return from Vietnam to the United States in 1973, I was asked by U.S. Navy Public Affairs to fill a few speaking roles. As one of the most junior of the returning prisoners of war, and certainly one of the youngest, I was not normally the first choice when officers far senior to me were available in the San Diego area to speak. Schools, scouting groups, and business groups were the main audiences. I soon came to appreciate the genuine interest shown to a central theme of our endurance—what held American POWs together while living in such poor conditions? Several early books have been published that helped explain some of the torture techniques, attempts to use POWs for propaganda, and the communication system we used to keep in touch with each other.

But what was the *glue* that held us together?

The short answer is the Code of Conduct,[1] solid military training, and faith in and love for our fellow POWs. As time passed, I realized that COL Ted Guy's attempt to start court martial proceedings against a group we called the Peace Committee, and RADM James Stockdale's similar efforts against three officers who caused pain and suffering for

---

1 The Code of Conduct was enacted August 17, 1955, to provide standards for the behavior of American service members held as prisoners of war. The Uniform Code of Military Justice is federal statute, but the Code of Conduct, although followed by POWs, is not. In 1974 CDR John McCain (USN), published a research paper for the National War College that documented the experiences of his and other Vietnam POWs and made recommendations for revision.

other POWs, were neither fully understood by the pubic nor reported accurately on by the media. All too often former POWs were cited as violating the Code of Conduct instead of the Uniform Code of Military Justice.

The other conclusion I came to is that most Americans could not find Laos on a map, even if you gave them three chances. Not only did most Americans have no information on Laos, but they often told me they didn't care: "It's all ancient history now Jimmy; move on with your life."

When I started to work for a credit union as a military liaison and point of contact, I soon was being asked to speak to military groups about my experience as a POW. At these events I received rousing support and confirmation that they were eager to hear my stories and were encouraged, if not inspired. I was told many times that I should write a book. At the same time, my father passed away and left several oral history tapes that explained our early family history. A cousin and several nephews urged me to write our Bedinger family story. One even reminded me that I was the one who traveled to Gettysburg, Pennsylvania in 1963 on the 100th anniversary of the famous battle in search of a grave or marker in memory of my great-uncle, Confederate Army CAPT George Rust Bedinger. And I'm a direct descendent of Daniel Bedinger, who fought in the American Revolution. He was one of 2,810 men held in a British prison ship where only 800 survived.[2] My family was touching a part of me that needed to be expressed more clearly.

When my working career started approaching a natural ending time, my wife, Laura, kept telling me every time I went out to speak to a group about my experiences, "Write your book!" She was correct, of course, and it reminded me of one of my grandfather's favorite sayings: "A happy wife makes for a happy life."

---

2 "Daniel Bedinger," Historic Shepherdstown & Museum, http://historicshepherdstown.com/portfolio-item/daniel-bedinger/.

So I have attempted in this work to clarify what I saw, heard, and experienced that was unique to me and our small group of POWs who were captured in Laos and held in Hanoi, Vietnam. We called ourselves the LULUs—the Legendary Union of Laotian Unfortunates. We were only ten in number and were almost left behind at the end of the war.

This book relates my family history, both in the stories told to me by my father and history written and published by family members through the years. In the end, I think of this book not as some singular achievement or goal I reached, but instead as a collective salute to all who came before me and provided examples of service to country and faith in God. They are the true heroes and long may their stories be told.

LT William M. Bedinger (left) and Ens Henry J, Bednger (right) just after Ensign Bedinger was commissioned at NAS Pensacola FL in August of 1967

CHAPTER 1

THE BEDINGER FAMILY'S AMERICAN REVOLUTION

If you are held captive, a prisoner of war held by a dangerous enemy, you search for something to sustain you—something the enemy could never take away. For me it was the values and beliefs that are uniquely American. My captors took every material possession, including my wedding ring, but they could not take my sense of history, my professional calling, my spiritual beliefs, or my feelings for my fellow POWs. My strength came from knowing about my many ancestors who overcame great odds to live in America. Those previous generations inspired and sustained me during a terrible time in my life.

★

The *Mayflower* set sail in 1620 and within less than a decade, word of the New World and a fresh start was spread not only in England, but in Europe, too. In 1630, seventeen ships met off the Isle of Wight and set sail for the Massachusetts Bay Colony. In the next eleven years it is estimated that more than eighty thousand people from England[3] alone left their home country. It was the first Great Migration to the New World and more waves of migration from the British Isles followed. The third wave that began in 1675 and extended into the middle of the next century has been called the "Friends Migration" because of the

---

3   David Hackett Fischer, *Albion's Seed: Four British Folkways in America* (New York: Oxford University Press, 1989), 13-17.

large number of Quakers who came to the Delaware River Valley from 1730 to 1750.[4] In the summer of 1737, from the port of Rotterdam, Netherlands, Adam Budingen with his wife and seven children went aboard the "good ship" *Samuel* and departed for America. They arrived in Philadelphia on August 31, 1737, and became part of this third major wave of migration to America.

Adam Budingen was a man of substance with some documented family background linked to the Isenberg-Budingen family from the region of Durstle, Alsace. A granddaughter of a later Henry Bedinger related playing with the family crest and described it as "the arms of Budingen, a rampant griffin, and for a crest, the helmet of a knight."[5] The family bought a large and fertile tract of land in York County, Pennsylvania and did very well over the ensuing years. Adam Budingen (the name is also found in early York County records as "Bietinger") changed the spelling of his name to Bedinger and revised the German sound of the "g" to a hard "g" to make it sound more like English. He lost two wives, married a third time, and had a total of ten children.

As waves of more immigrants arrived in Philadelphia and moved westward, the second generation of Bedingers, along with their neighbors in the York area, heard rumors of new unpopulated lands to the west and south. Three families composed of Henry Bedinger (married to Magdalene von Schelegel), the Morgans, and the Swearingens, moved to a sleepy little West Virginia town on the Potomac River that was once called Mecklenburg, but later renamed as Shepherdstown after Colonel Thomas Shepherd who had served in the Indians Wars. The first home of the Bedinger family was in the center of town and they moved in around 1762.

---

4   Fischer, *Albion's Seed*, 420-41.

5   Danske Dandridge, *George Michael Bedinger: A Kentucky Pioneer* (Charlottesville: Michie Co., 1909), 27.

The Bedingers at first were Lutherans, but in the early 1760s joined the Protestant Episcopal Church. Apparently the Lutherans in the new town had a dispute over which language the scriptures should be read in during Sunday services. Henry Bedinger was progressive and wished his children to speak and read in English, so the decision was made to support the Episcopal Church that was still tied to the Anglican Catholic Church of England.

Henry and Magdalene had seven children as follows: Henry, 1753; Elizabeth, 1755; George Michael, 1756; Daniel, 1761; Jacob, 1766; Sarah, 1768; and finally Solomon, 1770. Henry moved from the stone house in town to a bigger property with both grazing and farming benefits. The property had two natural springs and one was called Bedinger Springs for a few years, but after two meetings, first in 1775 and then in 1776, the natural spring became commonly known as the Spring of '76.

On May 25, 1775, Patrick Henry issued a broadside to the western regions for every man with a rifle to come aid in saving the gunpowder at the Colonial Armory at Williamsburg. At the young age of nineteen, George Michael Bedinger, along with his close friend George Morgan, took off to fight for their country. George Michael's younger brother, Daniel, who just turned fourteen, desperately wanted to join his older brother, but his recently widowed mother and the oldest brother, Henry, strictly forbade his leaving. And he respected their wishes.

As it turned out this early call was premature and their group returned soon after to Shepherdstown. But the siege of Boston was under way with George Washington commanding the Continental forces. He needed help and a call to arms went out again to all who had a musket, powder, and shot to add to the forces. On June 10, 1775, a town barbecue was held on the Bedinger property to gather support. Henry Bedinger, the first son of Henry Bedinger and older brother to George Michael and Daniel, was one of the speakers that day. As night drew dark, the group heard the nearby Daniel Morgan gathering in Harpers Ferry,

West Virginia, shoot a volley. The entire group rose to reply with a volley of their own and it was heard in all the surrounding areas. Then while everyone was still standing, the group pledged to meet again fifty years later to the day.

Again, Daniel Bedinger wanted to join his two older brothers in this march to Boston, and again he was told in no uncertain terms that his widowed mother needed one man to help run things on the Virginia farms and protect the women. In this part of Virginia there were still occasional parties of Native Americans looking for "winter food on the hoof." On July 17, 1775, the Virginia Rifle Company, under Captain Hugh Stephenson left the town and made a feat remembered as the "Beeline March" to Boston. They joined Washington and the American forces on Friday, August 11. The group took part in skirmishes and several defenses, but their most significant action was the defense of Dorchester Point in early March of 1776. Shortly thereafter, the British forces evacuated Boston and the Virginia Rifle Company was sent to New York City. The rifle company under the now Colonel Stephenson was assigned then to Staten Island where British squadrons had encamped at Sandy Point.

On one patrol just before George Michael's enlistment was up, he and Joseph Swearingen were almost captured by a much larger British force. The pair beat a retreat by rowboat across the choppy Jersey River, but by the time they returned to the Manhattan headquarters, George Michael was officially discharged and started the long trip home. He later recalled how he walked through the night and arrived at Philadelphia early on the morning of July 4, 1776, only to fall asleep and then be awakened by bells and loud cheering. He arrived home on July 15, 1776, to find out that a second town meeting had been held at the Bedinger property on July 4 and that it had been an even larger gathering than the barbecue of 1775.

This time George Michael was going to stay behind while Henry Bedinger would return to the Continental Army. Col. Stevenson had died in June from wounds in Boston, Abraham Shepherd was promoted to captain, and Henry to lieutenant. Before the company left there were several weeks of daily exercises and training. Daniel was caught up in the spirit of all this and continued to plead his case. After all, he was a year older and a better shot than most. The answer remained the same: he was ordered to stay home and told he was too young for this mission.

The Virginia Rifle Company marched north and then east. By the middle of August 1776 they reached Bergen, New Jersey. Two days later a fifteen-year-old boy asked an outer sentry where he might find a Lt. Henry Bedinger. It was Daniel, and his brother Henry was furious, but it was too far to send the lad home by himself and they needed every rifleman they could get. And several noted that young Daniel had "an eagle eye and a steady hand that made him a superb marksman." In further talking to Daniel, Henry learned that Daniel had left in the middle of the night and covered his trail so George Michael couldn't follow him. Daniel was one determined fifteen-year-old who heard the fife and drum and answered his country's call to arms.

The British forces had established positions on Long Island and Staten Island while the Americans held Brooklyn, Manhattan Island, and other northern parts of New York City. The battles for New York started on August 27, 1776, with heavy fighting around Brooklyn Heights. Pinned down by the British Navy with their heavy guns on the East River and the overwhelming mass of land forces facing them, the small band of Virginia Riflemen were assigned as rear guard where they would defend on a line of redoubts and then leap-frog to the rear and next line of defense. The situation looked bleak on the afternoon of August 29, so Washington met with his staff to discuss a possible retreat during the night across the East River. The boats were ready and that night under a steady rain, the American units were told to make ready to change positions.[6]

But then as if by divine intervention, the weather changed and a heavy fog developed that persisted to the next day. Under the cover of a hazy-gold morning fog, most of the

---

6   David Hackett Fischer, *Washington's Crossing* (New York: Oxford University Press, 2004), 100-101.

American forces were moved to southern Manhattan and the Americans on Governor Island were also saved. This was more than a minor victory for the Americans, but it was not to last. In middle September the British Navy amassed many vessels in the Hudson and East Rivers and attacked southern Manhattan at Kips Bay. Skirmishes and other battles delayed the final assault and gave Washington time to move his many forces to the north to what is now Yonkers, New York, and some of the headquarters staff crossed the Hudson River to reinforce Fort Lee, atop the Palisades in New Jersey.

The last position in New York City was Fort Washington on the very northern tip of Manhattan. The Virginia Rifle Company, now under command of Captain Abraham Shepherd, was assigned to man the eastern defenses along a ridgeline with a series of terraced redoubts up the slope. On November 16, the British and its Hessian forces (professional German soldiers hired by the British) closed in for the final assault. The American objective was to hold out as long as possible to ensure the American forces would have time to protect their current positions to the North.

Words from my ancestor, Major George Michael Bedinger, were read by me as a very young boy in elementary school—and they were read not once, but many times. Whenever my friends and I gathered to recreate another war in the woods, I was always allowed to be Daniel Bedinger. So these words as follows had much meaning to the man I would become:

> Captain Bedinger's younger brother, Daniel, then a little past fifteen, shot 27 rounds in this engagement, and was often heard to say, after discharging his piece, 'There, take that, you devils!' His youthful intrepidity and gallant conduct, so particularly attracted the attention of the officers that, tho' taken prisoner, he was promoted to an ensigncy, his commission dating back six years.[7]

---

7 Dandridge, *George Michael Bedinger*, 25-26.

The commanding officer of Fort Washington, Colonel Robert Magaw, had little choice but to surrender the fort to the overwhelming forces surrounding him. They were short of supplies of every type and had neither the powder nor the cannons to mount a defense. The Hessian troops, who had taken heavy casualties that day, were first into Fort Washington and behaved most cruelly. David H. Fisher described how George Washington viewed the harsh treatment and execution of some of the Americans at the hands of the Hessian soldiers: "As the full weight of the disaster fell upon him [Washington], he turned away from his lieutenants, and began to weep 'with the tenderness of a child.'"[8]

Although Daniel's life was spared, he was still a private in the eyes of the British and he was separated from his brother. The officers were billeted with English families in the Flatbush and Long Island areas and were allotted rations. On the other hand, Daniel was taken around midnight to southern Manhattan where he was confined in one of the infamous Sugar House prisons. Danske Dandridge in her biography, *George Michael Bedinger: A Kentucky Pioneer*,[9] states that "he saw his companions die from starvation every day."[10] The British treatment was indeed harsh and Americans were lost in great numbers. Dandridge reports "in the space of two months, 1,900 of the 2,673 privates were killed." Fisher also discusses in *Washington's Crossing* at great length the difference in how well American forces treated their prisoners as a general rule and how cruel the British acted toward the enlisted ranks of their prisoners.

Daniel was finally moved to a prisoner-of-war ship where he was overcome with fever, dysentery, and a great loss of weight. In the end, Daniel was one of only eight hundred men to survive on board the ship that imprisoned two thousand ten men. The British were notorious at this time and place for arranging prisoner exchanges with the Americans and choosing those most likely to die in a few weeks for exchange. Daniel's spirit and health

---

8 Fischer, *Washington's Crossing*, 113-14.

9 Dandridge, *George Michael Bedinger*, 27.

10 Dandridge, *George Michael Bedinger*, 26.

were so low by December that he was selected for exchange in a church near Newark, New Jersey. Then Daniel and few others were carried to Philadelphia where he became lost in the many places for the sick and wounded American soldiers. His next older brother, George Michael, took off in search of him.

Wartime Philadelphia was astir with rumors and finding one returned private was a difficult task. A nurse in the central hospital suggested to George Michael that he visit the parish of the Episcopal Church in the Germantown section. There he found Daniel in a corner, half-covered by straw and rags. Daniel was too weak to ride or even walk. George Michael took him in his arms and carried him to a wagon where he went a short distance to a Quaker family who took them in. Eager to get going, George Michael placed Daniel in a chair with a few pillows and attached leather straps to hold him in place, and then fashioned a backpack sling so that he could carry Daniel west, closer to York, Pennsylvania, and the original Bedinger family tract.

Daniel's condition slowly began to improve, but George Michael was eager to get to Shepherdstown. So with one horse in tow, George Michael let Daniel start walking, slowly at first to get his strength back, and then with each passing day they covered more miles. They wanted to be home for Christmas. All I know for sure is that they made it home.

George Michael immediately reenlisted to serve another three months with another Virginia Rifle Company and in early March 1777, fought in the Battle for Piscataway, New Jersey. It was during this time period that the most pivotal battle of the war took place when on Christmas Eve of 1776 Gen. Washington led his forces across the ice-filled Delaware River and attacked the Hessian forces at Trenton. An early winter blizzard and the freezing night may have covered the Americans' approach, but they overcame all the odds and achieved a total victory. Two days later after marching through another night, Gen. Washington and the Continental Army attacked the British forces at Princeton and completely routed them. This was the first battle that the world-renowned British forces had lost in any part of the world in more than forty years of almost constant warfare. The world's strongest army, composed only of veteran professional soldiers, had been beaten by an American ragtag militia, all volunteers, led by a country farmer. This was a turning point for sure. Moreover, the American victories at Trenton and then Princeton, New Jersey, caused a stir in every major European capital for the next decade.[11]

When the news of victory reached the western frontier of Virginia, Daniel's spirits were visibly uplifted, but he still had weight and strength to gain. There is no record today of exactly how long he was still weakened by his captivity or when he rejoined the Continental Army. I remember as a youth hearing my father and another Bedinger relative discuss this on a visit to Rosebrake, the Morgan-Bedinger-Dandridge family estate in Shepherdstown, and it was clear by 1778 that Daniel was back with the Continental Army and served three years as a private and then a corporal. In February 1781, a board of officers at Chesterfield Courthouse in Jefferson City, Virginia commissioned the young Daniel Bedinger an ensign, and on May 7, 1782 he was promoted to lieutenant. I have been told that the records of the Society of Cincinnati (formed after the Revolutionary War to recognize commissioned officers of the Continental Army during the War for Independence) list Daniel Bedinger as the youngest officer of the society. The most important thing, perhaps, is that once Daniel rejoined the American forces, he remained and never returned home like his brothers.

When Gen. Charles Cornwallis surrendered the British forces to Gen. Washington at the battle of Yorktown on October 19, 1781, Lt. Daniel Bedinger was there to witness it all. Shortly thereafter, he was assigned to another unit that was sent to the southern campaign. He served until he was discharged in April of 1783.

As a small boy I was fond of my father's stories from this timeframe and have included as much as I could remember, but what I remember most were Daniel's words to "Stick to the fight, you must never quit," and "Always finish what you start." These two

11 Fischer, *Washington's Crossing*, 259-62.

values helped to carry our young nation through difficult times and through the challenges that lay ahead.

Daniel later moved with his family to the Norfolk, Virginia area and was employed as a port official in the U.S. Custom House where he worked for more than thirteen years. After John Adams was elected president, Daniel was passed over for a promotion and in July of 1798, moved with his growing family and wife Sarah back to Shepherdstown where he settled into "a fine old house in the center of town." He bought several properties and on the one near the Spring of '76, a tributary of the Potomac River, he began building a beautiful estate house they called Bedford, from the first three letters of his name and the last four letters of his wife's maiden name, Rutherford.

Both Daniel and Henry Bedinger played roles in the 1800 presidential election. They were named as Virginia delegates when the states were called to resolve the tie between Thomas Jefferson and Aaron Burr. After Jefferson was inaugurated, Daniel was appointed to the position of commander of the Norfolk Naval Shipyard where he served until 1808. He then returned to Bedford in Shepherdstown and engaged in writing, traveling, and business opportunities. He was a strong and active participant in his community, but he suffered from lingering lung disease, probably tuberculous, a lasting scar from his captivity on the British prison ship. He died at home in Shepherdstown on April 1, 1818, at the young age of fifty-eight years.

Daniel's brothers Henry and George Michael survived and kept their original pledge to return fifty years later to the Spring of '76 exactly on the date of their July 4, 1776 rally. A monument just south of town on the eastern edge of the road commemorates this meeting in 1826. Although Bedford would later be burnt to the ground by Union Troops during the Civil War, another family home was built and called Rosebrake. It still stands today, with numerous room additions, about one-hundred yards up the hill behind the marker. As a small boy visiting Rosebrake, I used to reenact the Revolutionary War and I always saw myself as my direct ancestor, Daniel Bedinger, the youngest commissioned officer of the Continental Army and with each shot at the enemy, I would yell, "There, take that you Devils!" That Spirit of '76 still is alive in our nation. It shall never die as long as we produce men and women who cherish freedom more than life and who will not tolerate the slow undoing of the values upon which this nation was founded.

CHAPTER 2

A HOUSE DIVIDED

The Bedinger family prospered in Shepherdstown, West Virginia and just north of there in Maryland. In the 1844 elections for the 10th Congressional District, Henry Bedinger III, nephew of George Michael who found Daniel after he was freed from the British prison ship, was elected and served two terms until March 4, 1849. He continued in private law practice until he was appointed by President Franklin Pierce as the chargé d'affaires and later minister to Denmark, serving a total of more than five years in these postings. He was credited with helping to negotiate the first Treaty of Jutland and was often seen playing chess with Hans Christian Andersen. He returned to Shepherdstown in October of 1858 where he succumbed to an ongoing case of pneumonia and died on November 26, 1858. He was remembered as a fiery orator, determined litigator, and a seasoned diplomat.

Henry's oldest son by his first marriage was George Rust Bedinger. When George Rust turned eighteen he enrolled in the University of Virginia where he became a good student who was well liked and known for his humor and great skill on the guitar. When the War Between the States began, the Bedinger family, like our nation, was deeply divided. Some believed strongly in the Union and were living in Maryland and Pennsylvania, while those around Shepherdstown were more aligned by marriage and feelings to the tidewaters of Virginia. George Rust was quick to enlist as a private in the Shepherdstown Hamtramck Guards of the Confederacy and assigned to the Company B, 2nd Virginia Infantry under Gen. Thomas J. "Stonewall" Jackson, which later joined with Army of Northern Virginia under a distant relative, Gen. Robert E. Lee. George Rust served with an artillery division under Gen. James Longstreet. George Rust's cousin, Edwin G. Lee, was a lieutenant in this company and first cousin of Gen. Lee.

The Virginia Company quickly was thrown into action at the First Battle of Manassas and the succeeding battles fought by the Army of Northern Virginia. For conspicuous bravery under fire at the Battle of Sharpsburg/Antietam (even today this battle is called Antietam in the North and Sharpsburg in the South), George Rust was commissioned a captain of Company E, 33rd Virginia Infantry on November 19, 1862. Then in December, George Rust led his company—then known as the Emerald Guard—in the battle of Fredericksburg. After four days of heavy fighting the Union's Army of the Potomac under Gen. Ambrose Burnside, launched a heavy frontal attack on the center of the Confederate line and was soundly repulsed. The North suffered twice as many casualties as the South and quickly retreated from the field and the region. To this day the battle is considered the most one-sided victory by the Army of Northern Virginia.

In the following spring these armies clashed again in a series of battles that took the Army of Northern Virginia north across the Potomac River. Gen. Lee split his forces and led his larger army to confront the main Union Army at Chancellorsville, while Gen. Jubal Early's 2nd Corps of 12,000-19,000 men went to Winchester to confront Maj. Gen. Robert Milroy's division of 7,000 men. Letters from George Rust confirm that his unit first engaged in Chancellorsville fighting in which he reported on the tragic death of Stonewall Jackson by his own Confederate sentries. The battle was won early and a series of retreats by the slow and hesitant Union Gen. Joe Hooker allowed George Rust to take his company to shore-up the left flank of the 2nd Corps. Another letter confirms that the Union forces were overrun and suffered more than four thousand four hundred casualties with many captured. Yet, the loss of Stonewall Jackson was deeply felt and it was at this time that the Emerald Guards, led by George Rust Bedinger, petitioned the Confederate Congress to change the Guards' name to the Stonewall Brigade.

At Gettysburg, Pennsylvania on July 3, 1863, the Confederate forces amassed a large force of what today is estimated as an army of more than seventy-one thousand men. The newly appointed General of the Potomac, George Meade and his Union forces were estimated at more than ninety-four thousand men. And on that fateful third day there was a call for volunteers to strengthen Maj. Gen. George Pickett's Division. George Rust and the Emerald Guard (the new name of the Stonewall Brigade had not yet been approved) were the first to volunteer for this charge. It was the largest frontal assault of the war and it was long and deadly.

More than one hundred fifty Confederate cannons along the two-mile Seminary Ridge volleyed and thundered, and finally the Union artillery replied. Clouds of smoke filled the air and began to float gently in the wind from the West toward the Union lines. And around 3:00 p.m., approximately fifteen thousand Confederate forces began a one-mile march into the center of the Union's position. Initially covered by the fog and smoke of the cannons, the lines slowly began to emerge about a half-mile from the Union forces. Every cannon and gun along the mile-and-a-half of the Union lines began to fire and fire again. And yet the long gray line of Pickett's Charge moved forward. They actually reached the Union line at a stone wall that took a turn, and that was the point where the most vicious hand-to-hand fighting occurred in a pitched battle of almost a half-hour. That spot today is marked at the Gettysburg National Military Park as the Bloody Angle. There is no grave, no marker, and no way of knowing exactly where George Rust Bedinger fell that day, but several relatives on the Union side were said to have looked a week for his remains, which were never recovered.

The culmination of three days of fighting resulted in what is still described to this day as the largest battle fought in North America. The Gettysburg Foundation estimates that more than one hundred sixty-five thousand soldiers were involved and that and estimated fifty-one thousand were killed, seriously wounded, missing, or captured. There were so many decomposing bodies that the stench of death hung over the entire town for months. More than a thousand horses were killed in action and their carcasses burned just south of town. Human bodies waiting to be buried were stacked like cords of firewood, row by row and column by column. When Congress finally appropriated money to buy land and build a National Military Cemetery, it was already October 1863. President Lincoln came the next month to dedicate the newly authorized Soldiers National Cemetery and delivered what is considered one of the greatest speeches in American history—the Gettysburg Address.

One-hundred years later on July 3, 1963, the largest reenactment up to that time of any battle ever fought took place at Gettysburg. President John Kennedy was in Europe; so Vice President Lyndon Johnson was the keynote speaker that day and became the first Southern-born speaker at a northern Civil War event.

But the real excitement was palatable in a crowd of more than two hundred fifty thousand as we waited to see the events of Maj. Gen. Pickett's charge reenacted. And two in that crowd were there for one young Confederate captain who was a direct descendant of Daniel Michael Bedinger, lost that day in 1863. The two were my father, Henry Bedinger, the son of George Rust Bedinger who was named after the Confederate captain, and I, as an eighteen-year-old. We had come to see, to remember, and to wonder if we could find a marker or monument in the farming fields still being worked that might mark the spot of the Emerald Guard's last stand.

When the cannons began to fire around noon that day, I jumped. We were standing behind a stone wall about two hundred yards north of the Bloody Angle with a front-row seat on the now well-trampled grass. The Union guns were to our left, in front, and to the right of us. I thought of Alfred Lord Tennyson's poem, *Charge of the Light Brigade*, when he described a battle in the Crimean War as follows;

Cannon to the right of them,

Cannon to the left them,

Cannon in front of them

Volleyed and thundered;

Stormed at with shot and shell,

Boldly they rode and well,

Into the jaws of Death,

Into the mouth of hell

Rode the six hundred.[12]

It was just not the loudness of the guns, but also the smell of cordite that got my attention. I had never seen, heard, or experienced anything like it in my life up to that time. And across the way, coming out of the gray clouds and wall of fog, came the Confederate Army, slow and steady while many fell, minute by minute. And then a bugle sounded and the Rebel yell was taken up and the long gray line began to run into the Union line. Fighting with fixed bayonets, pistols, rifles swung like clubs, the Confederate gray melted into the masses of Union blue. Confusion and noise all around us made it so realistic that I actually ducked and tried to squirm because it was so horrific. And this was just the reenactment.

The loss of Captain George R. Bedinger was mourned by his entire family for some time. His cousin, Maj. Edwin Lee, published an obituary in the July 21, 1863 *Lynchburg Virginian* and later in the August 8, 1863 *The Richmond Whig* that said in part: "He entered the service as a private, earned his promotion upon fifteen battlefields, and at last has fallen where brave men love to die, leading his men up to the cannon's mouth." E. A. Moore of the

---

12 Avenel Book, *A Treasury of the World's Best Loved Poems* (New York: Avenel Books, 1980), 117-18.

Rockbridge Artillery added: "Gay, brilliant Bedinger, whose presence imparted an electric touch to those around him; I shall ne'er see his like again."[13]

How deeply moved my father was by the events we saw! We talked a little of why it might be so hard to have a monument for George Rust and the men he led because those who did survive reported that many of the Emerald Guard fell closest to or on the enemy lines. And my dad, in awe, said to me with tears in his eyes, "No wonder they never found George's body; there were too many others who fell on top of him on that day."

One of my lasting impressions from the reenactment of that day in history in 1963 was that our country was still divided over the issues that led up to the Civil War.

---

13 Alexandra Lee Levin, *This Awful War: Gen. Edwin Gray Lee, C.S.A. and His Family* (New York: Vantage Press, 1987), 66.

CHAPTER 3

MY JOURNEY BEGINS

Shortly before I entered Union College in Schenectady, New York, I enlisted in the Naval Reserves as a seaman recruit. I knew I wanted to be an officer, but wanted to serve my country in the summer before I graduated. I also worked with one of the first master chief petty officers of the U.S. Navy and a senior chief, his assistant in recruiting officers in the Philadelphia area. These two men could turn any job, no matter how intrinsically unpleasant the task, into a competition that was both productive and fun. It was that type of leadership I wanted to be a part of; plus, I wanted to do something for my country as I got my college degree.

When the Navy started the Aviation Reserve Officer Candidate (AVROC) program, these two chiefs helped me get all the paperwork, and medical and dental work completed so it would fly through. And it did and I was selected. While the Vietnam War was heating up I was going into officer training and finishing college. To my surprise my older brother, Bill, had taken a leave of absence from college and had suddenly become a pen pal of the local draft board. So he went to these super chiefs and used his two completed years of college to qualify for the Naval Aviation Crew Cadet (NACC) program.

In my junior year of college, Bill completed training and was assigned to a Phantom F-4 squadron that was deployed to the Tonkin Gulf. The year was 1966 and he was flying combat missions at the same time as I was attending Union College where Senator Wayne

Morse (D-OR) spoke to the college on why he voted against the Gulf of Tonkin Resolution two years prior, one of only two Senators who voted against it. He described Vietnam as "a revolution of home rule and who should rule at home." This was exactly what historian Carl Becker wrote about the American Revolution. Somehow I thought it was a huge stretch to put Ho Chi Minh, the communist leader who organized kangaroo courts to convict and kill tens of thousands of small landowners in 1954 to achieve land reform, in the same league. And it was not just the adults who were executed, but all their family members, too. I never could connect how communists like this were acting in a way that was consistent with how our founding fathers had acted. It sparked some great discussions both in my fraternity and in some of my history classes.

I graduated in 1967 and was surprised when my senior project was awarded the Smith Prize for the best and most original history research for that year. It was a work on the ongoing litigation surrounding Girard College in Philadelphia. Girard was a prestigious orphanage established by the "will and last testament" of Stephen Girard. I showed in my research how the weight and interpretation of law was on only one side—the side that wanted to change the "poor, male, *white* orphan restriction" on the admission standards. In 1968, the courts finally ruled in favor of the integration and I felt a little bit better about winning the prize.

There was honor in winning an award that had been presented each year since 1865. Also the $150 award was a lot of money in 1967. No one at that time would lend me money to buy my fiancée a diamond ring, so it worked out just perfectly as I was able to present Laura Yepez a small, but elegant diamond engagement ring before I left to complete my AVROC training in that summer of 1967. I was very proud that I didn't have to ask anyone for a loan; I had earned it.

I achieved my gold wings in May 1968 and traveled across the country to San Diego with my new wife, Laura, with her almost half-karat, blue diamond ring and white-gold matching wedding ring. The navy's move benefit covered a lot of things, but the most valuable things such as my flight gear, naval dress sword, and stereo had to go into the back seat of my brand new Volkswagen Beetle. It was truly a sight to see when we pulled into each stop at night. The insects at that time of year were swarming and our little VW lived up to its reputation as a "bug smasher." That practical little car never stopped through a tornado, through the heat of the dessert, and all the two-lane roads that were the way west in most places before the interstate highway system was completed. I was the only member of my class to make the trip without one car repair. And I had to remind my classmates when they tried to tell me a VW Bug would not hack it as a Fighter RIO (radar intercept officer). It was a great group with a lot of talent that kept me working overtime.

Having trained in the F-4 replacement group of the first class to fly the F-4J with the pulse-Doppler look-down/shoot-down radar, we all had swag and pride in our achievements when we graduated to the fleet squadrons. We were the first class from the F-4 RAG (replacement air group) that had deployed to Marine Corps Air Station (MCAS) Yuma for two weeks of air combat maneuvers (ACMs) and bombing training. This was a concept that helped the F-4 RAG develop what later became the Top Gun school. We all felt special.

I was assigned to Fighter Squadron 143, the Puking Dogs. They were just returning from a combat tour and were to transition to the brand new F-4J Phantoms. I had time to go to Communications Officer School, Classified Material Handling School, and a short course on cryptology designed for surface warfare officers. It was a time to study, get better in the cockpit by learning various systems, and fly air combat training missions. This flying including dropping both practice bombs and live Mark-82 five-hundred-pound bombs on the Chocolate Mountains and other ranges to the east of San Diego. I can never forget my first night mission when we dropped four M-82s at night and the entire sky lit up for a brief glorious moment—and when the rake target spotter came up on the radio with one of the few "Bullseye" calls of the night.

Meanwhile, on the East Coast, my brother Bill was assigned to an F-4 fighter squadron preparing to deploy to the Mediterranean Sea. There were last-minute visits and lots of paperwork to get through before I would be deployed.

In February of 1969, LT William Bedinger (Right) flew a Phantom from the east coast to NAS Miramar where he flew newly promoted LTjg Henry J. Bedinger (Left) on a two hour sortie to the Chocolate Mountain ranges and back to San Diego. It was the first and only time the two brothers flew together

One of the Puking Dogs squadron's traditions was to play our sister air wing F-4 squadron in a game of softball. It was a tied game and I was on first with a runner on third. The batter hit a hard ground ball to shortstop and it looked like an easy double play. I made it a bit more challenging by changing ever so slightly my forward progress to wipe out the second baseman as he was attempting to pivot and throw to first base. It was what we used to call in football "a perfect cross-body block." For the record, the Puking Dogs beat the Ghost Riders of VF-142 by a score of 2 to 1, but I never finished the game. My collision with the second baseman resulted in pain in my right wrist and swelling that quickly seemed to be getting worse. So I was replaced in the game by my roommate on the upcoming cruise who felt football had no place in the game of baseball. Later that evening, the pain got so severe that Laura persuaded me to let her drive me to the navy hospital in San Diego to have them check me out.

The verdict was not good. I had broken my navicular bone in my wrist, which has a very low blood supply and is known as one of the slowest healing bones in the body. And to make matters worse, the only way to cast my wrist in this area was a large plaster of Paris clunker that went from my finger tips to my arm pit.

The next morning broke gray and dull as my wife drove me to the pier where the *USS Constellation* was being loaded with the last things for the long cruise. I was quick to get aboard and check in with both the commanding officer and the administrative officer of our squadron. They both told me not to let the fighter doc see me for a few days and to lay low. I became the duty officer, so others could bag all the fight time. The maintenance control officer, a very creative mustang lieutenant who knew how to fix anything, made a few modifications to an extra-large, green flight jacket to cover up my cast.

We were scheduled for our operational readiness inspection (ORI) in Hawaii and would maintain a shore detachment at the Naval Air Station Barbers Point while the carrier and the air wing operated off the coast of Hawaii. It was a perfect job for a broken-winged RIO. The day before we hit Hawaii, the fighter doc heard some rumors about my encumbered arm and flew into our ready room to find me. He got in my face, pronto. He asked me which bone and practically exploded in front of me. He immediately sought out the skipper (great name for commanding officers in the navy) and recommended that I be immediately sent back to San Diego. The RAG in San Diego was being heavily taxed at that time to fill all billets and both 1966 and 1967 had been years of great losses in the skies over North Vietnam. The skipper thanked the doc for his professional opinion and recommendation and then assigned me to fill two upcoming needs: special envoy for VIP visitors in Hawaii and officer in charge of the ground detachment ashore. Then the maintenance officer and the mustang officer both told me that I could visit my great aunt Margery Bedinger, who was now fully retired in Kaneohe, Hawaii. The shore detachment was composed of our best troubleshooters and Phantom fixers, so they really didn't need me at NAS Barbers Point.

The VIP visitors were several TV celebrities I didn't even know and a seasoned U.S. Senator, along with several senior air force generals. I was glad to be able to explain the role of the air boss and how his office was positioned so that he could see everything on the aircraft carrier's flight deck. They all got a laugh out of the two rules for the air boss. *Rule #1: The Air Boss is never wrong. Rule #2: When the Air Boss is wrong; quickly refer to Rule #1.* And that still holds true today. The group was with us for one day of operations and I had fun explaining all the phases of the activities they were observing. The best comment I heard late in the day was the senator turning to the air force Lt. Gen. and saying, "If the air force ran an operation like this, they would have a Maj. Gen. as the commanding officer and a Brig. Gen. as the XO (executive officer)."

When the *Constellation* deployed with my air wing for the four-day ORI the next week, I was sent ashore and taken by pickup truck with a week's worth of clothes and some other necessities to Kaneohe where I was put up at the seniors' residence where my great-aunt, Margery Bedinger, had a beautiful apartment on the top floor. We could eat there or in the main dining room, which was pretty good and very well appointed. One day an elderly gentleman with his wife got on the elevator and my great-aunt formally introduced me to him as if she, too, had been to military protocol school. And she addressed him as a full colonel, so as a lowly lieutenant junior grade fighter RIO, I was duly impressed and made sure to say the required things like, "Nice to meet you, sir." But he said next to nothing and obviously wanted nothing to do with such a low-ranking naval officer. He just walked off— and that made a much more enjoyable lunch for me. When someone mentioned how they thought the army needed better manners, I was quick to speculate that he was probably having a bad day or maybe had a mild headache. Margery replied that people don't change or have bad moments when they grow older, "They only become more so. He was a jerk thirty years ago and he's a bigger jerk today."

I have never forgotten the sparkle in her eye and the smile she beamed at me that day. It was another life lesson from a Bedinger gal who had been the first woman head librarian at West Point Military Academy, had worked in libraries from Butte, Montana to Denver, Colorado to Cape Town, South Africa to Istanbul, Turkey. Margery's lifetime specialty was metallurgical engineering and her hobby was collecting Southwest Indian silver. After retiring, she wrote and published a complete history of how early Spanish settlers taught the Navajo tribes the art of metalworking and encasing special stones in jewelry. She was so proud of how it turned out and that her book, *Indian Silver*,[14] had outsold Dr. Alex Comfort's *The Joy of Sex*, in the Arizona and New Mexico areas. Margery took me to her favorite spots and around Hawaii to places to this day I would never be able to find. She was a remarkable woman[15] whom I think would qualify as the "Auntie Mame" of our family.

The *Constellation* was on the move to Yankee Station (a fixed coordinate off the Vietnam coast) in another week and I was again elected by unanimous consent of the officer wardroom to be the permanent duty officer. We were a great squadron and I had a lot to learn. So I kept my ears and eyes open and was getting quite good at using the various

---

14 Margery Bedinger, *Indian Silver: Navajo and Pueblo Jewelers* (Albuquerque: University of New Mexico Press, 1973).

15 For more information, please see: http://www.bedinger.org/margery-bedinger-355.html

means of communication that each ready room was equipped with. I started to develop a lower tone and calmer voice so well that other ready rooms started asking, "Who's the new guy in the Puking Dogs ready room?" In fighter squadrons today it's not what you say, but how you say it that makes or breaks you on the radio.

When we were half-way between Hawaii and the Philippine Islands I was summoned to the ship's message center for a special message—"CO's Eyes Only". This was most unusual and only Communications Officer LTJG James Bedinger (that's me), or the CO could pick up the message. Since the skipper had just returned from flying, I was quick to get my roommate to take my duty while I retrieved the message and delivered it to the CO's stateroom. This was the first and only message I handled like this, and I wanted to make it perfect. Once I delivered it, I returned directly to the ready room for the rest of the duty day. No sooner had I sat down at the duty officer's desk, than the sound-powered voice system came on with the CO telling me to "get my butt back to his stateroom." He didn't sound happy and I wasn't sure I had not messed up the envelope or the receipt chain, which I had returned to the ship's message center on the way back to the ready room. Several other officers overheard all this and gave me a very sympathetic look.

It didn't take me long to get back to his stateroom. When I knocked the skipper opened the door very slowly and simply said, "Come in Jim. I've some very bad news for you and as long as I've been in this business, I've never found an easy to way to do this. Sit down and take a sip of this." It was Jack Daniels on the rocks and illegal as hell on any vessel of the U.S. Navy, but some naval aviators back then surreptitiously brought it on board for a small taste of the shore on dark and stormy nights at sea.

As I opened the message I first thought that my mom or dad had died. At that time they were both going through divorce proceedings and my mom had just learned to drive at the age of sixty-five. I overstate the case by saying she was "learning" because she was often going off the road and was so short, she needed a pillow to raise her enough to see under the top of the steering wheel.

But then it jumped out at me: "Regret to inform you that LT William M. Bedinger crashed and was killed at MCAS Cherry Point on take-off, September 2, 1969." I was stunned, and for once in a blue moon I was speechless.

The skipper kindly put his hand on my shoulder and said, "Anything you need, Jim? You just ask." Then he told me how the aircraft carrier was too far from land to launch the carrier transport plane, an aging C-1, so I would have to wait a day-and-a-half before they could get anyone off the ship. Since my brother's wife, Doris, was pregnant with their second child, her doctor wished us to have a quick memorial service and burial. Bill's squadron had requested me to be his official escort from Cherry Point, North Carolina to Gettysburg, Pennsylvania where he was to be buried at the National Military Cemetery. But there was no way that could happen because it would take too long for me to get home—I'd be lucky to make the funeral.

A thousand thoughts flew by me, but then I looked at the drink in my hand and smiled because it was one of my brother's favorites. All I could think to say then was, "Thank you for the drink, Skipper; this was one of Bill's favorites." It was then I saw for the first time, tears in CDR Bill Alberson's eyes. He sipped his and I sipped mine. Then the ready room started to call for me, and the skipper just turned and told them to carry on without me. I asked the skipper if I could be relieved of being duty officer as I didn't want my squadron mates to see me cry. He just nodded and said, "Done!"

When I left his room, I had to stop in one of the enlisted men's heads and put myself in a corner and cry. My older brother, my hero who taught me sports and a bunch of other things, whom I always used as a measure of how well I was doing anything, was gone. A voice I loved was gone. And all I could think of was, "I'm going to bag a MIG for Bill."

I had attended St. Peter's School in Peekskill, New York, and so did Bill. If he played football, I played football. When Bill was a senior, I was a freshman. The other students called my brother "El Toro" because of his speed and ferocious blocks on much larger opponents. So I played and finally lettered in my senior year in football as a pulling guard in an off-balance, single-wing offense with direct snaps to the tailback. I was the lightest guy on the team and when we ran fifty yard wind sprints, I was usually last, no matter how hard I tried. But the coaches and students all knew I was trying harder than anyone else and was actually improving all season long. Bill was my role model in the best of ways because he made me better than I thought I could be. And his standards made losing him that much harder.

By the time I returned to my stateroom below the main hanger deck, I had few tears left; my throat was sore, and I had a real pain inside me. I then slept for twelve hours and awoke to eat a late breakfast in the flight suit wardroom. I learned that the transport C-1 would launch at 6:00 a.m. the next day and that I had to be packed and report to preflight by 5:00 a.m. I made a special point of telling the XO these arrangements, and he told me the skipper wanted to see me before I left. That night when the ready room was full of officers for the traditional movie (What made watching a movie in the ready room on cruise were all the fighter pilots' comments throughout. Sometimes we had to stop the movie, reverse it some, and restart because no one could possibly hear what was said after the last smart remark was made.), I met with the skipper in our squadron admin office where the communications officer usually hung out. It was late and the only person there was the leading yeoman petty officer. The skipper told him to check out the ready room mailbox for the next ten minutes. It was a difficult time for the skipper, and I knew he might be concerned because of my being the sole surviving son in my family. My parents had lost their first son as a baby and now Bill, the second son, had died. President Lyndon Johnson had announced in 1968 that no sole surviving son would be ordered to Vietnam and if one son died, the sole surviving son of that family would be brought home immediately.

I told the skipper I was hoping I could make the right connections to get to Gettysburg in time for the funeral to be held with full military honors. He nodded his head and said he was extending my emergency leave from ten days to fourteen days, but in two weeks he wanted me back on the *Constellation*. He then confided to me that he was having problems with some of the lieutenants in the squadron who didn't take their officer ground duties very seriously, but he and the XO agreed that I was one junior officer they could count on to get the job done. It was then I told the skipper of a "stupid dream" I had where I was trying to eject my brother in the front seat and I couldn't reach the ejection handle. And I told him there was nothing more than I wanted to do than to shoot down a MIG for my brother Bill. He wanted me to promise that I would be back in no more than two weeks. I looked him in the eye and shook his hand while saying, "You can count on it, Skipper, I shall return."

It was difficult to sleep through that night and I was up the next morning before the alarm went off. I didn't want to wake my roommate, LTJG Mick Enright, but he was awake and quickly got dressed. With my arm still in the clunky cast it was hard to navigate the passageways with the navy-issued canvas suitcase. Mick said, "Jim, I got your bag and I'm going to see it goes with you. If you need anything back here, I'll give it my best shot." He was true to his word. Although Mick had the reputation of being a bit of a goof-off and had lost some squadron equipment that was still being investigated in San Diego, he was superb in supporting me and had been the best squadron mate I could ever hope to get started with.

The first leg of my flying home was to Naval Air Station (NAS) Manila, but military airlift flights rarely landed there, so the pilot made the decision upon landing to take all the emergency leave people to the air force base, which was about a two-hour flight away. Everyone on this flight had lost a mother, a father, or other loved one. One man with two children had lost his wife in a car accident, so it made me think a lot about life and death. But I still wanted to bag a MIG for my brother. I simply had to honor my commitment, return to the ship, and get back into the fight.

Once we arrived at Clark Air Force Base (AFB) on Luzon Island, we were ushered into a large terminal and told to quickly move to a gate where a plane was about to depart to Kadena AFB in Okinawa, which increased our chances of getting a plane sooner that was going back to the U.S. It was a long flight with almost every seat filled. I was lucky to get a window seat so I was able to watch the day grow long and the edge of night start to arrive. Once at Okinawa, I and one other person were immediately told to bring our bags and hop on a cart. We were taken rapidly to a gate on the other end of the terminal and embarked immediately on what looked like a commercial airliner. It was under contract to take troops to and from Vietnam and was returning no more than half-full to the States. It was again a window seat and I watched the sky get ever darker with more and more stars shining brightly. It was a long flight at forty-one thousand feet above sea level, and the only comfort I had was the USO telegram that I had been given at Kadena AFB telling me my wife would meet me at the USO station at San Francisco International Airport where she had reserved a flight the next day to take us to Baltimore, Maryland.

Everything worked like clockwork. The dawn broke bright and beautiful over the blue Pacific. Breakfast was my first meal since leaving the ship the day before. Of course it tasted just great. When we started our descent and approach into Travis AFB, just to the east of Oakland, we were told that the Golden Gate Bridge was coming up on the left. I looked out and there she was, just as beautiful as a postcard, with puffy white clouds hanging around it. Once on the ground, I was met by an air force corporal who was holding a sign with my name on it. He said I was scheduled to take a bus to the San Francisco airport where my wife was already waiting to meet me.

At this time there was a growing peace movement and lots of demonstrations at various airports where troops departed and arrived. When I, wearing my service dress khaki uniform, got on the bus, I saw some long-haired, scruffy looking protesters outside and couldn't wait to get on the road. The bus was already loaded with many civilians, but few military; we sailed right by the protesters. And the same thing happened when we arrived at the airport in San Francisco. There were signs directing folks to the USO—and no protesters. And right there in the lounge was my wife, Laura. I was so happy to see her and overcome with tears both of grief and joy. She had an inner strength that helped me through this difficult time.

The funeral was scheduled for the next day and our flight was a nonstop to Baltimore with an estimated arrival time of 10:45 p.m. Laura had received a phone call earlier in the day that informed her my parents would meet us at the airport. When we arrived, we met my brother-in-law, Hank, and my father, who said my mom was too upset to travel tonight. Hank was a research scientist working on a cure for some African fever and he was starting to get the sweats and had a few shakes going on, too. It wasn't malaria, but apparently he was now infected with the fever and the cure was working too slowly. Yet we made it to Gettysburg by midnight.

When we checked into the small motel with a coffee shop attached, we were surprised to see all the lights on in the coffee shop. My whole family and all of our in-laws from my brother's wife's family were there. My cousins from New York and Tennessee had arrived and, of course, my mom was there and immediately started to cry all over again. She was just certain that I would be staying home now and not returning to my squadron. That is not what her son Bill would have wanted at all. But I knew that we'd have to discuss it at another time. My step-grandmother Sheila, who was George R. Bedinger's second wife, was there, too. I was amazed, but somehow not surprised that despite her advancing years, she had made it to see my brother buried at the National Military Cemetery.

The next day was another hot, humid, early fall day in Gettysburg. The funeral home's parlor was a very good place to have a memorial service with a closed casket. I couldn't speak and could hardly swallow. I was in my tropical-white-long summer uniform (white short-sleeves with shoulder boards) with a matching clunking cast to the fingertips on one arm, so I was a sight to see, The next phase was to move the casket to a hearse and form a funeral procession to the cemetery that went a lot faster than I had imagined. Funerals were rarely done on weekends at Gettysburg, but because of Doris expecting their second child and the shock of her loss, the powers that be made an exception, and we were now going through the center of town where five major roads all came together, just as they had in the 1860s. It was here that an older gent with a straw hat, a long piece of straw in his mouth, and denim bib overalls saw the flag-draped coffin in the hearse and came to attention. He removed the straw from his mouth and then took his hat and put it over his heart. At least twenty or thirty other people did the same thing. Those war protesters in California needed to visit this old Civil War town to see how patriotic Americans honored their fellow countrymen lost in war time.

That is one picture that sticks in my mind still today. Complete strangers in the middle of a busy Saturday morning paying their respects to our nation's flag and my brother. When we arrived at the cemetery I was amazed to see we were only a few hundred yards from where my dad and I stood six years before watching the reenactment of Pickett's Charge. I noticed some leaves had started to change color and one maple tree close to the driveway was turning red. I had tried not to cry and kept telling myself to stay in control. But our best plans often can be turned aside by nature and memory.

As the solders finished the rifle volley, the bugler played *Taps* and a wind stirred some leaves into the air. I turned to the west and remembered how those Confederate forces walked over a mile across farm fields with no walls, no fortifications, and no protection. I thought of my brother here and my great-great-great-uncle, Lt. George Rust Bedinger, who had probably fallen at the Bloody Angle just to the south of us. And then I saw my Dad looking there, too. He had large tears falling down his cheeks as he looked over that battlefield. Then the last restrain of *Taps* echoed from another bugler farther away: "God is nigh." And that's when I simply lost it with tears and sobs for what we had lost and how my brother Bill would be from now on so very close to our great-great-great-uncle George.

When we were returning to the cars, my dad came beside me and shared that he was thinking of how we saw the reenactment just six years before and now Lt. George Rust Bedinger CSA, would have another relative so close by, LT William Michael Bedinger, USN. At the very moment of the final strains of *Taps*, father and son were thinking the same thing, and I knew when it came to returning to my squadron, my dad would understand and support my decision.

That afternoon the two officers from Bill's squadron who attended the funeral had to leave for Norfolk, but first they were required to explain the sole-surviving son policy and have me sign a statement that they had explained the policy to me. There was no rush to make me decide one way or another, but I told them that I was going to go back to my squadron and do my best to shoot down a MIG for Bill. One of the officers looked at the other and simply said, "It must run in the family."

There were a number of partings and travel to my home town of Hatboro, Pennsylvania. My one constant was Laura at my side, observing and gently holding my hand when I needed it most. The issue of whether I would return to the *Constellation* was the number one topic for two days until I finally said that my duty was there and I was going back, no matter what. This issue was made all the more difficult because of the divorce proceedings my mother had started against my dad. So, like our nation, our house was divided, and I had to spend time with each of them at their respective places.

———————— ★ ————————

After returning to San Diego, my first order of business was going back to the naval hospital to see if my wrist was healed enough to have the clunker cast removed. Because of my combat status and orders to return to my squadron in just a matter of days, I was given a high priority appointment with the head of the orthopedics department. The corpsman who took me to the x-ray section explained that the doctor had ordered the cast to be removed so the x-ray results would be as clear as possible. I was hoping that my prayers were answered and that I was healed. At first, I thought something was wrong, because the head doctor ordered other x-rays at several different angles. Finally I was ushered into his office and informed that I was the exception to the rule and that in only six weeks, the bone had completely healed. He cautioned me to slowly start moving it and gave me the usual rubber ball to squeeze and the routine of using the ball that gave the best results. When an arm is not moved for six weeks, there is some pain and discomfort in just the slightest of movements, so he wanted me to use the sling for at least one week before I started a list of prescribed exercises. That was the plan.

Laura had to buy extra milk because I had kept up my routine of drinking at least two glasses at every meal and one before bed. I think that helped in the healing, too. I was soon packing and getting ready to make the trip back to the ship and my squadron. The tickets were all set and the time seemed to fly, but Laura and I still got to visit some of our favorite places in San Diego. When it was time to go, I remember very distinctly how proud my wife was of her driving and how she drove our VW Bug to all my appointments and on our short trips around town.

When Laura dropped me off at the airport she insisted on parking in the lot and coming inside with me. I was glad she did because, as it turned out, I would not see her again for more than three-and-a-half years.

CHAPTER 4

RETURN TO THE "CONNIE" AND THE "DOGS"

My flights to Los Angeles, then to Hawaii, and then to Manila in the Philippines went without fanfare or note. My primary concern the entire trip was to get from the civilian airport in Manila to the Naval Air Station at Cubi Point, a part of the Subic Bay Naval Complex. I was advised to take the "jeepney service". A jeepney is a colorfully decorated and modified minibus that is now manufactured in the Philippines as a new vehicle, but back in 1969, most were created from old leftover WWII vehicles modified and expanded to work as a shuttle van or minibus.

After landing in Manila I noticed several other American sailors looking for the same trip to Subic Bay so we combined forces to find the jeepney stand and bartered a good rate for the small group. We were on our way over mountain passes, through switchbacks, two-lane roads into beautiful broad valleys, and then back over another mountain range. We had several close calls, but nothing like a nighttime catapult shot in a Phantom jet off the "*Connie*," the common nickname for our ship, the *USS Constellation*. When we got to the naval complex in Subic Bay, the jeepney took those going to the ship piers first and I was the last one off at NAS Cubi Point in front of the base operations center. I checked in with the duty officer with my emergency leave orders and his eyes got a little larger when he saw I was due back before midnight of this date. So he told me I had the first plane going back.

Just then one of our mustang maintenance officers saw me and rushed over. He advised me that the *Connie's* shore detachment was flying back the next day in a brand new turbo-prop C-2 Greyhound. Its cruising speed was almost twice as fast as the older and tired C-1 Trader, and they would make room for me so I could stay that night. Also, there was a big party planned with about thirty people plus invited guests (young single gals). I really appreciated the invitation, but I had given my word to the skipper and I knew I had to get back this day and not the next. The Cubi Point operations clerk advised us that there was one C-1 scheduled to leave very soon with an A-7 Corsair engine stowed in the back that I could hop a ride with. It might be bit tight for leg room and it would be definitely colder at high altitudes in the back of the C-1, but comfort features were not a priority to me at this time—my word and the time were my first and only concerns.

I was not at Base Ops very long before I was summoned with my canvas USN-issued suitcase to get on the manifest and get my bag taken care of. That meant getting a tag on it and carrying it onto the plane to occupy the web seat next to me. There were no seat numbers on this flight; I was the only passenger and the entire center of the back cargo area was occupied by that A-7 jet engine. I was ready and the last thing I was told that they had no headset for me. The enlisted crew member who rode in the cockpit would open the door and let me know when we were starting our approach to land on the *Connie*. They also estimated our flight time would be approximately 5.5 to 6 hours, depending on winds aloft and the final position of the carrier when we arrived. They actually told me the newer C-2 usually made the trip in 3 to 3.5 hours. I did the math and knew that we might land somewhere between the next-to-last and last recovery of the day, which meant I might be on board just before midnight.

The trip was probably the most uncomfortable part of all my travels because I lacked legroom to stretch and had to shuffle sideways to get around the engine to reach the relief tube in the rear of the plane to void my daily coffee and water intake. Fortunately, the crew had an extra winter aviation jacket that I promptly put on and wore for the whole flight. It was a true gift because we had been assigned to a slightly higher altitude than normal and the temperature probably got down to the high forties before we started to descend to warmer air. The time became a slight concern to me because it looked like the last recovery was running late. As it worked out, we landed at around 11:30 p.m. I had my orders stamped by the flight ops and quickly departed with bag in hand. Since my stateroom was on the way to the stern of the ship where our ready room was located, I stashed my bag and made it to the ready room at exactly 11:50 p.m.

The squadron officers had started gathering for the daily movie and spirits were running high. I tried to hover around the mail box at the back of the ready room, but the duty officer saw me and announced on the sound-powered phone to the skipper, who was still in his stateroom, "LTJG Bedinger has arrived, sir." I then learned that some of the officers had started a pool by one-hour blocks on when I would officially land on the *Connie*. It was nice to feel wanted, but then a bit puzzling to see most had chosen time blocks in the following two days. The first thing the skipper did when he entered the ready room was to come up to me and shake my hand. Not a word was spoken; then it was time to start the movie.

Since I was the communications officer with the collateral duty of coffee mess treasurer, my seat in the ready room was traditionally right next to the executive officer. When I sat down, the CO congratulated me and told me I was soon going to be promoted to material division officer and I would haven't have to move from my front seat in the ready room. I still think to this day that he and the skipper did that so that they could keep a close eye on me and give me some vectors if I began to stray. To me it was a blessing in several ways because I needed to be close to see and hear all the comments. That night was the first good laugh I had since getting the news that my brother Bill had died.

The next day started early and my first task was to report to medical with my most current X-rays and the orthopedic surgeon's recommendations for getting full strength back. By his timetable, he thought I would be safe to fly by this date. But it required the flight surgeon to sign-off on that decision and no one flies until an "up chit" is issued by him. I was so good with squeezing the ball they gave me that I started doing sit-ups and push-ups several days before I started my trip back to the Connie. But before our trusty fighter doc—who had been flying in my place since day one—would see me, they needed to take one more X-ray on the ship. After waiting a few hours I was told to come back that afternoon to see if they could fit me in. I was not too pleased as I walked into the ready room and my normally assigned pilot was there. He asked what was wrong and I told him. Apparently he was eager to have me in his back seat again, but maybe not as eager as I was to get back in the air and get my very first combat flight time. That was a big deal at that time, because no one knew how long the war would last and how the new White House staff and team would work to end this war. The new president was Richard M. Nixon, who had run on a pledge to end the war.

Much to my surprise, my pilot let the senior leaders know I was not getting in to see the fighter doc and getting a runaround at sick bay. It didn't take long for our squadron fighter doc to leave a message to report to sick bay at 1300 hours and get that x-ray. This time they were waiting for me and he was there with the *Connie's* head medical office to confirm that I had a miraculous recovery of a broken navicular bone in less than six weeks. When the x-rays showed that I had no fracture, I was left with the fighter doc in a small examination room. He was sure I was not in flying shape yet, so he asked me to show him how many push-ups I could do. After pumping out fifty on the deck of the exam room, he relented and said, "Okay, the skipper was right; you are the exception. Congratulations and here is your up chit." A month when the squadron was having an evening event ashore and the doc came up to me at the bar and told me he was darn proud of me and that he knew I was going to do well as a Puking Dog. And that was a measure of a true professional; he didn't have to say anything to me, but wanted me to know he was glad to have me back on board. I've admired his skill and insights ever since.

A few hours later there was a stir in flight operations and we heard terrible news. Helicopters were being launched to conduct a search and rescue mission. The new C-2 Greyhound VRC-50 from the Philippines was missing. It had started its approach to the ship, but never reported "Marshal." This is a mandatory checkpoint and voice report at five thousand feet when making an instrument flight rule (IFR) approach to land on an aircraft carrier. The C-2 transport was the plane carrying twenty-seven people to our ship, many of whom were air wing mechanics returning from the first longshore detachment to support all of us on Yankee Station. And this was the plane that the our maintenance officer at Cubi Point had told me he could get me a seat on, but I had chosen to return on time on the slower C-1 transport. It was October 2, 1969, and night was almost upon us. Maybe they would find some survivors, but time and circumstance were not in the odds at that time of day.

The next day wreckage on the surface was discovered from the air and a destroyer was sent to investigate the area in question. A launch recovered some small aircraft pieces and parts of luggage. One wallet was found; it belonged to a member of the VF-143 Puking Dogs who in our shore detachment. Numerous theories started to be spawned and spun, but the ship's skipper quickly came up on the voice system and told the crew that the search was coming to an end and that all twenty-seven lives had been lost. Flight ops would be suspended in a few days to conduct a memorial service and a simulated burial at sea for our shipmates. I was devastated not only because I knew several of these men, but also because I could have been with them on that flight.

I remember vividly one part of the memorial service. My roommate, Mick, and I had approached the hanger deck from below where our stateroom was located and were amazed at how many people were there and how well organized it was. We found our squadron's assigned area and started to fall into ranks. The service was fitting and very moving. There were twenty-seven cardboard coffins by the edge of the rear elevator and after the trumpeter had played "Taps" with someone on the flight deck above us playing the echo refrain of "God is Nigh," the coffins were tilted one-by-one and some type of elongated bag with weights was sent to the ocean below. It was all symbolic; it had to be, for not one body was ever found intact. And all I could think of was that I could have been on that flight that day. When I shared this with Mick he simply said, "God is working on a different mission for you."

★

Now that I was back on the flight schedule, there was some concern that I had no green time (combat flight hours are officially logged in green into an aviator's individual flight log), and I would have to be scheduled slowly into missions bombing over land. My first combat hop was a barrier combat air patrol (BARCAP) where two fighters are placed in the sector closest to the enemy forces and fly in an oval track looking for airborne threats to the carrier task force. Or as we called it in 1969, we were "drilling holes in the sky to show them we meant business." By 1969, the North Vietnamese MIG forces stayed mainly over land, but the BARCAP missions continued in case the enemy changed its tactics.

We launched, hit the tanker to top off our fuel tanks, and reported to our controller for the mission. It was a great feeling to be back in the air with my regularly assigned pilot who was an ROTC University of California Berkley grad and an all-around great guy. Once on station, I tuned up the pulse radar and set the mileage, azimuth scan, and altitude scan on the scope, and then switched into pulse-Doppler to adjust for that mode. After we made our first turn, our controller came up in an urgent voice and said; "Taproom 101, your vector is 010 at 125 miles, flight of four bogeys in pursuit of friendly 10 miles in front, over." I replied "Roger!" and made a few adjustments. I immediately saw high velocity target symbols on the scope and told my pilot I was trying for an auto-lock. This is a feature where the radar and in-flight computer automatically take the highest threat target and switch into single target tracking. At this time the controller raised the urgency by telling us that the two highest flying MIGs were closing on the friendly and we needed to hustle to their location. Then our radar locked onto the high MIGs and I told the controller the azimuth and mileage. The controller said, "Roger! You're cleared hot." My pilot wanted no confusion and asked over the UHF radio, "Are we cleared to fire?" And they immediately responded, "Roger." We told them we had the intercept so that they didn't have to keep giving us mileage and azimuth updates. We were on our way to bag at least one MIG for my brother.

Our speed along with my radar pulse were increasing when my pilot realized we were already above the speed limit for jettisoning the centerline fuel tank. He told me that we had to keep the tank on and might want to jettison the tank when it was empty. But that was never needed because about ten seconds after we told our controller that we had the intercept, I noticed the closing velocity on the bogeys was rapidly decreasing as was their altitude. With all these indications, we knew the MIGs were executing a split-S maneuver where the plane uses the vertical to turn around and go in the opposite direction. Our radar automatically dropped track and I switched to pulse mode so I could see both the friendly aircraft and all the bogeys. We saw five blips with only one coming toward us and the other four heading away from us toward Hainan Island, a part of Soviet China that forms the northeast corner of the Gulf of Tonkin. The controller told us to return to station at normal speed and that our vector was a complete success. It was good we kept the tank on the aircraft, because we needed all the gas to complete our 2.3-hour mission before we could return and land on the carrier.

When we landed we usually went to our maintenance control spaces to fill out the required gripes on the aircraft so that our maintenance team could quickly repair or address those concerns and return the plane for the next launch, which was a serious issue with F-4s at this time because sortie numbers and mission readiness were high-interest metrics to the U.S. Congress. We never wanted to miss a flight or Alert 5 requirement. Just as we were finishing this task, still in complete flight gear, the folks in the intelligence center were screaming for our debrief. This was required on all combat missions, but normally there was no rush and crews got out of their combat flight gear before going to the intel center to make their after-action reports. There was quite a stir about the "vector" and what exactly I saw on the scope to make me believe the MIGs had reversed course. I think our intel folks were still adapting to the new capabilities of the F-4J and its new AWG-10 radar and advanced avionics, but it was good to know that my training had come to good use Finally, the combined team of intel officers and air wing veterans had assessed our part as well-played.

There were a few more routine flights and then the *Connie* exited the Tonkin Gulf and transited to Sasebo, Japan for a little shore liberty and resupply. We were to resume operations in the Sea of Japan in response to the North Koreans' shooting down an EC-121 airborne reconnaissance aircraft in April 1969.

I wanted to visit the Navy Exchange to buy a stereo and other shopping. The exchange at Naval Base Yokosuka was bigger and better so I waited. Once there, I found the stereo section truly amazing and purchased some major things. Getting a reel-to-reel tape recorder and some other electronics was a top priority, and then a trip to the library so I could make tapes of my favorite Bach, Vivaldi, Mozart, Beethoven, and Brahms pieces, which took an entire afternoon. It was only years later that I was able to understand how amateur these recordings were, but it would serve me well for the cruise and beyond. And some of these items were packaged and mailed home to my wife, which was a real blessing for Christmas.

When we were in Sasebo, our air wing received detailed briefings on how two MIG-21s managed to shoot down the EC-121 recon aircraft with thirty-one American servicemen aboard and what the rules of the engagement would be for these operations. The *Connie* moved with ease from the new fuel pier into the waters dividing North Korea from Japan where we were to operate for a week. I flew three missions with my regular pilot before being diverted to Marine Corps Air Station Iwakuni on Western Honshu Island, Japan. At the conclusion, we came around the southern portions of Japan and traveled north into Naval Base Yokosuka for another shore period, serious shopping, and one formal party.

The squadron had planned a dining-in at the Officers' Club at Naval Base Yokosuka, which involved all the officers dressing in their formal mess dress with miniature medals. The club was fashioned after a traditional Japanese tea garden, complete with an atrium garden in the middle and solid-wood parquet floors. The executive officer of the *Constellation* was a former skipper of the Puking Dogs and was one of our guests of honor. The carrier air group (CAG) commander was also a guest. It was a night to remember as one petty rule after another was announced to the junior officers who were going to their first dining-in. The fines for violating these rules started the minute we were called from the cocktail reception to the sit-down dinner. When it came time for a short break to relieve bladders, the senior officers were excused first, then the lieutenant commanders, then the lieutenants, and finally all the junior officers who were LTJGs and ensigns. Of course, there was no space at any place and they were already sounding the recall bell. So I did the natural things I had learned in my college fraternity days and used the sink to relieve myself, wash my hands, and get back to the dining room before more fines would be issued. Needless to say, and much to my embarrassment, senior leadership was shocked at my conduct, which was promptly and accurately reported to the president of the mess and I was awarded a trophy and the annual Mr. Gross Award, along with a hefty fine for my "putting the lives of all who used that sink in jeopardy." I never did learn what happened to the little trophy after I departed the squadron, but it was so appropriate and fun for all, including me.

The night evolved into some friendly jousting on floor buffers normally used to wax the club's wood floors. One man would ride the buffer with floor mop and trash can lid in hand while his partner manned the controls of the buffer to mount it into a full-speed charge against his opponent. After several broken mops, two bloody noses, and much laughter, the event moved outside to get downtown to catch four cabs ordered to take us all to the Paramount Club for some more drinking and laughter plus a show. But even here the competitive nature of our air wing and squadron emerged. The entire gaggle was divided into four groups led by the XO of the ship, the CAG commander, our squadron skipper, and our squadron XO. The last group to the Paramount Club would buy the first round of drinks for the rest.

When the cabs arrived, it was a scene from the *Pink Panther* movie car chase. Every cab was so full that legs and arms and half-bodies hung out of the windows. Two cars were in the lead followed by several others. In 1969, Yokosuka still had policemen standing on little stools giving traffic directions at major road intersections. As we descended at high speed down the hill to downtown, the poor young policeman took one glance up the hill at this pack of speeding cars overfilled and overflowing with many different body parts, hurdling straight for him. He quickly and smartly abandoned his post and we all screeched by him along the side of the road at full=speed ahead. I still smile as I remember the arguments and discussions on whose cab was really last to arrive because it appeared to be a tie between our squadron's XO and the CAG commander. Military etiquette prevailed and the junior man, our squadron XO, was declared last. The Puking Dogs were truly smarter than what they looked like and how they usually acted on the beach. But the saying back then was, "You worked hard, so you have to play hard to let off steam." And the acronym ODF (Old Dogs Forever) on some of the coffee cups had new meaning to the youngest in the kennel.

The next day I had a mild hangover, but many others were really quite ill. I had learned that the pitchers of drinks from which all the toasts had been made were grape juice for the senior officers and wine spiked with vodka for the junior officers. Naturally it didn't take me long to add water to my glass so everything I drank was diluted.

The following week we prepared to return to Yankee Station in the Gulf of Tonkin as our mission in the Sea of Japan was complete and another task group had arrived to watch over North Korea and run operations in Japanese waters.

────────── ★ ──────────

The first flights off the *Connie* were on November 1, 1969, and my pilot and I were assigned a ground attack mission over South Vietnam. It was my first flight over land and I went over all the procedures many times as I didn't want to forget anything. I finally designed a checklist card to review as we went from feet wet to feet dry (over land). What I remember most were the twinkling lights around our target area. Afterward my pilot told me that they were not lights, but the muzzle flashes of various weapons firing at us. What a novice I truly was!

In the next two weeks, I flew with my pilot on thirteen combat missions. On one bombing mission over Laos, our bombs scored a direct hit on the road by a river and the result was the hill's slope sliding down and the river further eroding, making the road unusable. The forward air controller (FAC) was ecstatic and we would learn later that several A-7 Corsair flights and an A-6 Intruder previously had been assigned this target, but the road had remained usable. My pilot graciously gave me a lot of the credit for making adjustments in our bombing run and calling the right time to release the bombs. So both he and I were going to be nominated for a Distinguished Flying Cross. I learned four years later that the award was adjusted to a Naval Commendation Medal before the paperwork ever left the ship and then approved only for my pilot. Because of my absences and then being held by the enemy as a prisoner of war, it was considered too risky to call any attention to me. I was not at all concerned when I learned in 1973 about this decision; I had a lot of other things to work on at that time. But it did open my eyes to the differences not only within naval units, but also between the armed services on how they processed and approved awards.

Several days later I learned that a plane from VF-143 had to be launched to NAS Cubi Point in the Philippines so that required landing gear and weapons tests could be performed with the weight off the wheels. This maintenance can't easily be done on the carrier, and we had received some new personnel while in Japan to fill the positions lost in October. But the presidential election of 1968 and the start in 1969 of the new Nixon Administration had created more press about the peace process and how the talks had started in Paris between the four major parties of the Vietnam War—they even agreed that the table would be a square, one side for each party. I had not earned enough flying time to merit my first air medal (In 1969 specific points from O.5 to 2.0 for overland bombing missions were accrued and after one reached a certain point, an air medal was earned.), so my pilot and another RIO with plenty of combat missions were assigned to take the plane to the Philippines while I would be assigned to fly with different pilots in the squadron.

For the next week I flew several bombing missions and a number of BARCAPs, which were fairly routine. On November 19 I was assigned to fly an escort mission with our squadron maintenance officer who was a Naval Academy graduate, test pilot, and very dedicated officer who worked on the AWG-10's new radar for our F-4Js. I had asked several others on how to prepare for such a mission, but didn't get a lot of guidance. First thing on the day of the mission, the maintenance officer wanted to see my low-level maps and flight planning, but. I was so new I really had nothing to show him. So he told me to get to the RA-5C Vigilante ready room and get prepared; he was definitely upset with me. I found the RIO who was going to be in the RA-5C, who shared his pre-flight maps and a number of other useful things, including check-in and exit frequencies, and as the escort, what we should do if we got separated during the mission.

We over-flew South Vietnam, flew north along the Thrung Son mountain range, and then descended and accelerated to make our photo run of supply lines in the southern-most part of North Vietnam. The radar and missile warning indicators became alive (very active), and then without much warning from *Red Crown*, the cruiser off-shore that was our controller, the surface to air (SAM) missile indicator and tone went off. The RA-5C went almost instantly into afterburner and accelerated ahead of us and my pilot told me to lock him up. We had a center line fuel tank and were somewhat airspeed-restricted unless we slowed down and jettisoned the tank. That's not a very viable option with a SAM or two in the air, so we plowed on as fast as we could go. Then my pilot saw the general direction of the SAM threat and rolled hard one way and then another trying to pick up a visual. The only thing I was able to see were dust clouds on the ground from firing the two SAMs. We were able to follow the RA-5C in a loose ten-mile trail and finally get back to the water and out of both small arms and SAM danger. It was a ride that became more thrilling with each new account during our debriefing. I was excited but tried to stay as quiet as possible; I was so new that I felt I had probably missed a lot of the details. It happened so fast, and the best thing I was able to do was get our radar locked onto the RA-5C and help the pilot stay in loose trail.

During this period I was standing Alert 5 watches on the flight deck, which meant my pilot and I were sitting in a fighter attached to the carrier's catapult, ready to launch to counter any threat. I was also flying every day and sometimes twice. At 2:00 a.m. on the morning of November 22, 1969, I was assigned to fly with the admin officer on a BARCAP. He was still learning a lot about intercept geometry and what they were now teaching the fighter RIOs. We did three intercepts on our wing man where I had the time and radar to explain target aspect (the angle at which the bogey sees the interceptor), and how that was used to get the cutaway and the turn-back into intercepting the bogey. It was a good hop and I felt good about it.

I was to fly around 10:00 a.m. with another pilot on an overland bombing mission. The operations officer in charge of the daily flight schedule had noted that the two points from this mission would put me just over a total of twenty BARCAP points and I would be the last officer in our squadron to qualify for an air medal so I was looking forward to this mission.

From the briefing to the preflight there were some major differences in this mission. First and foremost, we were carrying a new fuse that would make these 500-hundred-pound bombs not explode until a set number of magnetic fluctuations was reached. In short, these bombs were being used as land mines to explode when a truck or a group of armed personnel passed nearby. Also, the drop height above the target and pilot's mil settings—what he sees on his windscreen—were different. The airspeed had to be greater to activate the fuse to work properly and my pilot asked a lot of questions in the briefing. We even had a pilot from the sister squadron VF-142 come to our ready room and go over the procedures. As a test pilot at NAS China Lake, California, he had just finished a special project that had successfully shown how to drop this ordnance from the F-4 Phantom. What I remember most was that he told us to do everything the same as a normal bombing run, but when we came to the point of dropping, just wait another "one potato, two potato" before hitting the bomb release. So that was the plan—for me to say, "One potato, two potato, PICKLE!" at the release point.

We passed through the airspace of several forward air controllers (FACs) flying westward over South Vietnam and Laos who told us there were some low clouds and bad weather in our target area. Our primary and secondary targets were completely covered by clouds, so we moved to another area with a very active FAC and he was ready for us with phosphorous rocket flares (they were often referred to as Willie Petes) to designate where he wanted our MK-82 specially fused 500-hundred-pound bombs to be dropped. Our flight lead rolled in, but my pilot had not seen the white smoke from the flare, so I began to "talk his eyes" onto the spot. He finally saw it and told me to call in "hot" while he tightened his turn and rolled inverted onto the target. This is a standard bombing run maneuver for navy planes; when the pilot achieves a 40-degree, nose-down attitude, he rolls the plane 180-degrees so the crew is going downhill with the sky above them and the ground below them.

The only trouble I saw was that it looked like we were going straight down when he rolled wings level and my quick check of the attitude indicator showed that we were in an 80-degree dive.

"You're too steep, 80 degrees nose down, PULL UP!"

He replied, "We've been hit in the tail; I've got no horizontal stab control."

A second later, passing eight thousand feet above sea level with some mountains three thousand feet high and with airspeed less than two hundred knots, my pilot ordered me to eject. I pulled the face curtain handle on the top of the seat that basically pulls a curtain over the occupant's face to protect from wind blast. I heard the bang and then passed out momentarily from the force of the ejection and I was, in that instant, on my way to a new journey. The mission changed in just seconds and little did I know then what was ahead for me, but life was one thing that would continue. I am forever grateful to my pilot for instantly recognizing his loss of control of our aircraft and ordering me to eject. He saved my life and then the rest was left for Divine intervention.

CHAPTER 5

MOVING FROM LAOS TO HANOI

The first thing I remember upon regaining consciousness after I ejected was looking up to see my fully-deployed main parachute. It had alternating panels of white and international flame orange for the whole world to see. Then I saw what appeared to be red tracers above my chute. I looked down and heard the sound of automatic arms fire and it was loud. Three anti-aircraft 15.3 millimeter guns were shooting at me. The tracers started out below me and then at the last minute went above. The only thing I could think of was to pull on the chute's forward lines, which might perhaps increase my rate of descent. I realized I had the wind-blast face curtain in my hand so I made an exaggerated gesture and dropped the curtain, which accelerated earthbound below me. Somehow I thought that might encourage the enemy to stop shooting at me, but I was wrong on that one. I then did the only thing my training, education, and religion had taught me: I recited aloud the Lord's Prayer. I had enough time to recite one verse and get half way through the second verse when I hit the tops of brushes and trees. I was on the ground and someone up in heaven must have heard my prayer; what else would explain how three gunners all missed me when I got so close to their positions?

I immediately got on my 2-way UHF survival radio and contacted the forward air controller (FAC). His first words were, "Don't move. You're in the middle of a minefield." It would take me more than four years to learn that my reply at this point was, *"Mama said there would be days like this. There'd be days like this, my Mama said."* Then I learned that I was "Taproom 101B" while my pilot was "Taproom 101A."

I could hear Asian voices and the sound of machetes chopping brush. I tried to get up and move away from my parachute, but still leave those highly visible panels stuck in the short tree tops so that the FAC could see approximately where I was. I saw a bush still intact about twelve feet tall with low hanging branches to the ground and vines growing up it. It was the perfect place to hide until the rescue birds were here. I stood up and tried to run, but got only two steps and fell flat on my face. My kneeboard had slipped down my leg to my ankle and tripped me up. I quickly released it and tore up the classified material sheets it held. I crawled on my back under the bush I had spotted and hoped not to find any animal—or worse yet, snake—sleeping there. Once under the bush, I found a lot of dead leaves and what appeared to be an old nest of some sort. I got out my ear plug for the survival UHF radio so no one else could hear transmissions from the FAC. I also heard the machetes working overtime. I told the FAC that I heard Asian voices and they were getting closer. He repeated his earlier advice to stay close to my chute and that help was on its way.

Just as I was taught in the navy's survival school, I lay covered with leaves and perfectly still with the shadows and my green flight suit all blending in. The first group of soldiers went directly to my chute, but a second group coming down the hill came right by my bush and cut away much of the top and sides. They were so close I could see the toenails of one of the soldiers passing by. I didn't realize how close they came until I saw the bush a little later with a flat-top haircut.

The fact that both groups walked by me gave me a chance to transmit a short burst on the radio to tell the FAC the enemy was nearby and everyone would know not to send the first rescue helicopter to my location.

I had lost my glasses in the ejection and my uncorrected eyes had 20/200 vision. In an eye exam with no glasses, when asked to read the lowest line, I normally responded with a B or E, as this was usually the first and largest letter on the eye charts back then. The first time this happened they thought I was joking around and were shocked that I was still in the aviation training program. However, as a naval flight officer (NFO), I was qualified to fly if I could see 20/20 with corrective lens. Without my glasses I really could not see very far and was almost blind trying to see long distances. That day everything looked like one green, blurry blob.

I was under a bush that was a short way up a hill above where my chute was still flapping in the breeze. The main group of soldiers had come down the hill and was now around my ejection seat pan and the parachute in the short trees and bushes that covered the area. Soon they started a circular search, but were moving generally in a direction away from my position. One soldier sat down to light up a cigarette; I guess every group has one who wants to rest. The others started to yell not only at him, but up the hill to their unit's leaders. I heard several angry voices above me yelling down and thought the smoker was getting more agitated. Then he turned and starting yelling something back up the hill. Suddenly he stopped mid-sentence, raised his AK-47, and fired a burst above the tree I was under. Others started screaming and several on the hill started firing down at my position. There I was in the crossfire with my Aircrew Smith & Wesson .38 signal pistol ready to shoot, but where to aim and for what purpose? There were at least eight of them and one of me. In this melee, one calm solder closest to me ran full-speed ahead and threw himself on top of me. It was at that moment when I was alive and not shot that I radioed the FAC, "I guess I am a POW. I'm okay and they've taken me alive." The soldier grabbed the phone from my hand and threw it toward the others who had approached our position with more caution.

The next ten minutes seem to go slow motion, but when two Navy A-7 Corsairs flew over and shot some 20-millimeter rounds into the area, the soldiers wanted to start moving up the hill. My anti-gravity G-suit had to be removed and one soldier raised his machete to chop it off my leg when I stopped him and showed him how to pull the zipper down. It was as if he had never seen such a thing before, but the A-7s got him moving very quickly. They tied my arms behind my back and tried to make it so tight that my elbows would touch, but I kept squirming and the overall tying job was fairly loose. Tripping, stumbling, and generally making a spastic fool of myself, our group slowly moved up the hill.

Once on top of the hill, I saw one of the three anti-aircraft guns that had been shooting at me. I also saw an entrance to an underground bunker we were headed for. Just as got to this spot, all the guns opened up and soldiers started yelling. I turned to see a Jolly Green Giant (Sikorsky HH-53) rescue helicopter flying at top speed, nose down, and so low that the trees seemed to be moving out of its way. Behind and above the Jolly Green the sky turned red and black while more and larger anti-aircraft guns fired. But the soldiers could not depress some of the larger guns' muzzles low enough to get even close to the low flying Sikorsky screamer. In the doorway, I saw an aircrew rescue man standing with feet spread and tied into the plane. I knew this was a position that they took after picking up a downed pilot, so I knew at least my pilot was safe.

With a good deal of screaming and pushing, I got on a ladder and descended about ten feet down and transversed about twenty feet to another ladder that went even deeper. The air was not musty, but surprising cool for that part of the world. There were at least ten other soldiers who joined us there and after waiting about 15-20 minutes, I was pointed to the way back to the surface. Although everything was taken from me except my underwear and flight suit, another quick inspection was made. Then one of soldiers brought my flight boots, but no socks. We started walking as soon as the boots were on my feet.

We were a group of ten plus me; four walked in front of me and six trailed behind our group. After about thirty minutes of brisk walking we came to a base camp where there were a number of soldiers. The first thing they did was to remove my flight suit and boots and then place a blindfold on me. They led me to a tree and tied me to it, and this time the bonding was much tighter. Then they threw a rope over a low limb above me and hitched it to my bindings and attempted to lift me halfway up so I would not be sitting on the ground, but not standing either. It was most uncomfortable, but I was heavy enough that after a few minutes my rear end was on the ground.

A small group gathered and started sporadically throwing dirt clods and small sticks at me. It was their way of saying they didn't like me and my fellow aviators who dropped bombs on them and shot up the countryside with 20-millimeter cannon fire. Several hours later there seemed to be more soldiers arriving and a meal of some type was being served to them, but none for me. Many stopped by to look at me and laugh at my very white skin. I had red hair and probably most of them had never seen a fair-skinned redhead before. There was no formal attempt to question me or provide any food or drink to me. This was not in keeping with our intelligence briefings so I started wondering if that meant anything.

After about three hours in this position, I began to feel something tickling my left side. I moved my head enough to shift the blindfold and much to my horror, I saw a blood trail down my left side and a line of ants vigorously in pursuit of the origin of what would be a nice dinner for them. A centipede tried to interfere with the ants, but the greater number of ants quickly won the contest. I started to try to squirm, so I could sit on some of the ants. All that did was to attract the attention of several soldiers who corrected my behavior with a hit from a stick. When they realized the ants were ganging up on me, they started laughing, but found a shovel and started to beat them back.

A flight of two A-7s flew by and dropped a few five-hundred-pound bombs to see if it might get the Vietnamese to shoot and give away our position. What I remember most was the quiet of the engines fading away and the sound of the bomb fragments bouncing off rocks and leaves that sounded like a heavy rain storm. Several of the soldiers were pointing at the sky and cursing.

Around dusk the routine of the camp started to change. Although still blindfolded I could see out the sides and sometimes down my nose by subtly lifting up my head. The soldiers were getting ready to go underground for the night. Before it was completely dark, a fire was started to prepare dinner and I was untied and led to a semi-bunker that was half below ground and half above with bamboo and leaves on the sides and overhead. I was made to lie on my back on a bamboo rack that would keep me off the ground, but not very high. Then one soldier crawled underneath and cleverly tied my hands and binding to the bamboo so that I could not sit up or move around. This was going to be a long night.

As full night fell upon us, I noticed a symphony of sounds. A few birds, but mostly insects, rodents, and probably wild dogs made music and it wasn't too long before I started to doze off. That lasted until the first night bombing raid hit. It was probably centered about five miles away, but it was loud with extremely bright flashes of light. On one sortie the bombs came close enough to shake the ground and again I thought I heard fragments pelting the jungle like a hard rain. As I tossed and turned, I realized I had to urinate and that I didn't want to wet myself. My jockey shorts may not have been much, but they were still basically white.

By turning on my side I was able to move one hand around more and get ahold of myself; now I could aim the stream away from me. It was a strong flow and made so loud a noise that the youngest soldier guarding me must have thought I was trying to escape because he started pounding a metal iron bar with another smaller bar. The entire camp was wide awake and a small army of soldiers stormed into the little enclosure. They were not happy campers. The result was that I was tied much tighter, and this time they used a type of insulated communication wire to tie my hands behind my back. Then they took a hard, rounded dowel and inserted it in a way so they could twist the entire wire into the tightest of binding. This tie-down with all my weight also on my hands, resulted in some real pain, but I soon lost all feeling and felt a numbness set into my hands. I do not remember sleeping from that point on, but on the hour, every hour, a soldier with a small penlight flashlight checked me and the tie-down. They did not want any more false wakeup alarms.

When the gray of dawn seeped between the bamboo and leaves, the camp came to life. Soon I was being untied and led outside to the tree that was my home yesterday. My hands were swollen and a weird bluish-gray color, but the soldier just kept pointing to the tree. It was an hour or so later that a new soldier, who I believe was an officer, came into the camp and looked closely at me and started mumbling something when he saw my hands behind my back. He called out in a very loud and firm voice and soon the man whom I had pegged as the lead sergeant for this group came trotting up. A discussion followed and I am certain that I heard the word Hanoi mentioned several times. I got the impression that the sergeant didn't want me to be taken away, but this was a disciplined group of the North Vietnamese regular army. Before the officer left the site, I had my blindfold removed and I was untied and led to a place to urinate. I found it a new adventure because my hands were so numb that I had to look down to make sure I had myself in control so I could aim the stream.

There was another commotion among the soldiers and one came forward to me with a bowl of rice and a metal spoon. It was the first food I had had in more than a day. He then handed me a metal cup of hot tea that helped me wash the rice down. Not knowing Vietnamese, but suspecting some knew a little French, I said when finished, "Merci beaucoup." That changed a lot of things. There were four or five excited soldiers speaking to me all at once in French and so fast that there was no way I could follow. When everyone settled down, another soldier pulled out a plastic bag of valuables and proudly showed me a picture of his family at the famous Lotus Pagoda in downtown Hanoi. He was saying in

French that I was the lucky one and I would "allez tout de suite Hanoi" (go right away to Hanoi). Just about then a soldier with a white smock and Red Cross-type of hat arrived. The party again was over.

The medic whistled several times after he repeatedly stuck a small needle in the back of my hands, which didn't get any response from me. The sergeant came over and gave the medic some order and he rose and ran off. Another soldier told me in slow broken French that I would be OK. About thirty minutes later the medic returned with a super-hot bowl of water with something like Epsom salts in it. I soaked my hands for a good half hour, but still had next-to-no feeling. But that didn't matter for I saw a small group of soldiers, maybe six or seven, getting their gear together along with rations of rice to feed them for a trip. They were to be my escort through Laos into North Vietnam, and then north to Hanoi. For them it was to be a short vacation and a visit with family, but for me there was the hope of meeting other American POWs and getting my name out to my wife so she would know I was okay and that I was in Hanoi.

The day was not quite half-over, but we got on the road. At the start, they returned my flight suit and boots, but no socks. We started walking at a pace that seemed fairly measured. These soldiers knew how to pace themselves and that was, hopefully, going to help me keep up. I was glad I had some rice and tea that morning because I needed the energy. We soon were on a foot trail about three feet wide. On both sides the vegetation was thick and the under-leaves were full of leeches and other blood-sucking vermin that seemed to be hanging out just for me. After what seemed like several hours we stopped in a clearing and the soldiers began inspecting each other for leeches. When they found one, they used two pieces of sharpened bamboo as tools to squeeze and remove them. Then one lifted up one leg of my flight suit and—what do you know—there were two of those little devils having lunch on me. He showed me how to remove the leeches and I thanked him. He nodded and smiled, which surprised me.

The afternoon of the first day we reached the first karst ridge (topography formed by soluble rocks such as limestone and gypsum that often result in caves and sinkholes) that was part of the foothills leading up to the peaks of the Truong Son Range, formerly known as the Annamite Range, dividing Laos from Vietnam. There are at least five peaks that reach over eight thousand five hundred feet in this range, but the average height around the 17th Parallel is about seven thousand five hundred feet, but the first ridge lines were much less. About half-way up this first climb, the lead soldier hollered out something and everyone turned around and started climbing back down. The foot trail had steps carved into the hillside, so going down was much like going down a set of stairs, but the heights between steps varied and one had to be careful.

When we reached the bottom of this first ascent, a line of soldiers with families and supplies came into view coming down right at us. It was a wonder to me to see this first group of soldiers on their march to South Vietnam. They had bamboo poles carried by two men with supplies hung in the middle. On one such arrangement there was a large, conical metal cooking pot with at least four or five large bags of rice; in the very middle of the rice was a baby no more than several-months-old, happily swinging back and forth. His eyes were so big and beautiful I couldn't help but smile and, of course, the soldiers noticed and smiled, too. As most of the column reached the bottom, the soldiers of my small group started a conversation and then more gathered around me. They seemed to be surprised by my fair skin, red hair, and blue eyes. Several said the words "Hoa Loa," which I was later to learn could be loosely translated into flaming forge. When they left us they began to chant in a cadence "Vietnam, tong nyet." I learned later that what I heard meant "Vietnam, together again."

When rested and it seem clear to climb, our small group started up the ridge step by step. I noticed our pace was a bit faster than during our first attempt. It was then I first realized that the absence of socks in my flight boots would cause some discomfort. When we reached the top, we stopped to drink some water and rest and I could look out toward the west where I saw mile after mile of rolling hills and rivers draining westward. And that is why they told us that Laos was largely a part of the Mekong Basin. What surprised me was how vast and how wide the vista was.

We pressed on because nightfall would come soon. We descended off that ridge line and into what appeared to be a narrow river valley with a wider trail that kept us away from leech-invested leaves. We stopped at a minor camp site at least an hour before sunset and two of the soldiers took off in search of some other local group. They returned with four other soldiers who looked me over and laughed at my sore feet that now were bleeding a little and growing some bright red blisters. They also had some canned meats for us that were for the next three days of walking. When darkness came, my flight suit was taken away and I was given a ragged old blanket to sleep on the bare ground. My one wrist was tied to the other wrist and the rope was tied to a tree. I was going nowhere that night in my not so white jockey shorts.

Somehow the walking, the fresh air, and the bowl of rice all helped me fall into a deep sleep. It seemed like just after a few minutes when one of the guards awoke me, untied me, and gave me my flight suit and boots. We had compacted rice balls that served as a quick breakfast and a cup of hot tea. We were walking by the gray of dawn's first light and were now definitely on a course and time schedule to make another campsite closer to North Vietnam. At one point on this second day where the valley seemed to get very tight, the guards suddenly stopped and told me to get me to get down. One of the lead soldiers came back and started a routine of shaking wires on the sides of the trail and then moving forward forty or fifty feet, stopping, and then again shaking the wire aligned with the side of the trail. My only thought was this was an area where U.S. aircraft had dropped the magnetically fused bombs and they were trying to make sure they would not become the trigger to set one off. I never knew for sure, but the process slowed our progress. Once through that part of the trail, we picked up the pace and didn't stop as frequently for water or rest. The second night we camped beside a fairly swift moving river at least one hundred to one hundred-fifty feet wide. In the far distance I could hear a waterfall and knew that we probably would be climbing more karst ridges the next day.

The next day started much like the day before, but this time, one of the soldiers checked me for leeches again and removed one that I could not see. It was fat and full of blood. It was on this day five groups going to South Vietnam passed us. Some groups were only about two hundred in size and others` were over five hundred in numbers. I had trouble counting the groups because I didn't want the guards to know I was observing everything. This day we also encountered some local hill tribespeople foraging for food. They had different facial features and spoke some Vietnamese to the soldiers, but used a different language among themselves. I could tell they were trying to tell the soldiers it was too far for us to get to their village. I also observed one of my guards engage in bartering with these hill people for some tubers that looked like wild sweet potatoes, which made for an extra topping that night on our rice bowl dinners.

On the fourth day we came upon a road at least twenty-five to thirty feet wide that went up the side of what appeared to be one of the highest hills. As we went up, the soldiers almost together all stopped and went down on one knee. So I did the same. A few moments later a flight of two U.S. jets screeched overhead doing at least five hundred knots. I have often wondered how they knew those planes were coming our way.

Once the sound of their tailpipes faded into the west, we were up and moving again. The view was spectacular from the side of the mountain, but as we came down the other side, we entered into a wider valley with denser vegetation. And the road seemed to narrow the more we progressed. Soon we were back to a narrow foot trail, but it seemed to have wider sides, so we were not constantly scrapping against the plants and all their bounty.

That night I noticed the soldiers were counting rice balls, but not making any more. I thought maybe by tomorrow we might get to some place more permanent.

The next day started like all the others until we came to what appeared to be a small hamlet. The houses were on stilts and all located under tall trees, some of which I believe may have been teak trees. The tall trees and shrubs were so thick that only very mottled beams of sunlight came thought the canopy. It was here that I once again became the center of attention as both men and women closely inspected my hair and noticed my whiskers that had started to show through in a deep-red natural color. Now that really got all the women's attention. Then I suddenly jumped. It felt like a bee had stung my toe. I looked down and found a small boy about four-years-old at most, looking in awe at the fine white hair growing out of the top of my large toe. When everyone saw me jump, the boy suddenly moved and a large united roar of laughter broke the strain. It was obviously the first time this young boy had seen a Westerner and for most, the first time they had seen such a fair, a redheaded American.

I soon learned of another tradition in Laos. Several of the young girls, probably teenagers, took to throwing stones at me when the soldiers weren't looking. They were not throwing them hard, so I thought they were just trying to get my attention. But again I was later to learn that the way a young Laotian girl lets a man know she is interested in him is by throwing a stone at him. One of the guards in pantomime later made that very clear to me. That night as they took my flight suit away and made ready to tie me to a tree, one of the girls brought a fairly new, clean burlap bag for me to put under me while on the ground. That bag made the ground not so cold and allowed me to fashion the ragged blanket to cover most of my bare skin. Temperatures at night were dipping into the mid-40s, so keeping a bit warmer at night was a help. It was during this time I realized that I was developing a rash and sores in my groin area from not bathing. So that night I did my best at pantomime to see if they would let me wash, and they led me to a stream where I took my first and only full bath on the road to Hanoi.

On the sixth day of walking, the trail started to widen and I detected the faint smell of diesel fumes. We started passing many more groups going to the multiple foot trails that spread out to the west and then south. In what must have been only an hour, we approached the official border of North Vietnam. There were no welcome signs, no flashing lights, and no inspection station, but there was about a mile-long line of trucks in various stages of being off-loaded and supplies being organized into groups. I witnessed about two-hundred soldiers approach one mountain of supplies and start to load them onto their bamboo poles with two men to one pole. It was an ongoing process and no one seemed to care that I was watching the operation. My only thought was that it was too bad the folks talking peace in Paris could not get "film at eleven" of this operation.

Once inside North Vietnam, our small group was directed to a spot where we went through some type of registration process. A long discussion went back and forth between the leader of our group and a much older man wearing a faded Army uniform. I later was to learn he had officer insignia on his shoulders. We then walked a good half hour to a rather large encampment that had huts in some type of arrangement by units. I was taken to a small hut attached to the larger hut that my group would sleep in. I could tell from the faces and the actions that my group of soldiers was relaxing a little, but they were also upset. It turned out that we would have to wait here for a few days to get transportation by jeep to meet up with the minibus Hanoi was sending to pick me up. So these days got boring. They didn't let me go far, and I was not allowed to bath as the river was too far and had a strong flow at that time. I did get to take a large metal can of warm water and a rag to wipe myself off on the third day, and I really needed that because I had started to react to the food and had a series of bouts with explosive diarrhea. The leaves were plentiful for wiping, but not very effective. Nothing could have been better at this point in time than a little soap and water, and at least I now had half of that treatment.

After about four days at this base camp, two jeeps arrived for our group. I was placed in the rear seat of the first jeep and the others in no particular order all piled in. I could tell from the banter that they were all eager to get home to see their families after I had been dropped off in Hanoi. But Hanoi, by my calculation, was a long way off. We drove for several hours out of the mountains on switchbacks and rugged dirt and stone road surfaces. When we passed several high points we saw other soldiers digging and leveling land for anti-aircraft emplacements or surface-to-air missile sites. The talk in the Western media was about the peace process, but the actions in the Trường Son were all about the next phase of war and the American bombs that would surely come with those battles.

Once out of the mountains we stopped at an official army post of some kind. I was blindfolded and taken inside to a hut made of cinderblocks with a tile floor. It had several windows covered by wooden bamboo screens that tilted outward and gave some ventilation to the small space. There was a rice mat on the floor with one blanket that would augment my ragged blanket and burlap bag, but on this night only my boots were taken away and I was able to sleep in my flight suit. I had a small plate of some type of canned fish in oil and a bowl of hot steamed rice. It made for a better night's sleep, but I awoke several times because of the cold night air.

The next morning my flight boots arrived and I was allowed to use a latrine and quickly threw cold water on myself. I noticed that my flight suit had started to smell like feces, so I washed it as well as I could, which improved it a lot—and it didn't take long for my body heat to dry it out—but it did result in my starting to shiver again. One of the soldiers saw that and brought me some strong hot tea in a tin cup. Then I was taken to a picnic-type table and given bacon, eggs, and a small loaf of French bread. This was a very good breakfast and I suspected they had nothing else to give me, because the soldiers had used up all the rice balls and were all eating the same food, but in much larger portions.

After breakfast, I was blindfolded and led to a mini bus. There were three steps up from the rear that were hard to mount. So they took off my blindfold to let me see the handles and pull myself up into the rear passenger seats. There were about eight rows of seats, and the front-left row had a dark green plastic sheet arranged like a booth, so no one could see in or out. That was going to my seat and means of transportation for a few days. It didn't take me long to find that the rivet work around the windows was quite rough and I punched a hole in the plastic that left the top portion intact. This way I could lift the bottom like a flap to look out and then quickly let go so the flap would drop down and the soldiers would not know what I had done. It worked like a charm all the way to Hanoi.

When we were on the road again I began to smell the familiar salt air of the ocean. It was a cold, gray morning where the clouds hung low and a foggy mist shrouded the coast. Around mid-morning we stopped and most of the soldiers took off. One soldier brought me an orange and motioned for me to keep very quiet by placing his finger over his lips. I looked beyond him as he held up the main opening and saw the soldiers were splashing in a saltwater bay not far from the end of the truck. It was a great break from a long and arduous journey for them, and I enjoyed a fresh, juicy orange. I was curious as to where we were, but didn't want to look out and get caught or draw attention to myself. I sensed that this was a small side trip not authorized by higher authorities in Hanoi.

The morning dampness started me shivering again, and when I looked at my shriveled privates, I saw at least a dozen sores oozing lymph and puss. I needed some type of medical attention and worried that it might be something besides impetigo. The brown crusts and itching had me convinced it was some other type of dreaded disease. I started to think of God and if I was forsaken here. Would I ever return and see my wife again? Would I die of some disease? With all this on my mind, I heard the soldier guarding me talking to someone at the rear of the truck, so I took that moment to look out in the other direction to see if I could figure out where we were.

In the distance there were mountains with many overlapping ridge lines, the Truong Son, and closer to the truck was one solitary hill that had been recently bombed. At the top of this hill three trees were still standing and the one in the middle was just a bit higher than the other two. As I gazed at this sight, in shivering chills, the sun suddenly burst through the layers of clouds and created a stream of rays that looked like a road to heaven. My chill was suddenly gone and I felt a soft warm glow through the glass of the window. Somehow I knew I was not alone. I remembered my sacred studies from Saint Peter's where I had spent four years of high school and knew right then that no matter what suffering or torture may lie ahead for me, Christ endured far more on the cross to save us all. I also thought to myself that I was not the first from my family to fall behind the fight and that I would survive to meet my love—my wife—once again.

There on the road to Hanoi, with water buffalo pulling carts, dozens of bicycles loaded like pack mules and many people walking in both directions, I was in the midst of a main supply route, but the one thing my eyes focused on was the sun shining through the clouds to light up that one tree girded on each side by a shorter tree. I felt warm all over and actually started to relax. With all the traffic, all the soldiers, and all the dangers surrounding us, one stream of light on one tree on a hill gave one man a new hope, a new light, and a new life.

As the soldiers returned to dry off and get back into their uniforms, more oranges were given out and I could smell and hear them eating the sweet, fresh fruit. The remains of my orange peel were long ago disposed of by the one soldier left to guard me, and I wondered why no other soldier offered me an orange. This reminded me that I was still the enemy.

We reached our next stop just before sunset. Before complete darkness, I was still inside the minibus and given a plate of canned meat and a bowl of hot rice, which was much too oily and tasted almost sweet. A bucket was brought into the truck and left in front. Then the soldiers brought in three boards about eight feet long and placed them on the top rungs of the seats to make a level bed—my bed for the night. More plastic was used to hide me from easy viewing from outside. Once I was on the boards, I heard a crowd approaching and they did not sound happy. Two soldiers came inside and issued some quick orders to the one guarding me.

Chanting started outside and soldiers started shouting orders. This had been an area heavily bombed by American naval aircraft and I was one of the enemy. I think they wanted to punish me right there. The bus started to move up and down as the people outside were trying to rock it back and forth, but it was too heavy to tip over. As I turned to peek outside, a small boy on the roof of the minibus stuck a stick into the one-inch crack of the open window and caught me right in the eye. I recoiled in pain and tried to move more to the center of the bus. The soldier inside then got me off the boards and told me to lie on the floor between the row of seats. The crowd seemed to be getting louder, and one voice keep leading them in chants I could not clearly make out. Then a sudden staccato burst from an AK-47 stopped all the shouting. It was very loud and very close. It was then I heard all the other soldiers in my group getting into the truck with angry words back and forth. The truck started up and we were on the road again.

Early in the evening we soon came to a road stop. It was some type of security checkpoint and it took some discussion and checking to let us through. I noticed that our direction was turning back toward the mountains and that we were going more west than north. We traveled until what must have been about midnight. When we stopped, there was a discussion with what turned out to be an inn keeper. He actually came into the back of the truck to look at me and then nodded and said, "Okay." Then he started to make several points to the lead soldiers who simply nodded as he laid out his obvious plan. About a half -hour passed and I was summoned with no blindfold to what looked like a family dining room. There was a very large, square table that was designed to be used by sitting on the floor. Several soldiers were already there and squatting like they did around a campfire in the jungle.

I noticed over the mantel of the fireplace there was a large Roman Catholic cross. On one side there was a well-known portrait of Ho Chi Minh, and on the other side, a picture of Vladimir Lenin. To one end of the mantel was a small statue of the Virgin Mary with Baby Jesus and to the other end, a small statue of a Vietnamese soldier with his arm raised with a fist. I thought this added new meaning to the phrase "mixed blessings."

We were first fed a small bowl of fish soup and then a main course of some type of crispy fried fish with rice and vegetables. The meal closed with a small cup of hot green tea and a small round orange cookie. I ate exactly what all the soldiers ate and everyone seemed amused that I ate everything, including the soft bones of the fish. I had been told in survival school that bone marrow and fish heads were actually high in protein and vitamins and that we should eat everything we could to keep our strength up. I was then led to a side hut attached to the main house where I and two other soldiers slept that night on raised bamboo racks that kept us off the floor. I slept well.

The next day was a day of starting and stopping. We had to get through a number of security checkpoints and several times we seemed to have gone the wrong way and reversed course to get back on track. I think the altercation with the villagers and turn toward an inland route took us farther from the shores of the Tonkin Gulf into an area where we had not been programmed to go. But to the soldiers' and drivers' credit, they kept at it and were obviously getting us closer to Hanoi. That night I was allowed to sleep in my flight suit, but inside the truck on the boards. It was not so comfortable, but it was better than another poke in the eye. The one soldier who was always assigned to guard me was very concerned about my eye. It was obviously very swollen and I could barely see out of it, so I just tried to keep it closed and rest it. I later learned that was as good as I could have done under the conditions.

On the morning of December 7, 1969, the day hardly broke at all. It was a damp, dark dawn and the sky was gently weeping. I was dressed in just flight suit and flight boots and my soiled jockey shorts were long gone. On this day they made a show of tying my hands together and then to the seat. It took me a few minutes to get one hand free so I could continue to look out. We were definitely on the outskirts of Hanoi. Just the sound and smells of the city told me this was a major population center and the guards all became excited and were pointing out the sights to each other.

The rain seemed to be getting heavier and so was my heart. I had read the debriefing of former POW LTJG David Matheny and knew that my initial days in the Hanoi Hilton would be filled with interrogations.[16] I also had learned in the naval air training for POW survival that it was better to evade and diffuse answers than to be arrogant in refusing to speak. I felt the line of questions for me would be directed at classified materials, such as the capabilities and ranges of the new F-4J Phantom weapon systems and in the individuals of my squadron. I also had observed a piece of my plane that had the squadron insignia on it, so I knew from the start that they would know I was a Puking Dog. I was trying to prepare myself for the ordeal ahead. That made the ride seem longer and harder.

In the late afternoon the truck stopped for a few minutes. All I could see on my side of the truck was a large wall, but couldn't quite see the top of it. I also could hear hissing and popping sounds. After about a half-hour the truck started up and we did something of a K-turn to reverse our direction. While making this move, I observed the wall to be about eighteen to twenty feet in height with concertina wire and bare wire on the top. The very

16 Stuart I. Rochester and Frederick T. Kiley, *Honor Bound: The History of American Prisoners of War in Southeast Asia, 1961-1973* (Annapolis: Naval Institute Press, 1998), 366-68.

top of the wall seemed to sparkle and glisten under the spot lights in the drizzling rain and heavy fog. Then I realized it was broken glass embedded into its surface.

We had to turn around again and finally came to a stop before what looked like two garage doors that swung out. I cocked my head lower to look up again and noticed three strands of electric wiring strung about two feet below the top wires that produced the hissing I was still hearing. As several drops of rain fell between the electric wires, there was an arch and zap as the current flowed.

I was sure I had arrived at Hoa Lo prison—the infamous Hanoi Hilton—and yet no one seemed eager to take me inside. After about an hour, one of the two garage doors squeaked and squealed open. (I bet they had not been able to get any WD-40 in Hanoi for a few years.) As I looked out my little flap, I saw what looked like a very old man who had a beard at least twenty inches long. He seemed to be in charge and was asking the lead soldier a number of questions.

Hanoi Hilton

CHAPTER 6

ADJUSTING TO PRISON

It was Pearl Harbor Day and all I could think of was that the war was about to land on me in a very up-close and personal way.

"Good evening and welcome to the Democratic People's Republic of Vietnam. You are nothing but a vicious war criminal, but if you show good attitude, you will receive the humane and lenient treatment of the Vietnamese people. You must obey all camp regulations or else you will be punished severely. You must bow when meeting all Vietnamese people. You must answer all questions put to you. Violations of any of these rules will result in your being punished immediately. You understand?"

There was something very cold and sinister in his voice when he told me they could just as easily put my legs into stocks and throw ice water on me to clean me up—because that's exactly what he told me. I think he was hoping I would behave in such a way as to make it appear I had asked for mistreatment.

I knew this was the time to just keep it short and nodded my headed, still blindfolded, and said as politely as possible, "Yes, sir." That seemed to please all present, and so he ordered the guards to get supplies.

"You will receive two blankets to keep you warm at night and many other items to make you more comfortable," he said. "But first you must be taken to bathhouse to be completely cleaned off, because you stink very much."

71

I was hoping for some hot water and soap. I got only water that must have been about forty degrees. I tried to scrub as hard as I could with the remains of some type of brown pumice that had been left there. One of the soldiers noticed my sores and went out to tell someone. I was handed a towel about four feet long and two feet wide to dry off and given what looked like maroon and gray stripped boxer shorts and a T-shirt. Then there were the pajama-like pants with a drawstring and a loose-fitting top with strings instead of buttons to close the front. My flight boots were replaced with sandals made from old tires. I noticed right away there were just two front straps and no straps on the rear like the sandals the soldiers had, so these flip-flops were not going to go very fast or very far on an escape trek. But they would certainly do for the Hanoi Hilton.

I was blindfolded again and led down a long corridor through what seemed to be outdoors and into another building. Then there were more turns and outdoors again until I was stopped and my blindfold removed. I stood before a door with five steps leading up. It led to a single room about ten feet long and seven feet wide. I was taken into the room, which contained two sawhorses with a bamboo rack as a bed frame. There was one thin, soiled, woven-reed mat on the bed. One of the guards made a big deal of putting what looked like a brand new mat over the old one. The other guard had the promised supplies—two blankets, mosquito net, tooth brush, toothpaste, bar of soap (This really was a Hilton!), supply of folded brown coarse paper that was their version of toilet paper, change of shorts and T-shirt, and a second pair of pajama pants and shirt. I must not have paid too much attention to where I was supposed to put all this stuff, because one guard stayed behind and in pantomime tried to show me where to stow things. I soon learned that when the night got quiet, the rats would come to visit and soap was like a meat course and toothpaste their dessert. Luckily, a tea caddy basket kept the tea warm and protected some things from the rats.

What I missed and was desperately looking for was where the other American prisoners might be.

Although darkness was fast descending, a single lightbulb hung by a wire in the center of the room; it would stay on all night. They brought me a bowl of thin soup with a side plate of canned meat and a little half-loaf of French bread. The weak tea made it all seem like a nice reception. Later the guard helped me set up my mosquito net and showed me how to get into it without pulling it down. It was another cold night. However, what was on my mind was the old man with a sinister voice and continual threats. It was very quiet and I could hear my heart beating at a very fast pace. It seemed like a few hours went by before I could go to sleep. I heard a bell sound in the distance and counted ten bells, so it was ten o'clock at night. The sounds of the city outside the walls seemed to be getting very quiet, too.

I was awakened the next day by the sound of a metal pipe hitting a piece of iron bar. Then I heard speakers off in the distance and what sounded like someone leading morning exercises. The more I listened, I realized it was loud speakers from outside the prison and the voice kept repeating what sounded like, "Mot! Hi! Ba! Bong!" Not knowing the routine, I rolled over and tried to go back to sleep. That lasted all of about twenty minutes. A new guard opened the cell door and started screaming at me in Vietnamese. I had no idea what he was telling me, but tried to placate him by jumping out of bed and giving him a big bow. It worked and he seemed a bit confused himself, but another guard came along to see what was going on and he must have told him I was the new prisoner. The two guards started smiling and said, "Okay. Okay!"

Because of President Lyndon Johnson's successive, unilateral, and increasing restrictions on American bombing of North Vietnam, there had been no new prisoners arrive in Hanoi since February 1968, so I was the newest American in town. I quickly learned that when the morning gong sounds, I must get up, fold up my mosquito net and blankets, and sit on my bed at attention. I think the last part was an add-on from the old days because I usually started walking and doing some exercises and no guards ever corrected me.

After a morning breakfast of a half-loaf of French bread, a little sugar on a metal plate, and a new, hot teapot, I was led from my cell blindfolded and taken to another part of the prison where I was to wash, change into clean clothes, and then wash by hand the clothes from yesterday. I was just finishing up when another guard arrived with a chair, comb, and clippers to cut my hair. The clippers were hand-powered and it took him forever to cut my hair. My red hair grows quickly and was, at that point, a very thick head of hair. Then I was handed a razor and a small mirror and told to shave. That was difficult, because it was next to impossible to get the soap to foam up. I did my best and only had a few cuts when I was finished. Then it was back to one more rinse down and into fresh clothes. I was taken back to my cell area with no blindfold and saw that the bathrooms were in a central two-story array of offices and living spaces. Behind one was a long corridor that led to a small courtyard surrounded on three sides by more two-story structures. There was a single-story building next to my cell with a metal wire strung from it to my cell for hanging wet clothes. Once my clothes were on the line, it was back inside.

I was left almost all day with nothing to do, but was visited by what turned out to be an officer who basically just asked how I was. I told him I had a headache, which was true, and a rash on my groin. About an hour later another soldier sporting a white cap with a red cross showed up. I guessed he was the designated medic for the American POWs. He gave me two aspirin and had me sit on the steps to my cell where he took my pulse. He asked the guard several questions and they seemed to go back and forth. He said something else and went off. Later that afternoon after a light lunch of soup and bread, a much older man arrived with a blood pressure cuff and had me lie on my bed while he took my blood pressure. He looked very worried and said something to the guard, who quickly started to deny or protest something.

Late that afternoon I was taken back with no blindfold to the front shed and I thought I heard some coughing to my left and mentally marked this as a likely spot where other American prisoners might be living or working.

I was taken to a room where there were three officers behind a table and a single stool in front of them. I thought this might be a test, so I bowed very slowly and that seemed to please them. When we went through POW training in the navy we were taught to try to adapt to the captor's rules and customs. Bowing in the Far East goes back to the beginning of time, so it didn't seem like a big deal; it was just part of their culture. But I also sensed it was their way of trying to impose their will and political position on us and that was a very different condition.

The first question, which became a never-ending question while I was in captivity, was "How are you?" I told them I might need some medicine for my groin where I had a rash. That might have been a mistake, because when I was finally returned to my cell the medic returned with a bottle of iodine. He soaked a few cotton squabs and gave them to me. I tried it and almost screamed out loud in pain. From then on, it was only soap and water for that spot and lots of prayers for a speedy and complete recovery.

The senior officer of this small group spoke no English and had to rely on the youngest one to translate. I could tell the older officer had some experience in doing this and also noted that his left eye seemed to stray and was not focusing properly. I was later to learn that he was the officer in charge of the POW prison whom the Americans had named Dead Eye. He asked what squadron did I fly with, and what ship did I fly off of. Since I knew they already had this information, I simply told them the squadron and the ship. They all nodded their heads. Just like the three stooges, I thought.

Then the interpreter took a sheet of lined white paper and told me to write down the name of all the pilots in my squadron. I tried to resist by saying that I was bound only to give my name, rank, service number, and date of birth. This didn't surprise them and the senior one started in with a long spiel that no interpreter could keep up with. Then the younger officer looked down and started reading in English some official rebuttal to the Geneva Convention saying that we American air pirates were all war criminals, and that North Vietnam had not signed the convention and, therefore, was not bound by it. Being a history major and having some more details, I just couldn't resist citing an incorrect article number that supposedly said all nations, whether signatories or not, were bound by the definitions and treatment of prisoners of war. It took him a little time to translate and I could tell right away that the senior officer was getting agitated and aroused. But he just nodded and said something to the interpreter who told me I was taught too well and to go back to my cell and think more clearly about "showing a good attitude."

The second day of questioning started out very general and with them probing me to accurately determine how long ago I had left a college campus. I had graduated in 1967 from Union College in Schenectady, New York and so I was the most recent American by far whom they had in Hanoi who could speak to how the Vietnam War was impacting college students. But in reality, the year 1967 was closer to 1964 or to 1963 than it was to 1968 in attitudes toward the war. I, of course, made no mention of that and was fairly consistent in downplaying the size and impact of college unrest. But they were relentless and very demanding in trying to get anything. Finally, I told them of the only incident I had witnessed at Union College when eight students tried to interrupt the Air Force ROTC awards ceremony. One ROTC student's father stood up outraged, walked around the audience, and punched the lead protester squarely in the nose. And that was the end of the protest, I assured them. They looked at me very strangely and waited for at least a minute. It was like I had just let go the most silent and most malodorous flatus ever passed and they couldn't believe it was me. It earned me a quick trip back to my cell and another lunch of the same soup from yesterday with a half-loaf of French bread. When the bread was dipped into the thin soup it only tasted half as bad and I ate it all because I was very hungry and I wanted to keep my strength up.

On the third day of questioning an entirely new team of interrogators arrived. The lead two officers I had not seen before and would never see again. I think they were from headquarters and were very squared away. Their command of English was excellent and they didn't waste time with lectures of a political nature. They were "all military" and told me from the outset that they knew I was lying about what type aircraft I flew in. I played a little dumb and admitted I had not meant an old F-4, but I had indeed meant the F-4 Phantom. They told me that they had observed and recorded these new F-4s and they were not the same. The older officer let slip that they had read *Aviation Week* and *Space Technology* about the new F-4J Phantom. I nodded and said that was the one I flew in. I was again given paper and pencil and told to write notes on what the differences were. I wrote down a lot of publicly available types of data, such as bigger tires, stronger landing gear, a heavier arresting hook for carrier landings, and larger fuel cell capacity. When I threw in ground avoidance radar they jumped up and down and said something like, "that's it." The radios were improved some, but I told them the radios were much more reliable and had better tone controls so we could hear better. I said and wrote nothing about the new pulse-Doppler radar and weapon systems, which is what they had been obviously recording and analyzing. They probably knew more at their headquarters on that than I did.

The morning must have been a waste for them because they seemed to know the answers before they asked me questions. But the afternoon turned into a true war with me fighting back against questions about the types of information such as various ordnance, typical load-outs, and nuclear capabilities. My first and best line of diffusing these types of questions was that I was just a junior-grade lieutenant and was not given that detailed type of information. I insisted that the Phantom was not capable of dropping nuclear bombs and so I knew nothing. They kept trying to ask me how many nuclear bombs were on the *USS Constellation* and I told them I had no idea. But they asked again and again how many, so I told them that there might be some nuclear bombs on board because Marines with loaded M-16s would stand guard during some of the exercises in two of the areas marked as nuclear ordnance magazines. This answer was partly true, but mostly false, as I never really witnessed any kind of exercise on the *Connie* except what we had prepared and conducted off of Yankee Station. It all seemed like they just needed to take something back to their bosses that confirmed aircraft carriers were indeed carrying nuclear bombs off their coast.

When the day was done, I was more tired than I realized. I guess it was the constant battle to not give them classified material, which I tried to stick to, and to reformulate names to protect my shipmates. One of our pilots was actually named Whitehouse, so I changed his name to Blackhorse so I would remember it later. In other cases, I just changed the first initial of the last name to something still sensible like Marris instead of the real name, Harris. I had heard that the Vietnamese officers knew first-hand the names of the 1967 Green Bay Packers, especially Bart Starr, so using the Packers starting lineup would never fly as real names for any of my squadron mates.

———————————— ★ ————————————

For the next few days I was taken back to the original prison staff for attitude and personal history-type questions. I think some of this was just to get me to talk and to determine what kind of person I was. Plus, they displayed a genuine interest in what life was like in our country. They found it difficult to believe that we could travel anywhere in the nation without a travel permit or license. It took me several days to understand that the Vietnamese needed some kind of passport or travel permit to go from one part of their country to another, which explained some of what I heard on my way north to Hanoi.

The subjects of church and religion came up. They asked if I believed in Christmas. I had to smile and tell them I believed in Jesus Christ as my Savior and I knew He was with me on my journey. Now that really intrigued them and the oldest one, through the interpreter, asked if I would like to go to church this Christmas. In all the intelligence briefings and material we were told to do anything to get to a church service because that would get our names out. I was getting more and more lonely with each passing day. The fact that Laura might not know I was alive or she might think I was still in Laos—all this and more—troubled me. And I could not let them know I was that worried, so I played it as cool as possible and said that I would be very grateful to have the opportunity to go to the Christmas Mass.

Then they sprung the Christmas Choir question on me.

Could I sing? Did I ever sing in a choir? (I didn't tell them that it took me three years to finally pass an audition and make it into the Singing Peers Glee Club at Saint Peter's High School.) I told them I had sung in a very famous choir. Every year this glee club would travel by Greyhound charter bus down the East Coast and stop each night to perform a concert and/or evening service at an Episcopal church. The students were paired up and sent to stay at different homes to save on expenses, and to show people from New York to Florida that Saint Peter's students were polite, smart, and well-educated. We went all the way to Vera Beach and Fort Lauderdale.

The senior officer who spoke little or no English was confused by now, and so the interpreter disappeared for about ten minutes to find a *Rand McNally Atlas* of the United States. I literally wasted almost a whole day telling them about my senior-year glee club trip from Saint Peter's to Florida and how we sang both religious and Broadway show tunes. The senior officer wanted to hear, so I gave him a version of "There is Nothin' Like a Dame" from *South Pacific*. He smiled, laughed, and slapped his knee several times, so I think I sold him on my being a good candidate for the Christmas Choir that year.

Back in my little cell I was getting more and more concerned about my rash that had gone down somewhat, but was still present, and also about what seemed like migraine headaches. Each day I was taken to the front area and led into what looked like a cellblock with a latrine and several small bathing areas. I got to dump my bucket toilet, wash myself, and wash one set of clothes. And every three or four days I got to shave with what looked like a Gillette two-sided safety razor from World War II. The blades were usually very dull because others had already used them. So, I thought there must be other American POWs nearby, but the door was always locked and the guard was never far away. I would have to wait my time and hope that the Christmas Choir option would work out.

I was having trouble remembering the days of the weeks and dates at this point in time, so I recreated the calendar from December 7 on and started it on a Sunday, because I had remembered seeing and hearing church bells as we entered the city and thought it confirmed that I had arrived on a Sunday. This turned out to be correct and led me to see the differences between the Monday through Saturday routines and how things worked a bit differently on Sunday. The second Sunday in Hanoi, December 14, I had a different guard open my cell and lead me to the washing room area in the head shed part of the Hanoi Hilton. I learned later that the American POWs had dubbed this area "Heartbreak" because when POWs were being tortured, they were often kept here. On this particular day I finished washing a bit faster than I normally did and went to the closed door to wait. But when I hit the door, it sprang open. The guard had failed to put the crossbar on the outside brackets.

When I stepped through the doorway, a guard accompanying another American was approaching. He started yelling wildly at me, so I yelled out my name and rank. The other prisoner was about six feet two inches and very thin. The skin on his face was sallow and he had at least a week's growth of whiskers. His eyes stretched wide in terror. When I said my name to him from about ten feet away, he turned around and put his face against the wall and looked the other way. By this time the guard was pushing me back into the washroom and slamming the door shut. I heard him slam the crossbar in, so I knew I was locked up, but I peeked through a crack to see if I could see or hear more. I heard and saw very little. The other prisoner's expression and thinness haunted me for many nights and I prayed he would be all right. I learned latter that CAG James Stockdale thought this could have been Air Force Lt. Col. Ron Storz, who had been held at a special prison dubbed "Alcatraz" with the CAG Stockdale and nine other American POWs who were all severely punished for an escape attempt or for leading other POWs in resisting the Communists' efforts to extract propaganda from them. Lt. Col. Storz died while in captivity in 1970.

I was kept in the locked washroom for at least a half-hour and then led back to my cell. I wasn't served breakfast and instead was brought a bowl of sweet, soupy rice about mid-morning. The next time my door was opened was in the late afternoon when I was given the evening meal that was just like the one the day before—variety was not a big thing here and what we ate probably depended on what was in season.

The following day I was again taken to the same room and the same soldier who had been meeting with me the week before. This time he didn't seem happy and asked me directly, "What you do?" I acted a bit confused and wanted him to be more specific. I had been entertaining myself by mentally replaying the 1950 World Series, only this time the series went to game seven and the Philadelphia Phillies, with Robin Roberts pitching, won the game and the series. Mel Allen, the Voice of the Yankees, kept saying, "How about that." None of this made any sense to the interrogator so he said; "You try to speak to other prisoner."

Now there was no getting around that I did say my name, so I looked the soldier right in the eye and told him I simply said my name and the other one never said a word. He actually thought about what I said and replied, "Okay, but you must practice singing for Christmas Choir." This took me by surprise, because whenever a guard heard me verbalizing my play-by-play broadcasts, they would either bang on the door or tell me to keep quiet. Now this officer was telling me to practice singing. He saw my confusion and told me that in the afternoon I would come back and try to sing along with last year's choir. He told me to practice "Shylent Night" and "Oh, Holy Night."

When I returned in the afternoon the camp officer in charge (Dead Eye), was present and of course, had to ask, "How are you?" I said the two aspirins each morning had helped my headaches. Then he said something to the younger officer, who told me I had very high blood pressure and that it was probably causing my headaches. He said I must learn not to worry. I had had several blood pressure readings and no matter who used the cuff, they meticulously wrote the results in a little book, but never showed me anything. At times I could hear my heart pounding, but I had no good way to measure short periods of time and I couldn't even guess what my pulse had been, let alone my blood pressure. The rash was almost gone and the daily soaking of both my hands up to my mid-forearms had been helping to heal the wire mark scars on my wrists from when I was first captured in Laos, and the feeling was slowly coming back in my fingers. So all in all, I had nothing to complain about.

He then told me in very short sentences that I had to work very hard to be selected as a member of the Christmas Choir; I had to practice and show a very good attitude. The younger officer would assist me and set up a time for a jury to come and listen to me sing. All I could think of was that I had to give it my very best shot and get my name out for Laura. She had to know I was all right.

I was returned to my cell fairly early and went to work trying to remember all the verses and words to both songs, but soon learned that the first verse was what they would ask me to sing. The next day I was taken to another room very close by, but smaller. It seemed to be divided in half and on the table was a very old reel-to-reel tape recorder. The young officer explained that he would play a tape of the War Criminal Choir from last year and I was to sing along as best I could. He arose and very carefully made sure the machine was set and then told me to stand up. He explained the choir "must always stand to sing louder and better." The first song was "Silent Night." The choir had a simple guitar accompaniment—and half of the choir sounded a bit flat—so I jumped right into the project and gave it my best shot. Then it was time for "Oh, Holy Night." He asked to listen first so he could hear the song without my singing. He gave me a pen and paper so I could write down all the words. When the choir reached the refrain of "fall on your knees," the voices seemed strained and in pain. This was not what I had expected and my face probably winced in pain. Then the officer had the gall to smile and say, "The machine is not so good and the choir sounded much better last year."

During the next few days this routine was repeated again and again and there were only two Christmas songs they wished me to sing. Near the end of the week I was told just before going back to my cell that the next day the jury would come to hear me sing and I must do my best; I said I'd be ready. To prepare, I had taken to reversing my pajama tops and bottoms and inserting them between the two rice mats of my bed. In this way my weight would press a crease in both the tops and bottoms so I would look like a squared-away sailor. Little did I know then that no one would actually see me.

I was taken to the same room the next day and left there for some time with the old reel-to-reel tape machine with the music I had been singing along with. Finally, with much fanfare, the officer entered and said the jury would be ready in a few minutes and I should stand and get ready. He went back out and I heard several voices, but saw nothing. The officer reappeared very eager to get started and that's what we did. After one song, he disappeared and returned about five minutes later. He carefully explained that it was hard to hear and they were not allowed at this time to see me. He wanted me to sing much louder and more clearly.

I took up the challenge so they could hear me for sure this time. I sang as loud as I could and with a lot of spirit. This was going to be how I got my name out to Laura and I wanted to make sure others in the choir would hear me. After "Silent Night" it was time for me to do the solo and the chorus part of "Oh, Holy Night." I had relearned all the words and had them down pat, but the high parts in the chorus of this carol were really written for a first tenor and my voice was lower at second tenor. I told myself I had to try harder and I did. The officer came back and told me to wait a few minutes. Well, a few minutes turned into over an hour, so I got to moving around and trying to peek out into the main courtyard. There was some activity, but no sighting of another American POW. I had noted that the second room we came through had a table and several chairs around it. I guessed the jury must have been very old and maybe had a little tea while they listened to me. When the officer returned, he actually thanked me and told me a guard would soon take me back to my cell. And then he did something very strange. He looked really close at the crease in my jumper top and my pants. He tried to ask me how I did this. I didn't know what to say and so was quiet for a change. Then the guard appeared and it was back to my cell. I sensed the officer didn't want the guard to know what he had asked me, so I left it alone.

It was now Thursday, December 19, less than a week before Christmas. I was getting excited about going to a Christmas Eventide Mass and seeing other American POWs. Little did I know the plan was much different for me because I had been captured in Laos. The next two days I was kept in my cell except to wash and dump my bucket each morning. On Monday, I was again kept in my cell all day. I was starting to get worried, but I had planned my pajama tops and bottoms so that I would have the maroon and gray stripes clean for the night before Christmas and all Christmas Day with nice creases in the sleeves and pants.

On Tuesday, December 23, I was blindfolded and taken to another part of the prison where the officer in charge and several others were gathered. I was told that I should sing for them here and I did my first verse of "Silent Night" and it was clear from their facial expressions and body language that they were very impressed. The officer who worked with me was particularly all smiles and again thanked me for working so hard. I was then told that I should be prepared to leave my cell the next evening. I was going to church, I thought.

I waited and paced all the next day. I actually started counting the ten-foot and twenty-foot measurements as one lap and tracked my laps. I walked a little more than ten miles that day because I was very excited to go to church. Just around dark, a group of four soldiers and an officer gathered outside my cell door. When they opened it, they told me to bring everything, including the rice mats, blankets, and tea pot. Several helped gather the stuff together and then I was blindfolded. We went a slightly different way and turned left at the spot where I had heard coughing the week before. We made more turns before finally stopping and my blindfold being removed. I found myself in a fairly large courtyard with what looked like a line of lower wash stalls with overhead coverings that divided the courtyard roughly by one-third and two-thirds, with the larger part on my side. Then all my things were put by a door and I was ushered into the Christmas room.

It was a slightly larger room with poster-size Christmas artwork and a table with five officers sitting behind it. Dead Eye, the officer in charge, was sitting in the middle and was obviously very pleased with the room and the proceedings. One of the posters had a picture of Santa Claus leaning forward with what looked at first like a bowling ball. The caption read, "This Christmas have a ball." Then I saw the fuse, very small but lit, and started to laugh. The commander asked the interpreter to ask what was so funny. I didn't want to get anyone in trouble and wondered if there was any good answer. All eyes were on me. I replied, "This room and all the pictures remind me of home and I am happy there is some joy here." Now that was a winning ticket. I was then asked to sing "Oh, Holy Night" a cappella.

I wasn't sure, but I thought this would at least be a time to get heard by other Americans who might be close by and so I gave it my best. When I got to the chorus part of "Fall on your knees, oh, hear the angels' voices," I sensed a slight disturbance at the doorway and saw an American who was being pushed back into the room. He had gray hair and dark bags under both eyes. I stopped singing, smiled, and stepped forward to shake his hand and introduce myself. He smiled a bit tentatively and said, "Ernie Brace, civilian." We both were thinking there might be some kind of mistake here, and turned with questioning eyes to the men behind the table. They were all smiling and grinning.

The OIC spoke and the interpreter explained that it was indeed a Merry Christmas for us as we would now be roommates. I heard a lot of back and forth between Ernie and the interpreter. Then Dead Eye said a few words in Vietnamese and Ernie caught the meaning before the interpreter explained. He told us that Ernie was very experienced and that I was "young and innocent." Therefore, he was telling Ernie that they expected him to keep me out of trouble and to teach me all the camp regulations. Ernie was just grinning and nodding his head. I could tell immediately that Ernie was a crafty and experienced man who had a bit of an off-balanced stance, walked with an obvious limp, and had to reach out to the wall to reset himself occasionally. I wondered if Ernie was the "Count of Monte Cristo of the Hanoi Hilton?" I wondered how old he was and how long he had been held as a POW. I was guessing that he was at least sixty years old and wanted to ask him if had been captured in the battle for Bien Phu with the French in 1954, but that would have to wait. We were given some Christmas hard candy and mints and I noticed Ernie took a handful and stuffed most of them in his pocket, so I followed his lead.

This whole scene ended abruptly with Dead Eye trying to say in English, "Go back now." We were ushered out of the room and several guards picked up the pile of my things. The rice mat fell out so I picked that up. As we started walking, Ernie started coughing up a storm and I heard to my left from an obvious cellblock two very loud and distinct coughs.

The guards seemed very happy and I thought it was because they would soon be off for Christmas. I learned later that it was just a show for hidden cameras and potential photo shots.

We turned a corner and went toward the other side of the courtyard where Ernie had been kept. We walked up to the front of the one story building with a large two-story building abutting it to the rear. There were at least four doors on our little cellblock and each door had one window to each side. I noticed the windows all had bamboo screens that completely covered them.

My new home was in Room 3 of the Golden Nugget. This was the Little Vegas section of the Hoa Lo prison—the Hanoi Hilton as the American POWs referred to it—and it would be my second of many cells in this prison.

Interior Map of the Hanoi Hilton

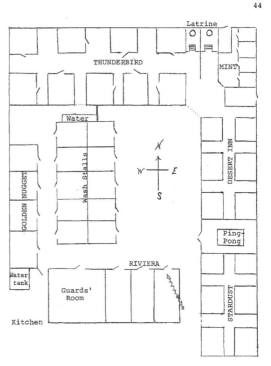

Map of Little Vegas

CHAPTER 7

ENDURING HARDSHIPS

The guards closed the door and I found myself in a cell approximately sixteen feet wide and ten feet deep. There were two bamboo racks on sawhorses on each side of the room. The mosquito net was already up on one bed that had blankets and what looked like a pillow. I looked a bit closer and Ernie explained that he had made it out of some old rags with a homemade bamboo needle. Wow! I thought this man was very ingenious, to say the least.

Ernie quickly told me how the camp was organized and that CDR Jeremiah Denton, USN, was the senior ranking officer (SRO) imprisoned at the time. He explained what the tap code was and asked if I had heard about the code in SERE (Survival, Evasion, Resistance & Escape) School. I told him I hadn't and was eager to learn it. He said it was a simple way to divide the alphabet into a five by five matrix without the letter K; we used C if the K was needed. He also explained that we had a hand signal code and a vocal code that was like the tap code, but coughs, sneezes, hacks, and spits were used to designate the coding. I was already a bit confused, so we decided to stick to the tap code, which I tried to use to say, "Hello, I am LTJG Jim Bedinger," But I didn't know the shortcuts and all the abbreviations commonly used by experienced tappers. We quickly agreed that I would be a good lookout and Ernie would do the tapping. He also took the time to tell me that he coughed out my first initial and last name to the Desert Inn part of Little Vegas where CDR Denton was kept. I was already amazed and said out loud, "Ernie, I think this is the start of a beautiful relationship."

Tap Code Matrix Used by American Prisoners of War in Vietnam

# of Taps	1	2	3	4	5
1	A	B	C/K	D	E
2	F	G	H	I	J
3	L	M	N	O	P
4	Q	R	S	T	U
5	V	W	X	Y	Z

Notes: (1) Timing of the taps determines which letter is being tapped. For example, "R" is in Row 4, Column 2, and would be four taps-pause-two taps, then a longer pause before tapping the first letter of the next word. (2) Acronyms and abbreviations were used for the common phrases or words, such as "GBU" for God bless you and "C/K" for acknowledgement. (3) One strong tap was No and two meant Yes. One loud thump was immediate danger.

Ernie showed me where the peep holes were on the door and how to pound once with a thump on the wall to alert tappers that a guard was close. Within minutes I was the lookout and Ernie was tapping on the wall to the man on our right and then to the man on our left. That's when I heard the POW to the left say out loud to "get to the sports page." Ernie got his empty cup, wrapped it in a T-shirt, and tapped on a specific spot. He began talking, yet I could hardly hear him. Ernie was trying to tell the other prisoner it was too dangerous because the lights were on inside and the guards in the dark outside could see everything we were doing. The POW to our other side thumped and the guard appeared around the corner and walked right up to our door. My heart was really racing now, but it was for naught; it was just a routine check on the new guy on the block. Ernie and I both stood and bowed and that seemed to make him happy.

Ernie had a hundred and one questions about the political situation back at home, the war, the peace protesters, and what our chances of going home would be if things worked out in Paris. I told him about what I saw on the road traveling north to Hanoi and some of the details that resulted in the 1968 election of Richard Nixon as president. Moments later a voice from the left cell asked who won the World Series, and Ernie tried to tell him in a low voice that we'd talk to him tomorrow when it would be much safer. Ernie and I discussed a lot of different issues and sports were not a high priority with us at this moment, but for the man next door, he had to get a few scores now. Every hour and every half hour he kept trying to get Ernie to talk sports—baseball, football, ice hockey, basketball, golf, and college sports, too.

I distinctly remember hearing bells a bit louder as they stroked two and Ernie explained that the Roman Catholic Cathedral was only two blocks down the street from us. It was very quiet, and then the same voice comes up and asks Ernie how the AFL merger into the NFL was going. Ernie was about to tell him to quieten down when a very tired and somewhat frustrated voice from the other side spoke.

"McCain! Go to sleep and that's an order."

Without a moment of hesitation our sports fan replied simply, "Aye-Aye, CAG." And we didn't hear from John McCain again until the morning broke bright and beautiful.

I had a lot of information that had not reached the other POWs at that time. For example, Ernie was ecstatic to hear the United States had landed on the moon and it was a naval aviator who took that "one small step for man, one giant leap for mankind." Ernie's smile was wide and his eyes were sparkling with joy. However, the news on the war front was not as encouraging as he had been hoping for. Although we got my mosquito net set up and I got under it, we never stopped talking all night.

I know this sounds strange, but I was Ernie's first roommate. He had been captured in May 1965 in the northwest corner of Laos, over three hundred miles from the North Vietnam border. When I told him I thought he looked like he was captured back in 1954, he told me he was fighting back then in Korea as an active duty marine corps pilot. He was only thirty-eight years old, but his three escapes and much torture as punishment had taken a toll on his health. He had been buried in a hole alive for over a week and lost all consciousness; he had been kept in stocks and, at one point, tied by ropes on his neck and wrists for more than two years and had lost some control of his legs. He hadn't been moved to Hanoi until the bombing halt of February 1968 and was put in a prison dubbed by the POWs as the Plantation. The first person to reach out to him was the ever-eager-to-talk John McCain.

Ernie told me about speaking with Seaman Douglas Hegdahl for over three hours one day. I had seen films of Hegdahl getting off a plane from Hanoi in Moscow in 1968 and later when he landed in New York. He was very quiet and made no statement except to say he was glad to be home. That was when I learned of how the Communist North Vietnamese were using the early release of POWs as a propaganda tool. All early returnees, except Hegdahl, had violated the SRO's orders and the Code of Conduct that instructed detainees not to take early release. But Douglas was ordered by USAF Col. Ted Guy, his senior ranking officer, to take the next early release offer and get the word out about the mistreatment of the American POWs in Hanoi. I told Ernie that this explanation made a lot of sense from what I had seen on TV. To his lasting credit, Douglas Hegdahl brought out more than three hundred twenty-five names he had memorized, some of whom were listed as killed in action (KIA) or as missing in action (MIA). This knowledge gave many families at home hope that their loved ones might also be safe, and more than several families had their loved one's status changed from KIA to POW. This brought up the topic of how my name and the news I brought with me would get spread to other POWs in the Hanoi Hilton.

───────────── ★ ─────────────

It was Christmas morning and before the guards came around, I could hear one cell wishing the cell next to them a "Merry Christmas." The Golden Nugget cells at that time held CDR James Stockdale, Commander (CDR) John McCain, civilian Ernie Brace, and now Lieutenant Junior Grade (LTJG) Jim Bedinger in that block.

The morning routine started with the bucket brigade. A guard opened the door and we were told, "Bucket." Ernie took our bucket and placed it outside and we were locked up again. Two American POWs came along and took all the buckets from the Golden Nugget into the building to our left called the Thunderbird. I asked Ernie about McCain's bucket, because they had not opened his door. Ernie explained that John had been caught so many times trying to pass messages in his bucket that the Communists made him dump his own.

When all the buckets were dumped and returned, most of the guards disappeared for their morning meal. One of the shortest and definitely one of the youngest guards came to get John and his bucket. I had the primary peephole and was watching closely. About two feet in front of our door, John swung his crutch (he was still recovering from injuries sustained while ejecting from his Douglas A-4 Skyhawk) forward and caught the guard right between his legs, who screeched something and ran ahead into the next building. John set the bucket down, hopped in front of our door, opened the guard's flap, and said, "At least tell me who won the Army-Navy game." I said, "I think it was Navy." He quickly closed the flap, got his bucket, and then yelled out to the Thunderbird, "It's a Merry Christmas after all, Navy beat Army." Well, the game actually was played after I had been captured and I confused it with the game a few years prior to 1969. It really didn't matter. What mattered was there was one American proud of his heritage who would never surrender and although captured, was determined to resist whatever the enemy wanted. I learned there was a lot more to this commander than just the urge to communicate and his feisty spirit to resist his captors. He was a thinker, and he had a vast number of stories growing up in the shadows of his grandfather and father. McCain was and will always be a hero in my eyes and not just because of this first introduction to his rather brash and flagrant violation of camp regulations, but because of the many times he put himself in certain danger to save others from being caught in the POW communication process.

After the bucket routine was finished we were brought the normal hot tea with a plate of sugar and a half-loaf of freshly baked French bread. Ernie ate his breakfast in a flash and was soon tapping on the wall to CAG Stockdale. My name and brief facts of landing in Laos, of my pilot being rescued by the Jolly Greens, and of my trip north to arrive on December 7 was all conveyed. After the dishes were collected, the wash routine was performed room by room. This is when Ernie showed me how we could look out and see the groups going in and out of the wash areas just in front of the Golden Nugget. He carefully told me names and ranks of all the prisoners we saw. It was a lot to remember for my first day, but what amazed me was the detailed knowledge Ernie had about each prisoner, including what prisons they had been kept at before ending up here in Little Vegas.

As activity subsided in the prison Ernie got his cup and T-shirt and rapped up John McCain. I was lookout as the two carried on what many would have considered a normal conversation. John asked questions about every sport, and especially the first two AFL-NFL World Championships and the merger that was being completed that year. John had seen the first game in January 1967 before he had been shot down and captured. He had missed the second game when the Green Bay Packers beat the Oakland Raiders and didn't know how the New York Jets, led by Joe Namath, beat as promised, the Baltimore Colts. He wanted to know if I thought the AFL was now on a par with the NFL and I told him that the way it was turning into one NFL with the AFC and NFC, there would be parity very soon if not already. The one answer I didn't have is why two original NFL Teams (the Colts and the Steelers) were placed into the AFC, which was comprised mostly of the AFL teams. He was amazed. Over the next few days, I learned a lot more about John, his escapades at the U.S. Naval Academy, his being selected as the top instructor pilot of all the naval aviation training commands, and about his wife, Annie, who had made TV ads for Ivory Soap. His enthusiasm and love of his family, his unwavering pride in our country, and his faith in God were contagious and inspiring.

It was shortly after noon when food started arriving at the racks just inside the Thunderbird area. They brought carts of plates stacked with some type of chicken or duck, potatoes, onions, and greens. Both Ernie and I could smell the food as it was brought by. After all the prisoners were served, McCain was given his meal and then Ernie and I were given ours. This was the best single meal I had as a prisoner. The North Vietnamese Communists tried to make the most of this type of event by filming and photographing the POWs as if this is how we lived every day. But the thought of a special meal on Christmas warmed my heart just a bit.

After the meal and the dishes were done and washed by two senior officers who were in the Thunderbird, the majority of the guards disappeared and the radio started up. After the normal "Hanoi Hanna" radio harangue to the sailors of the seventh fleet, an American voice announced that we would be treated to a recording of the Christmas Midnight Mass from the beautiful Hanoi Cathedral. There was the normal service, but when it was time for the offering, a Vietnamese voice in English announced that we would now hear two Christmas hymns sung "by the American War Criminal Choir." My first thought was that I had missed my chance to get my name out. Then I heard an out-of-tune guitar and a strong voice over the background choir singing with gusto and great volume the song—it was me. *Oh my God!* Ernie saw immediately the surprise and horror on my face; I never was very good at keeping a poker face. I told Ernie that I had been tricked. I recounted in detail the whole story about how they told me I might be able to go to church and sing in the prisoner choir, but I had to pass their review. I should have been astute enough to figure out that the officer had a second tape recorder and was taping my voice with the background music.

Within a short time, both CAG Stockdale and McCain were tapping at the same time on our walls. They wanted to know who the new voice was in the choir and if he knew the

SRO orders not to make tapes or announcements for the camp's radio. I was the lookout, and I was seething at being so naive and being tricked in this way. Before the day was over, I was able to talk to both CAG Stockdale and John through the walls and tell them how they had tricked me. It was then I learned that the young officer, who also was Dead Eye's interpreter, had been called "Rabbit" and "Maggot" by the prisoners. I remember both of the men telling me sooner or later, "We all get tricked into giving them something; the key is to wake up the next day and be proud to be an American and to rededicate yourself to resisting the enemy to the best of your own ability." I often thought after that day that as a LTJG in the United States Navy, it was hard to go astray when surrounded with great naval officers and leaders like this. As I put up my mosquito net that night, I said a short prayer of thanks and told Ernie I was thankful most for being with him and surrounded by men like Stockdale and McCain. Ernie nodded his agreement.

In the next three days I spoke with both McCain and CAG Stockdale in the morning's and afternoon's normal communication times. I was shocked to learn about how in October 1967, the CAG and ten others known as the Alcatraz Eleven,[17] were taken to a dark dungeon and kept in irons and handcuffs most of the day and all night. Each cell was about nine feet by three and a half feet. The ceiling was concrete and low; thus, summertime heat stayed above one hundred ten degrees and often rose to over one hundred twenty degrees in the afternoon. He told me of how he had disfigured himself so that they could not take him to a scheduled press show that would embarrass America and put other POWs in danger. Most of the Alcatraz Eleven were finally moved to Hoa Lo prison on December 9, 1969. They had survived the Alcatraz hellhole for more than two and a half years. Just hearing CAG Stockdale tell me of his time at this prison dubbed Alcatraz filled me with righteous indignation and an unending admiration for those who had gone before me. It also told me that the North Vietnamese who had tricked me were capable of horrible things.

---

17 Alvin Townley, *Defiant: The POWs Who Endured Vietnam's Harshest Prison, The Women Who Fought for Them, and the One Who Never Returned* (New York: St. Martin's Press, 2014), 189-208, 326-39.

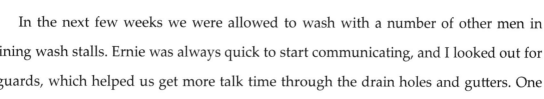

In the next few weeks we were allowed to wash with a number of other men in adjoining wash stalls. Ernie was always quick to start communicating, and I looked out for the guards, which helped us get more talk time through the drain holes and gutters. One day, LCDR Dick Stratton was in the next wash stall. I learned in SERE School that Stratton's zombie act and bowing in different directions was a perfect act of resistance that told the world the treatment was not what it was being touted up to be by the Commies. The coast was clear, so Ernie lifted me up the wall and I looked over and gave Stratton a well-deserved salute. When he saw my smiling face, my salute, and heard my good wishes, his whole face and body changed. He had been uncertain about how that press conference would be received back in the United States, and when he heard how I was taught by the navy about his resistance, he seemed both relieved and overjoyed that his suffering to resist the enemy's propaganda efforts was not in vain. He had, in fact, set a new standard for prisoners of war to resist the enemy's efforts to use POWs for propaganda purposes. His flat-top haircut, his bushy eyebrows, and his dark hair that had just started to show some gray peeking through—all these traits distinguished him and were firmly set in my mind.

Another day two senior officers from the Desert Inn were next to us. Ernie tried opening a dialogue with the fairly new cough code, but they were not hearing it all and tried several times to decipher what the coughs and hacks meant. Finally, in a moment of frustration a loud command voice said, "This is Captain Harry Jenkins, United States Navy! Say your names now!" At about six feet four, CAPT Jenkins was a commanding figure. His cellmate was CAPT Howard Rutledge, USN, who had served several periods as SRO in other prisons. They both were real leaders, part of the Alcatraz Eleven, so up the wall I went and gave them a big salute, too. They were almost in shock that any POW would be so bold and risk so much to render such military honors. But Ernie and I were already sensing that things were changing and we could get away with a lot more violations of camp regulations than in prior years. Plus, we wanted to be involved in everything the other prisoners were doing and talking about. One of things that Ernie told me on our first night together was that he was afraid the other POWs would all go home and they would forget about those of us captured in Laos and brought to Hanoi. So getting our names out and getting known by the other prisoners was a form of life insurance—we had to continue to communicate at all costs.

One of the very best meetings at the washroom was with my brother Bill's former XO, CDR Chuck Gillespie. My brother had been assigned as a radar intercept officer (RIO) to the Black Knights Fighter Squadron VF-151 and flew missions over North Vietnam. He was awarded a Distinguished Flying Cross (DFC), the Air Medal, and the Navy Commendation Medal for his performance in combat. CDR Gillespie had worked on several of his awards before he left the squadron to report to pilot training and did not know Bill had been killed in the new squadron he had been assigned to. So Ernie once again held my foot and I popped up the washroom wall to salute and talk briefly face-to-face with my brother's former XO. Gillespie was truly saddened and told me that Bill was one of the finest RIOs he had ever flown with. Then he said to keep up the fine work of getting the news out and thanked me for being a DFC—Distinguished Frantic Communicator. Ernie and I were already building a reputation for our communications.

This conversation got Ernie thinking of even more ways to spread good news. All the POWs needed some good news because the North Vietnamese Commies were always quick to broadcast all the bad news, especially every flood, riot, and hurricane that hit the U.S. So we secured (in a very clever way) some more brown toilet paper and pieced together several old broken pencils to make a writing instrument, which had to be hidden carefully when not in use. Ernie started writing about two to three notes each day. Then when it was time to pick up our meals, I would distract the guard and Ernie would drop one in the soup or stuff one into a piece of bread. We didn't know what to call these notes, but someone suggested *The Vegas Rambler* that rhymed with gambler, and that stuck. We even tried to explain the election of 1968 and how Governor George Wallace, running with retired Gen. Curtis LeMay, won forty-six electoral votes. Some said that swung the election; however, a careful reading of the electoral votes told a different story: the Nixon/Agnew ticket won over fifty-five percent of the electoral votes, so that ticket would have won even if all the votes for Wallace had been given to Hubert Humphrey. Most were interested in this because they were hoping President Nixon would make the rules of engagement less restrictive on U.S. forces, untie the military's hands, and finally end the war.

In the first few months we were put in a small exercise pen to walk and get fresh air, which was located at the dividing line of the central courtyard. On the other side of the screen were three POWs. However, only one was moving. Ernie told them who we were; then he recognized LtCol Edison Miller, USMC, who was part of his Marine Aviation Cadet (MARCAD) class for about two years. Ernie said on the next pass toward the screen, "Hi Slobbering Ed, Ernie Brace here. Good to see you." As Ernie turned away to make sure the guard didn't suspect anything, Miller said in a loud voice so all could hear him, "Good God Brace, you're supposed to be dead; your wife's already remarried." That was quite a reaction, I thought. Ernie, on the other hand and to his credit, wanted to know more. "Where is she and how are my boys?" he asked. It was at that point one of the other prisoners with Miller said something to Ed and then he told us again in a very loud voice, "I'll have to report you to the camp authorities if you keep trying to talk to us. It's against the camp rules to talk with each other."

This last statement really got to Ernie, plus the weight of his wife being remarried and not one word about his four sons. In over the three years that were to follow, that day was the first and one of the few times I saw Ernie Brace have tears in his eyes from the mental strain and concern for his family. When we returned to our cell Ernie immediately got in contact with John McCain to discuss what he could do to get news from home. CAG

Stockdale had made a courageous stand that he would not receive a package or write home until all POWs were allowed to receive packages and mail. So the tapping and talking on the walls was centered on trying to do more for all the POWs who were now left out of the improving treatment. The Desert Inn leaders all agreed that each cell block commander had to bring the issue up and see if we could shame the Commies into giving everyone something.

The month of February was almost gone when one morning Ernie and I were summoned to an interview with Dead Eye and Maggot, his interpreter. Ernie thought it was another "how are you?" attitude check and maybe a caution about our occasional loud conversations. Instead, there on a table were two small, opened boxes with address labels and some international postage stamps. Dead Eye went on for about five minutes and then Maggot condensed it all down to "the humane and lenient treatment of the Vietnamese people allows you now to receive a special Christmas package from your family." Ernie never had received any letter or package. He had been captured in May of 1965, so this was his fifth Christmas as a POW and not one piece of mail. What could explain this sudden change in policy? We didn't know, and when we got back to our room we were both thinking this was a mistake. We reasoned that we better hide the vitamins and eat the candy before our guards woke up and came back to our cell to take it all away.

Ernie and I examined every scrap of paper for hidden messages, but found little. Ernie did notice the return address on his package had listed Mrs. Brace in Arizona, where his parents had moved to when they retired. So he hung his head and said, "I guess that means my dad has died." I told him that his dad was in a better place now. He simply reached out and patted me on the back and said, "I hope so."

I also noticed in my package that there were two types of soup bouillon cubes in the small container, so I surmised that my wife had packed up the house and had maybe moved back east or to a small apartment. In early 1969 we had purchased a three-bedroom house with a beautiful used-brick fireplace in the center of the house. Before I left on cruise, we worked to paint every room inside and outside, including the wood siding, wood flashing, and all the stucco so that it would be in great shape to sell quickly or rent, just in case. I also found that all the items in my package had been opened to be inspected and was amazed that they let the pills all come to me. They were daily vitamins, which we divided into two stashes and hid. Ernie and I would use those later in the year when it got cold again.

The other prisoners had shared items from their packages with us in late December and early January, so now we could share with them. What would our neighbors like? What could they use? And the answer was always the same: "We got plenty. You keep and enjoy every item from your first Christmas package." Then one of the POWs from the Thunderbird cellblock sent us a note saying that our newsletter was the best gift of all and we didn't need to send them anything except some more news on NASA and our progress in space.

NASA was something that resonated with every POW we talked with. We even described how NASA sent live video back from the missions and showed the first official moonrise from earth. It didn't take long for a question to come back to us: "Since the light side of the moon always faces the earth, how does the earth rise from the moon?' Now that was difficult to explain without props. We drew two cups to simulate the mother ship circling the moon and the lunar landing module on the moon. Michael Collins stayed on the mother ship that would return the three astronauts to earth, and he circled the moon from the dark side to the light side repeatedly. One morning NASA decided to show the Apollo 11 mother ship's view of coming out from the dark side of the moon to the lighted side. As the spacecraft moved closer to the light, the earth slowly began to appear as if it was rising. That's why it's referred to it as "the first earthrise viewed from the moon."

Ernie and I never received another package and we never received a letter or any other news from home. There were no new POWs coming into the prison system in North

Vietnam and news from home was hard to get. Thank goodness for one South Vietnamese pilot, Max, who was very fluent in both English and Vietnamese and could often hear the guards talking among themselves, or sometimes hear the radio or street broadcasts. He was quick to pass on news of any type. Through Max we learned that news of the U.S. landing on the moon had not reached the people of Hanoi, and when it did in 1972, the story was a criticism of how the U.S.—with no regard to human life—"used their pilots like lab rats," while the Russians were able to build robots and remote controls to explore the moon's surface without risking even one life. Any positive news from the United States was filtered and blocked from us, and often from the Vietnamese people.

Several weeks after Ernie and I had received our packages, I was called to an interview by the Maggot. It started out as an attitude check with the normal "how are you?" questions and when I asked for a Bible, I was told that I was receiving "humane and lenient treatment." I thought the interview was going to end quickly; instead, we were joined by Dead Eye. The speech he gave me in Vietnamese lasted about five minutes and then Maggot put it into English. The gist of what he was telling me was that I was young and innocent, but the other Americans were "unrepentant war criminals" and I must never try to talk to them, because they were all guilty of committing crimes against humanity and, "One day they would all be tried and brought to justice."

I am not sure to this day what the purpose of this harangue was. At the time I was incensed by the thought of such an injustice. I knew I was not supposed to argue with our interrogators, but there has always been a part of me that wants to speak out against injustice. What better time and place to state my faith in God and in America? So I told him he was mistaken.

"These men all chose to serve their country, just like you and the North Vietnamese Army chose to serve your country. These men were engaged in war, wore the uniforms of their nation, and had ID cards to prove their status in the U.S. Armed Services. Someday this war will end and we shall all go home. There will be no trials as war criminals. You know this. These men are brave American war fighters, and although you have captured us, we have not surrendered. We shall never surrender, for that is not our American way. You may torture and subject us to pain beyond belief, and we may submit but never surrender. We are Americans and will always be proud of what that means."

To this day, I believe there was a part of CAG Stockdale and CDR McCain speaking from me at that moment.

Maggot translated all I had said, which took some time with Dead Eye asking him questions. The Maggot finished finally, and the COI was furious. He stuttered a few words and Maggot interpreted: "I am the camp commander and you will obey me or face hard punishment. *Go back!*"

As we stood up I distinctly heard two coughs. Some American POW had been listening, heard me, and liked what I had said. That made me feel a little better; I had no idea that others could hear. I guess I do have a loud voice at times.

I was returned to the cell and once again told to speak to no other American. I thought it was interesting that Maggot left out the criminal element this time. Ernie asked me immediately what had happened because I had been out of our cell for a long time. I told him all, he smiled, and said I did well. Then Ernie tapped to James Stockdale and then to John McCain. The news was that Dead Eye had tried to make the case to me about war crimes and I had raised the BS flag right in his face. Just a year ago, this prison commander would have had any POW who spoke like I did in ropes and bars. It was a significant sign that something was indeed changing.

After each meal a guard would take CDR Bill Lawrence, who had been flying with the Puking Dogs in 1967, and LtCol Thomas Kirk (USAF), to clean dishes. Each day after lunch and dinner all the other prisoners would listen closely for the message of the day. Lawrence was very fast and did most of the sweeping with a stiff bamboo broom in a rhythm that was tap code. On this day, his message was clearly based on the fact that he had been near the interrogation room, heard me, and coughed twice. It was a message that went something like this: "The new young pup (Puking Dog term for junior officer) in Golden Nugget 3 eats Commies for dessert. BZ and GBU!" Bravo Zulu is a Navy message from signal flags days that means basically "well done," and the GBU is how we ended tap sessions and translated it as "God Bless You." Ernie was beaming with joy and I was walking on air. POWs could have a nice day and that was one of them for me, thanks to the leadership and assistance I had been given.

Another incident that showed the news lag was when Ernie and I were put outside to exercise and get fresh air. Another POW was locked in a bath stall, so we introduced ourselves and started feeding him news items, as if we were talking to one another when we walked back and forth. No guard ever caught on to our technique. The person we were talking with was LtCol Sam Johnson, USAF, one of the tough leaders who had been taken to the Alcatraz prison in 1967 before being returned to Little Vegas.

When Ernie told him the Suez Canal was still closed, Sam asked, "Who and when did they close the Suez Canal? "I told him it was closed in the Seven Days War and he responded, "When and where was that war?" I later told him 1967, when Egypt attacked Israel across the Suez and Sinai Peninsula. The best part was Ernie telling him the reporter asking an Egyptian general what mistake the Egyptian pilots had made and an Israeli general replied; "They took off." That's the stuff of fighter pilots and many POWs enjoyed these types of news bits.

Our effort to produce a daily newspaper was paying off. Every two to three months the Communists made changes and reshuffled the prisoners into different cellblocks and sometimes changed the cellmate arrangements. CAG Stockdale got a roommate, but it wasn't working out. The new cellmate was convinced that we needed to start a psychological warfare campaign against our captors by yelling out slogans at all hours of the day and night. One night he yelled at the top of his lungs, "Ho! Ha! Ho Chi Ming!" Someone in the Thunderbird replied, "Hi! Low! Low! Looney Bin!" Ernie and I got a chuckle out of that, but we could tell this was a serious issue for our senior leadership and even CAG Stockdale could not control the behavior of his cellmate. Soon after, the CAG was moved to the Desert Inn with Air Force LtCol Robbie Risner and others like CDR Jeremiah Denton. In place of CAG Stockdale, we had a new neighbor, CDR Ernest Melvin "Mel" Moore, who was originally from Berkeley, California and had joined the Navy in 1947. He entered naval aviation training in early 1951 and was commissioned in late 1952. Like Ernie, he had flown missions in the Korean War and was a very experienced and highly decorated naval aviator.

One day we were talking about family and Mel offered to share pictures of his family with us. He was not tall enough, even when standing on a bed, to pass them through the bamboo ceiling, so Ernie passed him a five-foot piece of bamboo the next day. The plan was that I would hold Ernie up by one of his feet and he could reach through the bamboo thatch ceiling and grab the pictures on the end of the stick. Just as we were about to complete this operation, a pith helmet on a particularly short guard came bopping by our cells. We all froze as he just kept walking on. We completed the transfer with much concern that my vision was not as sharp as the 20/20 the pilots had because I had lost my glasses when ejecting from my Phantom, and that I had missed seeing this short guard turn the corner and start toward our cells. I offered to stand on Ernie the next time, for I had lost notable weight and was considerably lighter than I was just few months before. Ernie was taller and had better eyes to see any approaching guards. We did get the photos back to Mel and very much enjoyed looking at the family living room with decorations and Christmas trees. I think we talked for two weeks about the different Christmas traditions that we had enjoyed with our families.

——————— ★ ———————

In 1969, Easter came on March 29, the day before my birthday. By Good Friday, I was telling stories from Saint Peter's School from the Good Friday Stations of the Cross service to Night Watch to Easter Morning Sunrise services. Mel and Ernie were not very steeped in such formal religion, yet they remained interested and asked questions. And so it was that on Easter Morning, I just had to sing a few Easter hymns. Several times one of the pesky guards kicked our door and yelled, "Keep Shylent!" It was then that I just had to share my high school alma mater, "Rise up! Oh, Men of God," which had been given a new tune by our headmaster, and each verse had a slightly different tune. The song ends in a rising crescendo of "Rise up! Rise up! Rise up! Oh, men of God!" I didn't realize it, but Ernie was trying to give me the lower the volume sign, but it was just too late. There was a lot of yelling and several guards calling out.

It took about fifteen minutes before a tired and very angry Maggot appeared and said, "Bep! Long shirt and come now!"

I was taken away to an interrogation room and told that I had violated the camp regulations by singing loudly and why did I do that? I explained that just like Christmas, Easter is a High Holy Day with beautiful music and praise to God. I was trying to share some of the music just like I had done at Christmas and got carried away. Maggot thought about that and then said, "Yes! Yes! I think I understand, but now you need to stay for a few days away from other prisoners." I didn't respond, so he said, "Go!"

I got up to leave and then he remembered he needed a guard to take me to whatever cell I was to go to. A guard arrived and we were on our way. Instead of going to one of the other cellblocks, we went through the kitchen area, around a few corners, down a short corridor, and came out in the same small courtyard and the same cell that I had stayed in when I had first arrived. They brought a bucket and finally a new tea pot in a new tea caddy that kept the tea much hotter. But I knew I would miss Ernie and our communications. I also was concerned that they might be harder on Ernie since he was supposed to keep me out of trouble. After all the years he spent in solitary confinement, had I raised my voice in song only to get him more solitary confinement? I had found out where the red line was for these folks, but I also had turned their trick of taping me for the Christmas service against them and even their officer didn't refute my explanation of why I was singing.

The days passed and soon the weekend was approaching, but my routine didn't change—perhaps the solitary time of a few days was going to be a little longer. Fortunately, it was only eight days and on Monday, April 15, I was taken back to the Golden Nugget cell where Ernie was eagerly awaiting my return. All my things, including the two blankets and mosquito net, were still stacked neatly on my rack. The guards left us with strict orders of "No sing! No talk!" Later, in a very low and quiet voice Ernie said, "Let's lie low for a few days and give someone else the chance to tick them all off." I heard Mel in the next cell cough twice, which was our way of saying yes.

Soon John McCain was on the wall with Ernie and wanted to talk, but they were watching us very closely and Ernie advised against it. So John told Ernie to tell me that I had been nominated for a Grammy Award for the best spiritual of the year. He also advised me to save my singing voice for a time we could all celebrate together; after all, "Like all wars, this war will come to end. We'll all go home and these poor bastards will still be here chasing rats and picking stones out of their rice."

The man did make sense and he lifted my spirits more than words can express, even today. I used to kid him that he never met a glass half-empty.

CHAPTER 8

ERNIE BRACE

The weather was getting warmer by April as Ernie and I put extra efforts into a few newsletters. We had heard through the tap system that the Communists were on the lookout for note communications and were searching some weird places under tiles and nasty holes in the walls for notes. Ernie had devised a way of quickly slipping a note wrapped in plastic into the drawstring of a set of pajama pants left on the clothesline to dry. In this way the note was hidden in plain sight where no one would suspect it to be. When the POW got back to his room and pulled a little on the string, the note would drop out and give him some more news from home.

Early one Monday morning, Ernie had about six notes to drop. There were lots of pants hanging on the line from the previous wash time and, as usual, we were the first to go to the wash stalls. When we were let out of the wash stall and walked over to hang our clothes, the guard turned and walked away. This was strange behavior and Ernie was suddenly on high alert. With a clear view of the passage way from the Desert Inn to the Golden Nugget, John McCain in Cell 1 of the Gold Nugget yelled loudly, "Comm purge, Ernie! Ho, ho! Ho Chi Minh!" Then he started yelling other salty things about the Commies. By this time Ernie had swallowed two of the notes and given me two to eat while he went to work on the rest. I had no sooner swallowed and there was the Maggot with four other soldiers wearing latex gloves on their hands and cloth masks on their faces.

We were told to stand aside. Every pair of pants on that line was searched, but no notes were found. Then Ernie and I were searched, both on our outside pants and inside boxer shorts along the drawstrings. No notes were found on us, thanks to John McCain. We were quickly put back in our cell and they went for John. Being more senior and definitely the one who sounded the alarm for the surprise inspection, John was the only one who could see the inspection party coming toward us and had alerted us. He alone saved us from being caught red-handed with those notes. I looked out the peephole from our cell and saw John was being put into shackles around his ankles and old metal handcuffs. Then the guards led him away. He didn't return for about ten days when some other POW misbehaved and they needed the solo punishment room where John was to put for the next "unrepentant war criminal." It was at this time that I was told the POWs had named the room the Black Hole of Calcutta.

Within minutes Ernie had a cup with a T-shirt folded into it to talk with John through the wall. I was on my hands and knees looking under the door for any moving shadow of an approaching guard. We learned that John was kept in shackles both day and night and had his neck tied to an iron ring in the wall. John joked and said it took him two days to figure out how to use the bucket without splashing on himself or the rack he was attached to. Ernie questioned him about any physical blows or punishment like straps and bars. John said, "No, and maybe those days are behind us now." Ernie was not so sure and advised John to try to keep a bit lower profile. John replied in typical fashion; "Not my style, Ernie."

Ernie and I both agreed that we didn't know anyone else who would be willing to subject themselves to that type of punishing treatment to save us from getting caught. There are no words that adequately describe how we both felt that day about this man and how he would stand up for his fellow Americans, no matter what. We also had senior ranking officer (SRO) James Stockdale, who was made of the same stuff in spades.

The remaining question on all our minds was how did the Communists learn we were using the drawstrings? Prisoners from other camps confirmed that they had never heard of this method for passing notes. We were concerned, because it was a sign that, potentially, an American POW in the Hanoi Hilton had received a note in his drawstring and told the Commies about it. Ernie guessed it might have been a man in LtCol Edison Miller's group of seven POWs we called the Peace Committee (after the war they were accused by CAG Stockdale of being collaborators), but we had no way of knowing for certain. At least we knew we had to devise a new way for periodically passing notes and maybe decreasing the frequency and number of *Vegas Rambler* editions. We were getting to the end of items that we considered newsworthy anyway, so it made a lot of sense to avoid the drawstrings and stick to bread and soup for our delivery mode on more important note traffic.

Another action began and finished very quickly by the Commies was horizontally cutting in half the doors to all washrooms to make them into Dutch doors. When POWs were washing, the bottom door would be closed and the top would remain open. In this way the guards could watch and see everything we were doing. It was perhaps a great plan, but they forgot to put enough guards in place to watch us. As one guard walked back and forth from end to end, he could see only two stalls. So the POWs in the other stalls were rapidly communicating and swapping stories. Ernie and I were housed just across from the stalls and had a grand time all morning flashing the latest news to all who were washing.

Ernie also devised a way where we made long lines of string from the pieces of cords in our tire sandals and connected them to the little clothesline by the front window. We could slightly raise the line and tap out messages. It was a brilliant idea and it worked well while we looked out for each other, but one day Ernie was taken for an attitude check and I tried to use the string to say "EB at Q." The guard quickly noticed one of the washing POWs looking at our window too intently—I was busted. When Ernie returned, Maggot came into the room and had the guards remove all the pegs and screws in our cell, including the screws with which we tied up our mosquito nets. I felt like an idiot for several days, but Ernie was quick to see my remorse and tell me we all have to learn by doing. Moreover, it was good I had the initiative to communicate on my own, he reasoned, because someday we'd be separated and I'd need to keep communicating.

———————— ★ ————————

The Vietnamese seemed to be trying to make it look like they were treating us better. Our time outside was increased so we could get more sunlight. They converted the old Christmas room in the Stardust cellblock to a ping pong game room, which Ernie and I got to use once a week, but others were seen in there more often. Ernie had a great backhand, a good serve, and no trouble beating me all the time. There was another room set up in the Rivera cellblock with a Vietnamese-type of billiards/pinball game. Because it had pockets recessed under the table, it was a perfect place to hide notes. We tapped instructions to others around the whole prison and soon we each had our own drop box position on the table.

This system work fairly well until they closed the room and moved the table. Three notes fell out and camp authorities went ballistic. They focused on the most senior leaders, including CAG Stockdale, who had nearly died from self-inflicted wounds that prevented them from taking him to a press conference a couple of years previously. The direct result of that action was that Stockdale as SRO and now in the Stardust cell block, had decided to show the camp authorities that they didn't have complete control of everything., He ordered a three-day hunger strike to protest three men being kept in solitary confinement. We were ordered just to say we didn't feel well and couldn't eat that day. The senior officers, when interrogated, would tell them they must give each POW at least one cellmate.

I was losing weight rapidly by this time and my body was getting more heat rash as the summer began. Ernie had learned from some others who had been given an armpit thermometer when there had been a flu outbreak, that the temperature in most of the cells was one hundred twenty degrees by day and only went down in the Golden Nugget to one hundred ten degrees at night. That was because the cells in these buildings had concrete tile roofs that retained the heat of day and radiated it downward at night. Ernie told me that fanning myself would help, and that putting one mat on the floor and one blanket as a padding to lie on would allow me to put the other blanket, clothes, and mosquito net on top to serve as insulators. Even with this, Ernie was concerned for me and kept advising me to eat everything to keep my strength up. I had developed a case of what Ernie called "Oriental belly," in which I had some vomiting and continuing diarrhea. My weight had dropped so quickly that he could see every one of my ribs and the order to fast for three days started a discussion. If the other POWs were not eating, I told Ernie I would not eat. CDR Mel Moore thought that three days would not make a lot of difference to our total health and Ernie kept reminding me to make every day count. I finally told him, "The SRO has the final say and until he tells me differently, I am not eating." And Ernie didn't eat either.

The hunger strike lasted exactly two days.

Camp authorities quickly told our SRO that progress would be made to have every POW housed with at least one other POW. It was clear that conditions in the summer of 1970 were in a state of change for the better, but not so great as to bring our daily living conditions into anything close to meeting the standards set by the Geneva Convention. Yet Ernie was so delighted with every little change, and even some reports of progress at the Peace Conference in Paris, that I too was feeling very hopeful. In addition, several POWs did not fast and ate everything. I was amazed at how Ernie refused to taste the soup or take a bite of bread in those two days. He was a civilian, but he was the epitome of the adage, "Once a Marine, always a Marine." I was to witness again and again how Ernie Brace might not always agree with some SRO orders, yet he would embrace and cheerfully obey every single order because in his heart, he was still a "Captain, United States Marine Corps."

Shortly after our two-day fast, Ernie and I noticed some new guards who were being trained on what to do as they watched us. Ernie and I again were first to wash. We were put into the stall at the far end, which was right in front of John McCain's cell. As we stripped and started to pour the cool water over our bodies, a small crowd gathered in front of our wash stall. One of our normal guards started calling my Vietnamese name and told me to turn around. As I did so, several of the new guards starting laughing and pointing at my groin. My red hair was something they may have never seen before and they were having great fun making jokes about it. This was certainly nothing new for any redhead, but there were no other redheads at the Hanoi Hilton at that time. I turned around fairly embarrassed and went to work washing my clothes with a day's worth of sweat on them. Then all hell broke loose as John McCain, in a very loud voice, started calling the guards a number of names (that are no longer politically correct) and told them all to get back to their posts. The officer arrived fairly quickly this time and, of course, it looked like McCain was in trouble again. The officer looked at Ernie and me, and then asked Ernie what had happened. Ernie told him how they ordered me to expose myself while washing and all the guards were laughing at us and pointing at my groin.

I had been the center of attention several times on the road north to Hanoi, but the soldiers were disciplined and had never pointed out my differences to each other. I thought Ernie was going to get in trouble for being a bit too agitated and for raising his voice, but the officer, to his credit, just used his hands to signal Ernie to calm down and then said in a very level voice, "These guards are new and we shall make sure they are instructed not to conduct themselves again in such a way. I am sorry this happened." He then turned to John McCain's cell and carefully inspected the bamboo screens that covered the windows. He opened the flap and told John something we couldn't hear and then told the guard to put more bamboo over John's windows.

Ernie and all the rest of us were surprised that after the note incident, they didn't do anything to John for this new outburst except to try to block his windows more. In this effort they failed, because John found a fairly long nail that he had hidden and used it to make a new peephole through the newly added bamboo. American ingenuity and persistence would not succumb to the enemy's wishes, and as John told Ernie and me, "They will never win the battle to stop us from communicating."

Several weeks later Ernie and I were placed in the passage that led to the Desert Inn from the Golden Nugget. There was a screen at both ends of the area that allowed us to walk about twenty feet back and forth. On the southern end of this area there were large bamboo poles about eight to ten feet long and five to six inches in diameter. After a few minutes, one of the new guards—who was as mean and as nasty as he could be to all the American POWs—came into the area and stopped us from walking. He couldn't speak English, but he made it very clear that our task that day was to move all the poles from the wall on the southern side to the wash stall wall on the other side of the passageway. After several minutes of acting confused, Ernie said to me, "Okay, you take that end and I'll take this end; we'll make fast work of this."

Ernie's solution made sense, and we were completing this task much too quickly for the guard, so he intervened and motioned that Ernie and I had to each carry one pole by ourselves. The poles were very seasoned and dried out, so they were not very heavy. The courtyard was filled with a series of bamboo screens making small areas for each POW group to get sun and exercise. We knew that many could hear us, and I just couldn't resist making a very loud straining noise as I lifted the first pole. The guard put his finger over his lips to motion me to make less noise. So the next pole I placed between my legs and raised it vertically, as if I had suddenly had a monster woody. And of course I joked with Ernie; "The South shall rise again." Even Ernie started to laugh and I started wobbling back a forth in such a way that when the pole came down, it landed smartly on the screen at the end of our area and knocked it down. The crash started a chain reaction and all the screens in the courtyard staring falling down, one by one, like a string of dominoes.

I stepped over the first screen, introduced myself to CDR Charlie James, USN, and shook his hand. His smile was from ear to ear. Then I heard all the guards screaming and saw them running around yelling, "No talk! No talk!" and "No look!" Meanwhile, our guard was trying to pull me back into the area while Ernie, behind his back, was waving to all the other POWs in the courtyard. It took the guards some time to restore a small degree of order and get the bamboo screens raised again. But it took no time at all for them to take Ernie and me back to our Golden Nugget cell. One of the older POWs passed onto us that Lulu and Tubby in the comic strip *Little Lulu* could not have done a better job of screwing up the Commies' system. Ernie and I had done in just a few minutes what a whole team of Keystone Cops would take an hour to do. I think this was the first time I heard other POWs refer to us as Lulus and it felt very good.

The hot weather continued and my heat rash expanded to cover from my scalp to my groin. Blotches of my skin turned bright pink and itched day and night. If I scratched it, the area felt like a thousand pins and needles, hence the name of "prickly heat." The only relief came once a day when I was able to wash in the morning. I kept under my bed and fanned myself with a twelve-inch by fifteen-inch bamboo fan, but it was little help. Ernie and I talked about our diet and figured that caused some of the rash, too. One night that stayed as hot as the day I found it almost impossible to go to sleep. I would fan until I dozed off and then have a horrible dream of ants, centipedes, and leeches all crawling over my body like they did in the jungle on my first few days of captivity. Ernie noticed several times that I would suddenly awaken and start furiously brushing something off of me. Nonetheless, there was nothing on me. He suggested that maybe a little tea might help, so I tried that. It was no cooler than the room and did little.

I'm not sure how late it was when I half awoke and thought I had to knock myself out to get some sleep. As I got out from under my mosquito net, I went to the other end of the room near the door and turned around. I ran as fast as could in that short distance and hit the wall with a loud thud, right on my forehead. The next thing I know Ernie was on top of me yelling, "Bao cao! Bao cao!" This was the approved way to summon the camp authorities. There would be no second charge of the light brigade at this wall tonight.

It took about five minutes before the two guards and an officer arrived with keys and opened our door and cool air from the night started to drift into our cell. The officer had one of the guards get the medic who oohed and awed at my pink, puffy skin and continued to poke and then press his thumb down on spots, release the pressure, and then time how long it took for the skin to turn from white to pink again. The officer and the medic conferred and pointed to my scalp. Then I was ordered to get a towel and come out to the wash stall. I was allowed to pour cool water over the upper half of my body and soon I was soaked from head to toe. This treatment immediately relieved most of the itching. When I returned to the cell, Ernie looked relieved, and I realized that they had temporarily lowered the bamboo screens on the two windows to allow more cool air to enter our cell.

It took me only a few minutes to settle down and then tell Ernie how grateful I was that he so quickly stopped me from doing any serious harm to myself. I had one small bump and a slight scrap mark on my forehead and nothing else—I guess I did have a hard head after all. Before the next day ended the story was repeated to our neighbors and then to the Thunderbird cellblock. The gist of what happened was passed all around the camp by tapping on walls, floors, or doors. It was truly amazing how efficient the tap code was.

I was still having trouble getting the knack of both tapping and listening. I asked Ernie if there was an easy way to remember the first letter in each row of the Matrix. He smiled and said there was a Marine Corps way. And then he said that AFLQV was an acronym that was a humorous saying based on inter-service rivalry. I never forgot it from then on, and it also would be useful for explaining the tap code to new POWs in the future when we were placed next to a few of them.

The months of July and August brought some real changes for Ernie and me. First, we were moved to the corner of the Little Vegas prison with three small cells with stocks built into the concrete beds and an outer room that connected all the cells. A tall guard tower was located on the wall behind the corner of this location, and pigs were kept just outside between the cells and the outer wall of the prison. The smell of the pigs was compounded by having the main latrine area located just to the interior side of this three-cell section. The odor alone was enough to make one gag.

Besides the degradation of living comfort, this new area resulted in our being cut off from much of the camp communications. The only added benefit was that it gave me more time to ask Ernie detailed questions about his life. He was by nature a quiet and soft-spoken man. In several types of crises, he had remained calm on the outside; and his judgement of the Vietnamese was keen and usually very well-founded. It was not as natural for him to give his life story as it was for me to talk about my family, growing up north of Philadelphia, going to schools and college, and working in my father's tree and landscape business. But one day he reluctantly relented and began by telling me why he had run away from home in 1946 at the age of fifteen. When you live twenty-four hours a day, seven days a week with one person, you get to sense their moods and thoughts at times. And if you listen and ask the right questions, you really get to know the person. The more I was to learn about Ernie Brace, the more respect, admiration, and love in the purest sense of that word, I got to feel for him. It was only natural.

Ernie was born in Detroit in 1931. His youth was fairly normal until World War II started. His father was too old to serve in the military and wasn't that happy about it. As

Ernie got older, he was almost as big, and taller, than his father, who all too often stopped at the local tavern and came home after too much beer. He often would get in arguments with Ernie's mother and sometimes got physical. Ernie had been in Junior ROTC and wanted someday to become an officer, but his father never thought much of his career choice. Things boiled over one night and Ernie ended up punching out his Dad. He gathered up a few clothes in a bag and took off. It was then he decided to join the United States Marine Corps. It was a time of decreasing force strengths for the newly created Department of Defense, but the marines, being the youngest service, always needed to recruit. He soon was on a bus to Parris Island and Camp Lejeune, South Carolina. The first two weeks were the toughest, but he realized that his young age (recorded as sixteen with forged signatures of his parents) was working to his advantage. He soon was an outstanding recruit. He excelled at close order drill, military subjects from his Junior ROTC in high school, and all academics. Ernie is what we call today a quick learner.

Trouble began when two weeks before graduation he was allowed one phone call home. He didn't want his parents to know where he was; so he called his sister. The next day she told her mother that she had spoken with Ernie and that he was about to be a marine. His dad hit the ceiling and reported to a recruiting station that his son of fifteen had been illegally recruited into the marines. With only a few days before graduation, Ernie was called into the battalion head office and the truth came out. He had three weeks to go before he turned sixteen, so he was placed in a special hold battalion. His parents were contacted to determine if they would agree for him to sign a minority enlistment when he turned sixteen years old. They agreed, signed the paperwork, and a week after his birthday, Ernie Brace became a marine. He learned if he had not been discovered on his underage status, he would have been the distinguished graduate of his class, a truly distinct honor .

Ernie had a love for flying and was soon advanced to an enlisted aircrew training school. He qualified as an airborne radar operator and then started to take every correspondence course he could get his hands on. After a year, a staff sergeant suggested to him that he get his general education degree (GED), the equivalent of an official high school diploma. He passed all tests with outstanding scores. In fact, his scores were so high that he was encouraged to sign up for the next official USMC college equivalency test. When he took that test, he was certified as a two-year college graduate that made him eligible for the Marine Aviation Cadet Program. This was a two-year pathway to a commission and wings of gold. This is also where Ernie had met the not so friendly, future POW, LtCol Edison Miller.

Ernie not only survived, but he flourished in this training and in all things concerned with flying an airplane. His instructor pilot on his first flight told him afterward that in over one thousand student pilots, Ernie was the first to keep the plane in balanced flight at all times and phases of the hop; he was a natural pilot. Ernie was not quick to say this, but I learned from some of his friends years later that he was the smoothest guy in the squadron to fly wing on and that he was the rare man born to fly. By then Ernie was not quite twenty-one years old and was soon assigned to an attack squadron in Kaneohe, Hawaii. From there he was sent to Korea where the marines had set up the Pusan Perimeter defense near the end of 1950. Ernie arrived in early 1951 and flew over one hundred missions in the ensuing year.

In one mission, Ernie was the flight lead and took multiple hits to his aircraft soon after dropping his bombs. Dark smoke was trailing behind him and his wingman told him he'd have to bail out. Ernie knew he had a number of miles to go to get to the ocean that offered some degree of safety from being captured, so he stayed with the plane and steered to a ridge line where the updraft gave him more altitude. He knew that would convert to more miles at a maximum glide power setting. It was close, and his plane crashed within sight of land.

Ernie's wingman was high above. The Navy was notified and on its way, but so was the enemy. Three small fishing boats with soldiers were coming out from the shoreline. As Ernie floated to the top of a swell, four or five tracers soared by his raft. He immediately pulled out his Colt .45 and was ready to get a few shots at them. He had to time his shots carefully with the ocean's swells so that as he started up the swell, he would be set to fire three or four quick shots. In the middle of the fire fight, Ernie heard a larger boom and at the top of the swell, he saw three boats turning toward the shore as fast as they could. He thought maybe some plane had dropped a bomb. Then he turned around to see a navy destroyer, the *USS Kidd* (DDG-661), with its five-inch bow gun still smoking and bearing down on him at full speed ahead. No wonder the enemy had taken off. Ernie joked that at least the navy was good for a ride back to home base and then back to his squadron.

Ernie was selected from his squadron to attend a new aviation safety program at the University of Southern California (USC) where he spent a year in a professional certificate program. He was then sent to the Advanced Training Command in Kingsville, Texas as an instructor pilot and safety officer. After a few months of flying in the jet aircraft assigned for what at the time was a new jet pilot training program, he was put in charge of an accident investigation where a student had crashed and been killed. After extensive interviewing, reviewing maintenance records, and getting a number of eyewitness accounts, Ernie was able to use a new mapping technique he had learned at USC to show the end of this fateful flight. He proved and showed how the student was flying low to do an airshow for a girl friend who was a college student at Texas Agricultural and Industrial College in Kingsville. His analysis earned a safety award from the Naval Safety Center and was published in *Approach*, the official *Naval Aviation News* monthly magazine.

Ernie was next assigned to Camp Lejeune, where he flew several types of helicopters and took part in a number of exercises. My favorite story from this time was from a ROTC summer training exercise when the students flew vertical assault to support an amphibious invasion on a shore in South Carolina. The night before the early morning flight, Ernie had one too many drinks and had awakened in the shrubbery in front of his bachelor officers quarters (BOQ). He quickly showered, shaved, and got into his flight suit, but he was not feeling quite as sharp as he may have looked. His copilot had started the preflight and the crew was set to start loading the students after the engines got started. As Ernie approached the aircraft, one of the ROTC students had placed a small sign under the pilot's port side window, "It's what's up front that counts." This was a tag line to a popular cigarette ad campaign at the time. Yet it showed a lot of faith for the pilots flying the students.

As the aircraft engines started up on both sides, the aircraft started to rock which was normal. However, Ernie's stomach wasn't quite ready for this motion. Ernie promptly slide the side window open just as the students were approaching and lost what little coffee he had tried to drink for breakfast. The vomit slid onto the sign and down the side of the aircraft. Ernie looked up to see his ROTC squad approaching the aircraft to get aboard. Their eyes were all focused on the side of the aircraft and were as big as silver dollars. Ernie was sure they were already praying for their lives. Ernie let the copilot fly most of the flight and was glad to get the mission completed safely and back to the base so he could more fully recover from the previous night's revelry.

Ernie's total career and life changed when he started to attend Command and Staff College at Quantico, Virginia. While checking out a plane to perform proficiency flying, at that time a requirement for every aviator to retain flight pay, he met some men from another part of our government and became interested in the chance to help them on a special mission. The mission was a priority and its scheduled date had been moved up. It involved flying to the Miami area, refueling and loading some special supplies, and then flying about eighty miles south to support forces involved in a covert operation. Things went badly went he arrived at the destination and he aborted as covered in the plan and executed the instructions for his return. Off the coast of the Carolinas, he experienced some engine difficulties that were a possibility with this mission, and ditched his plane. As instructed, he buried his parachute and flight suit. He went by foot to a road in the civilian attire he wore under his flight suit and hitched a ride to civilization where he stayed in a motel for a few days.

Ernie reported that he had lost his way and then experienced engine problems. He remembers ditching by the beach and hitting his head. After the head injury while ditching, everything else was blurred. Neither the marine corps' central command nor the FBI was buying the story. They decided to try Ernie in federal court for deliberating destroying the plane. His contacts knew a very top-rated legal team of Alan Sperling and Ed Dragon; Al was a 1960 Harvard Law grad who was tall with silver hair and a great voice, while Ed wore strong thick glasses, walked with a limp, and was a very thorough legal researcher and a quick mind for fine legal points. They defended Ernie and he was acquitted. But then under the Uniform Code of Military Justice, Ernie was ordered to Marine Base Quantico to be tried by General Court Martial under Article 134, the General Article. The charge was really "conduct unbecoming an officer" by leaving the scene of an aircraft accident.

Ernie had so appreciated the services of Sperling and Dragon that he did not accept the military defense attorney, a major offered by the U.S. Marine Corps. Instead, Ernie wanted to use the same firm that had won the day for him in federal court. The rules at that time for the General Article were much less limited than they are today. On July 7, 1961 (the birthday of Ernie's son, Patrick), the court found Ernie "guilty of deserting the scene of an aircraft accident" and ordered him "dismissed from naval service." Ernie later told me it was a general discharge, but under honorable conditions, and he kept his top secret clearance. The general discharge, however, would be forever a red flag to any future employer. Ernie was on his own to make his way in the world, but if it didn't work out, he had a name and a number he could call in Virginia to get a little help in the job search department.

Ernie, with his wife, Pat and their four boys, moved back to Southern California to start a new life. But times were hard as the nation was coming out of a recession and jobs were not too plentiful for a former marine with a general discharge. When Ernie failed to make a sale of an *Encyclopedia Britannica* to a foreman on the tenth floor of an unfinished sky scraper being built in Long Beach, he moved his car to a pay phone in the construction parking lot and called his contact. He answered on the second ring and when he understood what Ernie was facing, he told him to stay at that pay phone for the next fifteen minutes and not let anyone else use the phone. After five minutes the phone rang and Ernie was told that he was to report the next day to North American Aviation to be the lead test pilot on a new stability augmentation system for helicopters.

I think Ernie and I spent a week going over his year on the project and how he and the lead mechanic took the first beta-test bird flying around the country. They started out by going to MCAS Yuma, Arizona. They flew the low altitude system and at that time didn't even have to file flight plans unless they were going to fly at higher altitudes with fixed wing aircraft traffic. The best part of this story for me was when it was coming to an end at Marine Base Quantico in Virginia. This was the base from which he was discharged by the marines. When he returned, his status as chief test pilot for North American Aviation was equivalent to being a general officer in the marine corps, so they had to send a specific type of message to Quantico from Fort Bragg, North Carolina before they took off.

When they reached the designated landing area, they called for clearance to "hover taxi" to the assigned overnight area, but ground control directed them to the front of base ops where a small crowd had gathered and a small marine band was waiting. After shutting down the engines and waiting for the rotors to stop spinning, Ernie and his mechanic noticed several marines undoing a red carpet and the base commanding officer (BCO) in Class A Blues waiting to welcome them. As they exited the aircraft, the band rendered honors and played "Ruffles and Flourishes" for a two-star general. The colonel who was the convening authority for Ernie's 1 court martial was the greeting BCO. Speaking into a microphone, he only got half way into the official welcome when he recognized Ernie and then he stammered, right into the microphone, "Good God! It's Ernie Brace! I thought we got rid of you last year." Ernie told me that he still could hear the chuckles of the crowd at that moment when recalling that trip. It was, in a sense, redemption from the past. At last the BCO recovered his composure, shook Ernie's hand, and told him that if he needed anything on the base in the next few days, he only had to ask. Ernie didn't ask.

When Ernie finished the test project the flying part of his job stopped, too. He didn't like the paperwork and felt a bit awkward getting paid and not flying, so when Dick Hart from National Helicopter Service in Los Angles contacted Ernie, he was eager to take a new job that would keep him flying. His first assignment was flying support for firefighting with special helicopters that could scoop water and drop it on specific hot spots of a forest fire. Then Hart wanted Ernie to fly power line installations coming from the East to Los Angles. National Helicopter had lost a few birds when the spool of electrical cable developed a snag and pulled the helicopter down. The pilot had to be quick to recognize a snag, come off with the power, and reverse literally though the air while being pulled backwards to take the tension off the line. Ernie was quick and had a feel for how the helicopter was flying. He also was assigned to support offshore oil rigs because if the navigation system failed, Ernie, by the seat of his pants, could fly the bird home from anywhere. Not all pilots had his acumen and presence of mind; however, Ernie would never say that. Those who knew him were forever glad to have known and flown with him.

In June of 1964 a friend in one part of the U.S. State Department called Ernie about his being considered for a more permanent job that would take him overseas and asked if he would be interested. The next day he was told he would receive a special delivery envelope with a ticket on Pacific Southwest Airlines to San Francisco where Ernie would be met by a driver and driven to an interview and returned to fly home the same day. He was also told that he could not mention this, even to his wife, as it was top secret. Off Ernie went and he said it was just like a James Bond movie.

The building he was driven to appeared to be an aging, nondescript, twelve-story building like a lot of other downtown San Francisco buildings. The driver gave Ernie a letter with instructions to the floor and room number. He followed the instructions, but he noticed that other offices on the floor didn't have signs and didn't seem like normal commercial concerns. When he got inside the assigned room he was led to a second interior, bare-bones office and there he met one of his old friends who explained the parameters of the operation and type of flying Ernie would be doing should he be selected for this position.

After a ninety-day probation period and training to become familiar with the missions, Ernie's family would be able to join him and live in a large house with a staff in Chieng Mai, Thailand. It would be a perfect place for four growing boys, and Patricia would be excited about the increased pay and all the benefits. Ernie was excited that he would get to fly a short takeoff and landing (STOL) type of airplane—a Pilatus Porter (PC-6A) made in Switzerland. Some missions would be more dangerous than others, but it was right up Ernie's love for being in the center of the action. He practically took the job on the spot, but followed instructions and got Patricia's complete buy-in to this job change.

In the summer of 1964 Ernie was on his way to Vientiane, Laos with his passport, a civilian right-to-work license, and all the credentials to fly in Laotian airspace. He officially was employed by Bird and Son Construction, a wholly owned subsidiary of Continental Air that had obtained a contract from the U.S. Agency for International Development (USAID). He passed every test they gave him with very high marks for navigation, airmanship, and headwork. Later they chose him to fly to Switzerland to ferry another Pilatus Porter to Vientiane. The operation was growing as the war in Vietnam was also increasing in size and scope of American involvement because, in reality, there was no real border between Vietnam and Laos. After three months the family arrived in Thailand and moved into a beautiful house along a river and equipped with a number of things that made life interesting, fun, and beautiful.

May 20, 1965 Ernie dropped off supplies to a group he called "Terry and his Pirates." They were making a lot of good progress at a site located north and to the west of the Mekong River. A case of beer was the promise made and a promise made was a debt unpaid. The next day Ernie was going to make sure that Terry and his men would get their case of beer. Ernie had no way of knowing that a full battalion of North Vietnamese regular army had been watching this site, looking for signals used and the pattern of flights arriving and departing. This site was always having radio problems, so the all-clear to land was usually an array of three flags laid out on the ground. Ernie had no good visual indicators that during the night the camp had been overrun. Terry himself was fortunate to escape with the clothes on his back, several weapons, and ammunition.

Ernie Brace wrote a book called *A Code to Keep*[18] that talks in detail about his capture, his transit across Laos, his two escape attempts, his stay near Diem Bien Phu, and his final escape attempt from within North Vietnam territory. He was buried vertically in a hole for more than a week. He lost consciousness and awoke with a Vietnamese army medic giving him a Vitamin B shot. He had survived! He composed a poem in his head that he kept telling himself every day. It ends by saying:

> *I'll leave here alive, I know that now,*
>
> *But I don't know when and I don't know how.*
>
> *And I'll see my family once again,*
>
> *But I don't know where and I don't know when.*

---

18 Ernest C. Brace, *A Code to Keep: The True Story of America's Longest-Held Civilian POW* (New York: St. Martin's Press, 1988), 148.

That summed up how many of the other POWs felt, and he put that feeling into words to keep himself going. But it also gave many others hope, faith in our country, and inspiration to fight and resist the North Vietnamese Communists.

———————— ★ ————————

By the late summer of 1970, Ernie and I had learned there were two other POWs captured in Laos and living in the Thunderbird. When we were moved into the Thunderbird block, on the north side of Little Vegas, we were placed right next door to them. They were Maj Walt Stischer and LT1 Steve Long, both USAF. We established almost immediate communications by flashing the tap code under the door to them. But that was truly the second order of business. Ernie always amazed me by getting his side of the cell set up so quickly with all our moves. He kept telling me that "Home is where you hang your hat; get used to moving as the Commies will not let you stay anywhere for too long."

After this move Ernie stopped me and pointed to a small hole just above his mosquito net nail. It looked like the old nail had fallen out and they didn't bother to fill in the hole, which then got bigger with time. I looked closer and saw a small head emerge. It was a little gecko lizard with suction cup type feet that we often saw walking on the ceilings or up the walls. This guy was very small, so Ernie took to catching a few mosquitoes and feeding the little guy. I was amazed that it didn't take long for the gecko to realize Ernie was his provider, and so he came out and made little squeaking noises at Ernie. Even the lizards in this prison liked Ernie Brace.

One week after our move, the guards took Ernie and me, along with Walt and Steve, out of cells together. We washed in the morning and were allowed to exercise together. What a mistake! Both Steve and Ernie were avid communicators as well. I think from the first day together, Walt was raising his eyes and thinking "here we go again." But we had better lookout coverage, so we didn't get caught right away. This day marked the start of our group known as LULU—the Legendary Union of Laotian Unfortunates.

CHAPTER 9

MOVING TO CAMP UNITY

The routine was quickly established that as LULUs we would be treated like many of the other POWs who were being allowed joint activities. Some were having card games with decks of cards they had received in Christmas packages, so Ernie got busy and started cutting the brown sheets of toilet paper into card shapes, three inches by two inches. Within two days and some secret use of his stashed ball point pen refill, we had a working deck of cards. The first game we all played together was called Shit on Your Neighbor (an extreme version of Crazy Eights), and I was the novice at it. It was a game I had to learn from scratch. Steve Long couldn't believe I had not played it, because it is so versatile and can be played with a large group. Steve had been a forward air controller and was very athletic. He had earned a four-year football scholarship to Willamette University in Oregon and played starting linebacker for three straight years. He really knew football and a lot of other things.

One of the first points of official discussion was seniority. The navy had advanced ensign to lieutenant junior grade (LTJG) after one year, while the air force waited two years to advance its new second lieutenants. So although I had been promoted before Steve, I had been commissioned almost a year later than he was. I personally didn't think that I was senior, and no one thought it was that important, but Steve and I would tease each other about it. Finally I told Ernie that we needed a junior ranking officer (JRO) to have some fun. So after consulting with a few other cells, I was proclaimed the first JRO of the Little Vegas prison section. My first policy (Yes, I was asked several times what my first policy decision would be.) was to start a sideburns' growing contest. The military had some strict haircut standards that, by 1969, had started to be tested by some of the more flamboyant fighter pilots. So it seemed like a good idea to let our sideburns grow longer and out more. Of course, the actual issue for how long and how bushy our sideburns would be was dependent on which guard would cut our hair.

On the day of the LULU's next hair cutting, we drew one of the more unfriendly and impatient guards. When it was my turn in the chair, he shook his head and bore down with clippers. The guard had to repeatedly open and close his hand to make the clippers go. My hair was thick enough to snag and make the task much more difficult than most. He started screaming at me as if it was my fault, then he got scissors and tried to cut, but this only made my hair more uneven and not very military at all. Finally, the sergeant, whom we called Pepe Le Pew, took the clippers and told the guard something. He nodded and watched closely. Pepe had a way of moving his hands faster and take a smaller cut so that the cutting went more smoothly. Once started, Pepe just had to continue, but at one point he stopped to rest his hand and tried to say in English that I had very thick hair. Instead, he said, "Bep, you have very thick head!" Ernie Brace started laughing and told me that Pepe Le Pew had me pegged. Walt Stischer and Steve Long were laughing as silently as possible. The end result was that not much was taken off my sideburns; the thought crossed my mind that I was too quick to take myself out of the contest. I didn't want to appear to be setting myself up to win my own contest. So I was not in the field for this one. I told Ernie that Pepe had probably given me one of the greatest compliments any Commie could give an American POW. However, I also knew that others had suffered much from these same guards.

After thirty days the judging began by each cell block nominating the best sideburns from their area. A few days later a panel of judges of our most senior officers was able to watch the wash areas and see each of the four potential winners. By unanimous vote of the judges, the winner had been CDR John McCain. He had so ticked off his two guards that he had missed some of his shaving days and never got a haircut. When he did shave, he made sure that he fashioned mutton chop sideburns that truly stood out, because his hair had turned prematurely white on top, while his whiskers remained fairly dark brown. He had a two-toned appearance that one would never miss, even on a crowded city street. We may not have accomplished much, but there were a lot of POWs laughing or smiling that night with the thought that some secret message got out and an aide had to march into the office of Admiral John Sidney "Jack" McCain Jr., Commander-in-Chief of the Pacific, and inform him that his son had just won the 1970 Annual Sideburns contest in the Hanoi Hilton. Of course, that never happened, but just the thought of it kept me smiling for weeks. In the Hanoi Hilton, simple little joys had to be savored.

As pumpkin season was now in full bloom, every meal had pumpkin soup and often a side dish of pumpkins cooked into a mush with some other type of vegetable. Ernie was sure it was turnips, but Walt and Steve thought it had to be something else. One week everything was flavored with curry and Walt was sure the NVA had so much curry sent to them by China that they decided to give the POWs some, too. It lasted at least three weeks and started Ernie guessing that the talks were going well. So we derived a new word for Webster and the good folks at Oxford: gastro-political, which was defined as the food which determines how well the North Vietnamese felt the propaganda and peace talks were going for their side.

One evening the guards were busy making short square stalls in the court yard. Ernie had seen this at the Plantation, the first prison in Hanoi he was held at, and said we probably were going to be shown a movie. He said even a bad movie was better than no movie at all. That evening the four LULU POWs were the last to be brought out to the courtyard. A large white cloth served as a movie screen and Bug, one of the more senior officers of the Vietnamese Regular Army, told us there was to be no talking and no coughing. At which point several guards starting coughing and all the POWs started laughing. The movie was a very slick Russian color film on the superiority of their COOP system and how the harvest was growing each year. The facts were very different in Russia, but who cared here. The girls looked beautiful and reminded me of how much I missed my wife.

After that film we were shown a black and white film on how the United States was using secret forces to infiltrate North Vietnam along the coast. But the ever-vigilant forces of the Peoples Liberation Army were on the sea and on the scene. The pictures showed a patrol boat manned by an all-woman crew of soldiers who had purportedly captured an American SEAL. In fact, it was Seaman Douglas Hegdahl. Ernie didn't have to tell me, because I had seen film of this man getting off a plane in Moscow and then in New York in 1969 before I deployed. Walt and Steve were amazed that both Ernie and I could both identify the man as Hegdahl, and many others who knew Doug at the Plantation could, too. I then realized that many people started coughing that sounded like "Horse-ship" and "Bull-ship." It was an interesting night and also was the first time that Ernie, Walt, Steve, and I were allowed to see the movies with the other prisoners. We had no chance to communicate because of the screens and the guards, but it was still good to be seen from time to time and other POWs clearly saw us being led back to our cells.

Ernie and I had been moved several times in the Thunderbird and landed up next to COL Robbie Risner, USAF. He was senior to CDR Jeremiah Denton and was now the SRO at the Little Vegas part of the Hanoi Hilton. He reaffirmed the previous SRO orders to make no tapes, offer no propaganda for the North Vietnamese war effort, and resist to your utmost from going to a peace delegation press show. One of things he started was a daily evening prayer time. Near the end of each day after the evening meal was cleared, COL Risner would thump three times on the wall and it would be passed to others. We were to stop all activities and pray for the POWs who were still solo and those being punished. Although there were some rules that had been relaxed, the conditions were still filthy, oppressive, and not close to Red Cross standards; our health was a serious concern for all. I remember one cell wanting to know if we had to get on our knees at this time and COL Risner said, "Please pray as you have been raised—standing, sitting, or on your knees—but please pray for these men and the end of them living in solitary confinement." And every day we prayed.

The issue of "date of rank" and being senior was probably never tested more than in Hanoi. The best example I can think of is when a long time air force officer passed a message onto Robbie that he had a date of rank to lieutenant colonel at least five years before COL Risner's date of rank, even though at this time we had learned Risner had been selected for general officer rank. The military system on establishing date of rank was based on the date of rank at time of capture, so the most senior at date of capture should take charge. The duration of this war was straining the logic of who was really senior, and Risner's reply to the air force officer's message sticks in my mind vividly. We were in a cell next to Robbie's and had to pass his reply down the passageway so it would get to the next building and the sender. COL Risner's reply was simple, "I am at your command, sir." And so the baton was passed, but nothing really changed a great deal until a prisoner in the cell with this new SRO was caught red-handed tapping on the wall to their neighbors. Another purge started and it was learned that the new SRO was issuing orders. As soon as he came back from interrogation, he passed the command back to COL Risner with the caution that he was under more restrictions now and extra guards were assigned to watch him.

About this time we received a curious message from the Desert Inn where all the senior leaders had been moved. We gathered that several were given an assignment to define the acronyms we used, so there was a list of common meanings. They wanted to know what LULU stood for and I tried to tell the others that it was a cartoon strip. Somehow that didn't sound too military. We discussed this for a few days and all agreed that LULU would stand for the "Legendary Union of Laotian Unfortunates."

When we were finally released in 1973 we learned that there were at least 600 Americans either missing in action (MIA) or killed in action (KIA) in Laos. And by 1973, our LULU group had grown to ten—nine Americans and one Canadian. We were, in fact, the most fortunate ones because we lived to return home in honor. But the name LULU stuck and was passed to many who ended up being moved to other prisons. I have always been somewhat amazed that many years later people who never had direct contact with us knew exactly what LULU stood for and still could recall our names.

In late autumn we heard a large group of Americans singing "God Bless America." This was incredible, and we were all speculating on what it could mean. Some thought it was a group getting prepared for release, but that didn't make much sense to Ernie or me. Soon after the guards moved a South Vietnamese POW near us. He was Capt. Dat Q. Nguyen, South Vietnamese Air Force, whose call sign was "Max." Dat had actually been trained as a pilot at Randolph Air Force Base in Texas. He had been imprisoned near Sgt. Chi Chan Harnavee, the Thai Special Forces man captured with Ernie Brace in May 1965. Ernie was delighted to hear that Harnavee was doing well and gathering a lot of intel for other POWs. Max told us there was a section west of us in Hoa Lo with a large group of Americans from a camp that had been closed down and were housed in one of the six or seven larger cells. Later we learned the Americans had called this section of the Hanoi Hilton, Camp Unity.

More news arrived just before Thanksgiving. Max heard on the camp radio and from listening to the guards talking to each other that American military had landed rescue forces at Son Tay, but found no prisoners there. They had all been moved just several days before the raid. Max also said he heard on the radio that a U.S. senator had said, "The U.S. will not stand to see our POWs mistreated any longer and would land special forces anywhere in the world, including the streets of Hanoi, to save our POWs, and no force on earth could stop us." I do not recall Ernie getting more excited about anything up to that point, and this was indeed good news—we were not forgotten. The rules of engagement had obviously been changed. Hope springs eternal.

> *But I'll leave here alive, I know that now,*
>
> *But I don't know when and I don't know how.*
>
> *And I'll see my family once again,*
>
> *But I don't know where and I don't know when.*[19]

Ernie's words seemed to ring increasing true and all hopes were really on the upswing now.

In early December, a number of POWs were taken for "attitude checks" and to prepare rough drafts of their traditional Christmas messages home. Many drafts of letters were written; few letters were sent. These prisoners reported that Dead Eye, Bug, and Maggot were telling Americans they were going to get a "big" present this Christmas, but the LULUs were told nothing. When Christmas Eve arrived we heard a lot of activity, but being stuck deep in the Thunderbird, we could see little. Finally, two guards appeared and took us to the Christmas room; we obviously were the last ones to visit. It was Ernie's and my one-year anniversary and we were hopeful for another package or some specific news from home. There was nothing, except for a few pieces of candy and instructions that we were going to be moved to a new location. At first I thought it might mean a big cell, but when we were led out of the Thunderbird, we were right back in the Golden Nugget where Ernie and I were last Christmas. But now it was different—we could not hear or see any other American POWs. It appeared that the Little Vegas camp had been emptied, except for the four LULU POWs. Without talking or saying very much, we were all a bit worried.

---

19 Ernest C. Brace, *A Code to Keep*, 148.

On Christmas Day 1970, our LULU group was brought together in a Golden Nugget cell for a small breakfast and then we were allowed to visit. The mid-day meal actually looked and tasted like turkey, stuffing, sweet potatoes, corn, and a type of relish that served in lieu of cranberry sauce. It was tasty and more food than my shrinking stomach could handle. It was good to spend all day with the LULUs and to play a game of Hearts and the perennial favorite Shit on Your Neighbor. What a Christmas!

It was not too late in the evening, but it was definitely dark when we started hearing sounds as if another group of prisoners was moving into other sections of Little Vegas. Steve Long reported seeing four women carrying what looked like a large container of equipment. The next day we saw at the wash stalls what appeared to be Vietnamese women prisoners. Most were quite young and all seemed a little too feisty to be POWs. It didn't seem like we would be here for long, but no officer or English-speaking guard came by. The days of our imaginary calendar kept turning.

One evening we heard a lot of prisoner activity in the courtyard and the splashing of water. Apparently Steve was first to spot the women, who were having their long hair washed and combed. The moon appeared to be rising, and all I could see were silhouette figures going through the motions of combing their hair. Ernie suspected that they were all women who had been caught engaged in the world's "oldest profession." Walt Stischer tended to agree, but said in his very reserved way, that they were all good looking. And then we heard one of them singing in a most beautiful soprano voice in French, the song "Plaisir d'amour." This song was made famous in the U.S. by Joan Baez. The first verse in English is, "The joys of love are but a moment long. The pain of love endures the whole life long." Walt whispered to Ernie and me to ask if we could get their attention and when the woman finished one verse, I sang softly the verse back to them in English. The girl stopped and I am sure she was startled to hear a man, an American man, singing her song in English. She sang another verse in French and I repeated it in English. Across the miles, despite a war that was raging across this land, two voices on that night came together and communicated a hope for peace and a prayer for lost love.

When she finished, Walt asked me to sing something that was "American." The only thing I could think of was "God Bless America." I tried to sing it slowly and articulate the words well. Steve and Ernie could see the women and Ernie said, "Keep singing, they hear you. They are all turning to look this way. Steve! Are you seeing this?"

"Roger, Ernie!"

When I finished I distinctly heard one gal say, "God bless you." Ernie and Steve reported that some of them had placed their hands over their hearts. I guess they didn't all hate us in North Vietnam. We tried several times to speak to a few of the women, who were close to our cells, but they didn't seem to understand us and we couldn't follow their Vietnamese. But they had listened to a simple song written by Irving Berlin on the eve of World War I and seemed to know that tune meant something special to Americans.

Just before New Year's Day we were told to gather up our things. Once we were out of our cells we were blindfolded and told to put a hand on the shoulder of the prisoner in front of us. Off we went—to where, we had no idea. After a series of turns and various sounds, I gave up trying to track where we were, but not Ernie Brace. He kept whispering what direction we were going and surmising that we are working our way toward the new Camp Unity. And as usual, Ernie's sense of direction and distance was spot on.

We stopped and waited a few minutes before our blindfolds were removed. We were inside a small compound with a wall that divided us from cells on the other side. We were taken into a one-story building and walked to a door at the far end, and then entered a long corridor with cells on both sides. The corridor angled to the left near the end where our new cells were waiting for us. This time Steve whispered for me to go with Walt. I did and no one said anything. So Walt and I were at the very last cell, and Steve and Ernie were just next door to us on the same side of the corridor. We could talk very easily to one another, and Ernie quickly made contact with a few prisoners whose cells we had passed.

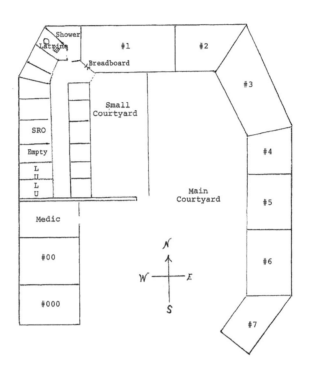

Map of Camp Unity

When in our new cell, Steve jumped up on the concrete rack with stocks built into it and asked out the window, "Hey! Any Americans here?"

"Yeah! John Flynn and Dave Winn here," we heard from the direction of the entrance.

Col John Flynn, promoted to brigadier general by the air force while in captivity, was the most senior officer captured during the Vietnam War. He was held along with three other USAF full colonels: James Bean, Norman Gaddis, and Dave Winn in Camp Unity. On the other side of the corridor about half-way to the entrance, were Max, the South Vietnamese pilot; SGT Harnavee, Ernie's Thai Special Forces man; and two other Thais. Ernie and Max had established some good communication procedures for tapping to them and said Max would act as a relay to the senior officers who had been kept in various hard-to-reach places for obvious reasons.

Within a few days we made contact with a group of about twenty in the cellblock east of our section called the Mayo or Block 00. Held there was Everett Alvarez, Jr., the first pilot shot down in the Vietnam War. When Alvarez was released in 1973 he had been held captive for eight and a half years—longer than any other American POW in history. After our return in 1973, we learned that Army Col Floyd J. Thompson was captured on March 26, 1964 and was officially the longest held military POW of the Vietnam War.

My cell block in Camp Unity was known as Rawhide or Block 0. The main tapper and talker in Block 00 was LT David Carey, who had been captured in 1967. My cellmate now, Walt Stischer, (who remained the SRO of our LULU group), was tall and could stand on the beds and get his voice to bounce off the exterior wall so the Block 00 group could hear him well. I was on the floor as lookout, watching if any guard came up the corridor so I could sound the alarm before the guard could hear anything. Steve and Ernie did the same thing toward the four colonels, but they were not talkers and only coughed to acknowledge. This reluctance to communicate tracked with what Ernie and I had heard when we were in the Little Vegas because their seniority resulted in more attention. I humored them one day by changing a well-known acronym, RHIP, which meant Rank Has Its Privileges, to Rank Has Its Pain. And that was true for the Hanoi Hilton.

The large group next to Walt and me had not heard details of the lunar landing, so one day when it was raining and appeared safe to talk, I stood on a pile of blankets and went through the flight and how Neil Armstrong stepped onto the surface of the moon and the video sent back to earth. I repeated his famous phrase, "That's one small step for man, one giant leap for mankind." I could hear Dave repeating this to his group and actually heard them cheering the news.

One of the most unusual questions we got from Dave was about a photo from home. He asked, "Is everyone wearing two-toned shoes with wildly colored shirts and pants? And are all the men wearing their hair like the hippies?"

The commies had been quick to show film of the peace demonstrations of 1969 and 1970 with American protesters making highly critical statements about the U.S. and its role in the Vietnam War. Walt whispered to me and I relayed to Dave that he shouldn't put too much stock in that and not to believe anything the Commies said. Then he told us he had just received a package from home with a picture of his family and his brother had long hair down to his shoulders and a shirt that probably was stolen off a circus clown. I didn't know what to say and finally said that the styles were all in flux when I left over a year ago, so it might be the popular style for a lot of the younger generation. I heard Ernie laughing next door and then finally Steve said "Now that's a good one."

The exit from Rawhide led to a small but long courtyard that was walled off from several large cells and the main courtyard. When we were taken to wash, two would wash and two would exercise in this small courtyard. At first the guards usually took a position close to the door that led to the courtyard, but soon they started leaving this small area and standing outside a larger courtyard. This allowed Ernie, in the wash area, to step back into the corridor of Rawhide and speak with the four colonels while Walt was inside and Steve and I kept outside watch. When any guard approached the outside door to our space, I would throw a homemade ball of very tightly wrapped rags to Steve, who would yell "I've got it!" This system worked well and we were never caught.

We learned from COL John Flynn that he was indeed the SRO, but he found it very difficult to communicate with the other cells. Ernie also sensed the other colonels may not have been as keen to be involved in all the activities, so the challenge for the LULUs was to find a way to contact the main group in the larger seven cells. Once again Ernie, ever-questioning and observant, noticed a strange add-on to the wall on the north side of the washing area—it looked like someone had bolted a breadboard onto the wall. With Steve and me outside watching for any guards, Ernie and Walt went to work on the four bolts holding the board in place. As they tried to undo it, they heard the distinctly American "shave and a haircut" call-and-response from the other side. It was Cell 1 who had contact with Cell 2, who had contact with Cell 3, and so on to the end at Cell 7.

The most senior officers who had been moved to Little Vegas in 1969 were all now in Cell 7 and had been acting on daily matters that required SRO rulings. CDR James Stockdale and CDR Jeremiah Denton, COL Robbie Risner, and a very senior USAF Col Vern Ligon were there. All four had served alone as the SRO in other prisons. Now we could pass a note from Col Flynn to Cell 1, which in turn would pass it onto the next cell. Eventually, after several days, it would get to Cell 7. However, any answer might take another few days to return to us for passing to Col Flynn. The LULU group went to work to ensure this communication chain was not busted and Ernie Brace, Korean War veteran, USMC, and longest-held civilian POW in the Vietnam War, was the center of it all. I think that being closer to the four colonels in age and having Korean War experience made it easier for the colonels to talk to Ernie directly, and we worked hard on a daily basis to make that happen.

One item we learned from the Cell 1 was that those with dental problems were being allowed to see a dentist who had been provided to the prison. Ernie had a small dental plate to replace several missing teeth from years ago. When he was beaten for his escape attempts, it had loosened and decay started to set in. By 1971 the area around the implant was starting to turn an ominous black with a distinct smell of something rotting. Being captured in Laos, we probably were their last concern; yet to our surprise, we soon heard from the guard that we would be afforded the care of a dentist in camp, The next day a guard came for Ernie to see the camp doctor who thought he needed penicillin before any oral surgery was attempted.

A few days later Ernie, still in great discomfort, was taken to the new camp dentist. The Novocain needle was repeatedly placed in Ernie's gum alongside the teeth, which were very painful. The Novocain was useless as it kept running off and down Ernie's throat. Meanwhile, Steve, Walt, and I were left outside and having a catch with a new and much harder ball Steve and Ernie had made with a large seed nut in its center that we had found in the courtyard. While Ernie was out of the area, we were working on making it curve and sink.

When Ernie returned he was white as a sheet and both eyes were swollen and very black at the bottom. He had a large cotton wad in his mouth that didn't look too tasty. They had yanked his dental plate out with a pair of pliers and then the dentist used a foot-powered drill to clean out the decay. Ernie said it was worse than torture. He was in serious pain and not even an aspirin was offered. Walt went to the guard to ask if the medic could give Ernie aspirin at least. Ernie was more interested in getting his clothes washed and getting some rest. When he came out to hang his wet clothes, my throw to Steve sailed high, tipped off his outstretched hands, and hit Ernie right in the mouth. Ernie was not only in pain, but he was also bleeding profusely from his mouth. I had this terrible sinking feeling that I was the cause of it all, but the guard seeing Ernie left the court yard area and quickly returned with the medic. A new cotton wad was prepared and he gave Ernie four aspirin and told him take two every four hours. It was a very uncomfortable night for Ernie, and also for me with my feelings of guilt and anger that I had thrown the errant ball his way. Steve kept saying, "If only I was a bit taller, I would have caught that one." Ernie finally silenced us all with, "Go to sleep; this too will pass." And he was right again.

After solid communication was set up, Ernie devised a new tool, a bamboo wrench, to work on the bolts on the breadboard. He wanted to see the Americans on the other side and particularly after we heard that LT Michael Christian (USN) had used a discarded handkerchief to sew an American flag with a bamboo needle. He had secretly procured threads and colored them red and blue with roof tile dust and ink from discarded ballpoint pens, which he painted onto the cloth with glue made from rice. The LULUs simply had to see that!

Within two days the board was off and we could look through the hole. We were in awe of this group. There were more Americans in one cell than any of us had ever seen. And when Mike showed us his flag, Steve and I acted in unison by standing a little taller and saluting it. Then we couldn't resist and recited the Pledge of Allegiance. We quickly said goodbye for that day and reset the board. We arrived just outside the wash area before the guard got suspicious.

I shall never forget that day when we saw the first American Flag since being captured. For Ernie it was the first time in six and a half years. Communication was the blood of resistance and an outward, visible symbol that America would never forget us, and we would never forget our fellow POWs.

★

We learned that Col Flynn's call sign had been "Sky," so we affectionately started to refer to him in notes and policy issued as Sky. One of the first notes from Cell 7 was to reissue what CDR Stockdale had called in 1967 the "Plums," which was a strong statement to all POWs not to help the enemy, to resist writing and making tapes, and to give your best to resist in helping with anything the Commies asked of you. The officers with LtCol Edison Miller had been put into a small group just to the east of Cellblock 00, so we called their cell Triple Zero. Ernie was adamant that we had to encourage them to come back into the fold and start resisting and stop making tapes. Because the three officers from Little Vegas (Miller, CAPT Walter "Gene" Wilber, and CDR Robert Schweitzer) were all senior officers, they had a lot of influence on younger officers. In fact, in my first week of captivity while still not in contact with other Americans, the Maggot had played a tape of two Americans being interviewed and talking together on how "any new POW should obey all the camp regulations and answer all questions put them by the Camp Authorities." This tape was played to many other POWs and was also played on camp radios so often that other POWs referred to it as the "Bob and Ed Show."

When we tried to enlist help from Dave Carey and Cell 00, they told us they had already sent word to the officers in Triple Zero about the Plums and what the new SRO was ordering us to do. I shall never forget the look on Ernie's face when he heard that Miller said the only authority here was the "camp authorities." Ernie proved the expression of "Once a Marine, always a Marine" true when he got on his bed during a rain storm that helped to dampen voices and yelled out to Triple Zero, "Hey, Miller! Square yourself and your group away. You're still a U.S. Marine, for God's sake!" There was no answer from Triple Zero.

The LULUs stayed very active in passing notes and got a first look at SRO notes back to the Cell 7 leaders. As the month of January passed, it was obvious that younger junior officers and some of the hard-nosed senior officers wanted to push back and actively resist more. Walt Stischer expressed what many others were passing onto Col Flynn:

"Sir, this setup is the best I've had since being captured, but they still have the straps and bars in storage as well as the leg irons. We need to proceed with some caution."

The thing about Col Flynn is that he listened to a number of various suggestions and then tried to maneuver a middle course. However, that guidance was hard to keep control of when the guards started to stop POWs from conducting prayer services on Sundays. Several incidents in early February resulted in more questions for the SRO. In his replies Col Flynn had a professional and compassionate concern for all. He wanted to prevent a big uproar if it was at all possible.

On Sunday, February 7, 1971, the proverbial bubble burst in Cell 7 when a group of large guards rushed into the cell to break up religious services and take the most senior officers out of the cell. Nothing worked well for either side, and soon Dead Eye and Bug were issuing orders. That evening as we were getting our mosquito nets up, we heard Cell 7, and then other cells joining in, singing our national anthem, the "Star Spangled Banner." The LULUs didn't have a clue at this point of what had happened. However, it was clear that every prisoner in the larger cells were on their feet and singing the anthem and military service songs. The LULUs joined in and sang as loud as we could. Between songs we could hear the loud speakers on the street now playing at a very loud volume in an attempt to drown out the voices of some four hundred American POWs and several Thai POWs.

The last song sung that night was "God Bless America." Those stirring words fortified many for the repercussions that were sure to follow. We then heard a group shouting, "This is Seven! This is Severn! Where in the hell is Number Six?" Of course, the next cell and each cell in sequence picked up the chant. Our group was so small that some POWs found it difficult to hear us. Then Cell 00 sounded off loud and clear. After that there was a prolonged silence awaiting the group of around ten POWs in Triple Zero. I quipped to Walt, "That's Triple Zero or strike three as we say in baseball. What a group of losers!" What we didn't know then, but learned later, is that both LtCol Edison Miller and CAPT Gene Wilber ordered their group to "sit down and shut up."

We had a quick conversation with Cell 00 who told us the guards were amassing in force and some POWs had already been put in handcuffs and led off to the Heartbreak—the cells used for torture. I had just fallen asleep when guards opened our doors and told us to pack everything. Our stuff was taken by guards while we were blindfolded, our hands tied behind us, and we were roped in a single line. We were led out of our little prison courtyard to a truck already running and ready to hit the road.

While we headed westward we all kept trying to peek out the back of the truck. Ernie was best at sensing that we were on a main road leading out of the city. After about an hour, there was darkness around us and we could peek out the open end of the back of the truck to see the glow of the Hanoi's lights fading on the horizon, much to east of us now. Ernie feared we were being taken back to Laos and whispered for us to look for a time to escape. No time like that appeared, and we never stopped until we arrived at another North Vietnam Army camp.

We were roughly taken out of the truck and our senior guard was our old friend, Peppy Le Pew, who instructed the other guards to tighten our blindfolds. We were then led in the dark over uneven ground and walked a fairly long way. When we stopped we heard the squeak of a rusty door hinge crying for oil. I sort of stumbled and brushed against the man in front of me, causing my blindfold to slip. It was so dark that it was hard to see anything, but I did see a guard tower about twenty feet high that had one light in it illuminating a small building in front of us. We were led one-by-one at this point. I was put into a single cell with a bucket and my clothes, mosquito net, and bamboo mat. Peppy Le Pew held an oil lantern while another guard removed my blindfold and untied my hands. The walls were a very course concrete type of stucco, and it was hard to see how I was going to get a mosquito net up. The guard took the mat and then helped me hook the net up to small screws that were very hard to see and blended into the wall. The floor looked like hard, compacted dirt, and it wasn't until the next day that I realized it was all concrete. Then Peppy Le Pew said very sternly, "No talk!" He abruptly turned and left me in the dark to figure out how to get in bed and finish fixing my mosquito net. There was one window with bars on it and I could see lantern light from the other side of the building—and again heard Peppy Le Pew saying, "No Talk!"

When Peppy and his lantern left, it was completely dark. I held my hand up and could only see it when I stood in front of the window that faced directly out to the guard tower to my right. There were no lights and no noise from a camp radio. Ernie began tapping on the floor and we all answered his "ring." He said the good news was that we were not in Laos or near the China border. He also said that wood rats were very common in the countryside and that we needed to tuck in our mosquito nets under the bamboo mats very tightly. If we didn't, we might wake up with company in our beds. Walt Stischer was now our prison SRO and it didn't look like there any other Americans here or near to us. He finally tapped to all of us that he hoped we had a good night's sleep and welcome to "LULU's Hideaway."

The name really had a double meaning. One of Ernie Brace's greatest concerns was the main body of POWs would be released, be flown home, and we would be left behind. He was never one to sit back and let others do the heavy lifting with communications or any other activity to resist the enemy. Now we were undoubtedly removed from the other POWs and really didn't know where we were. The POWs we had left in Hanoi would awaken the next day only to know we were no longer where we had been the night before. In a very real sense, we were missing in action again. We also knew we were not constrained by the prison system and would probably fall more under regular army control. Both Walt and Ernie made it clear that the next day we had to get a good fix on where we were and what kind of treatment we would now receive.

One thing was for sure: the North Vietnamese had repeatedly denied having combat troops in Laos. They hid us away because each one of us was living proof that the NVA was in Laos and, in fact, that was who had captured all four of us. So in short, they wanted us hidden away from Hanoi and any other POWs held in that urban area.

CHAPTER 10

THE LULU'S GROW

The next day was a new start in my captivity. Before the sun ever appeared, I could see the gray dawn gradually turning the sky into a lighter hue of gray. Looking through my mosquito net, I could look out the window and up into the sky for the first time in many weeks. I had no idea when or how we would be notified that it was time to get out of our racks. Ernie soon whispered that the soldiers were usually awakened with a metal piece of iron being hit by a metal bar. He advised we stay in our racks until we heard the gong or until a guard came into our compound. I had already risen to use the bucket to relieve my bladder and when I looked out my window, I realized that I was in the only cell with a view of the door used to access our small compound. I spoke up and let them all know that if a guard came in, I would greet him with a cheery "good morning" so that they all would know we had company. Meanwhile, Steve, Walt, and Ernie whispered and wondered more on where we were. The Legendary Union of Laotian Unfortunates began their work.

Just as the sky was turning blue, the sound of the gong signaled the official start of the day. I noticed a guard soon relieving the soldier who had been on duty in the tower. About an hour later I could hear keys rattling at the compound door, and then Peppy Le Pew strode into our little world and I yelled out a greeting. He opened my door and told me to wash. The basin of water was on the north side where Walt could look out his window and see me. Peppy told Walt, "No talk." Walt told him that he had spent many days and nights with me at the Hoa Lo prison and asked why we couldn't talk to one another since

151

we all knew each other. Peppy walked off to the other cell where Ernie was being held and told him no talking. Ernie had such a pained looked, Peppy further explained to him that this was new place run by the army and a new place meant new rules.

Ernie nodded his head and said, "We understand, but if we just whisper and keep our voices very low, no other soldiers will hear us." Peppy stood there for about a minute, nodded his head, and walked around the building. Soon another guard joined him and he told the guard to let the other prisoners out. They all came to the basin where I was washing while wearing my boxer shorts because I didn't want my red hair to start any entertainment show for an army base. Peppy quickly stepped up and told us that we had to stay apart by at least twenty feet.

"There is no gathering or exercising in a group allowed now," he said. Obviously, I thought this a blowback from the earlier song fest, but didn't want to push him today. He looked like he had not gotten but an hour or two of sleep and was not very pleased to be away from Hanoi.

Soon our breakfast arrived: four teapots of tea hotter and stronger than what we had in Hanoi, and four plates with a type of pancake about six inches wide and thin, sweet syrup poured over it. It actually tasted quite good, by Hanoi standards. With much pride, Peppy told us the food here was Vietnamese Army food and that made us all smile.

On the first day we were not allowed outside very much, and Ernie astutely observed that Peppy was probably the sergeant in charge of us now and he needed to feel comfortable we would not cause him embarrassment or loss of face. Walt grumbled something, but agreed that we needed to remain at a low profile. When our mid-day meal came, it was hard to believe. We had rice, boiled vegetables, and a few grilled peppers, along with some canned meat. We had a similar dinner, but instead of canned meat, we had some type of grilled fresh fish that was crispy and simply delicious. Ernie told Walt we were all going to get fat eating like this and we should probably start a mandatory exercise program. Steve said he already had a good daily routine that included thirty minutes of running in place, and one hundred each of pushups, sit-ups, and squat jumps. I couldn't resist and added the navy had doubled my tea ration in order to exercise my right arm more.

After a few days in our new camp, we determined we were in a place that probably had been another POW camp and we were staying in the four punishment cells for troublemakers. We later learned that this prison was called Briarpatch, which had been completely emptied of American POWs and moved back to Hanoi's Hoa Lo prison in 1970. We were imprisoned here because we were all captured in Laos.

After a week the guards starting letting us out together to wash and exercise. We completely ignored the former directive to not communicate and started walking together. I was surprised no one said anything. I could sense that Ernie was getting restless and started talking about the chances of escaping from here. He had spotted a metal reinforcing rod about three feet long that was hanging loosely in the barbed wire on his side of the compound, and we all spotted it on our next loop around the inside portion of the outer wall. Steve was eager, but Walt and I questioned Ernie on whether the risk would be worth the attempt if the U.S. and North Vietnam were talking peace in Paris. Ernie felt the Code of Conduct set a moral standard to attempt escape at every chance, and he was right about that. So, in a few days Walt and I distracted the guard in the tower when no guards were inside our compound and Steve lifted Ernie up to grab, yank, and finally procure the metal rod. Ernie also had discovered that in his cell there was a four-foot by three-foot patch of dirt. A five-inch layer of concrete made up the rest of his floor, while the floors of the other cells had no dirt. This would make a great hiding place and by night fall, Ernie had the rod buried six inches deep.

Ernie started making plans for the escape. Because I lost my glasses when I ejected, I had trouble seeing anything beyond fifteen feet and asked Ernie if I would be more of a hindrance than a help in such an escape. I didn't realize it at the time, but Steve Long was also having some doubts about the efficacy of escape from this place. There were few American planes over North Vietnam since the bombing halt started by President Johnson in 1968, and we really didn't know how far and in what direction would be our best chance of getting seen and rescued by American forces. Walt was our SRO and said that he would not stop an escape, but he would not join in it. He had felt his heart murmurs increasing of late and didn't want to risk the stress on his heart. He would bless our trying if the time was good for an escape, and Ernie thought we could get far enough away in the first night as to not be caught right away.

Each night it would get very quiet about an hour before darkness completely descended on our compound. Ernie, Steve, and Walt were not singers and liked to hear me on occasion sing a melody of patriotic songs or songs from the 1950s and '60s. "Yesterday" by the Beatles and "As Tears Go By" by the Rolling Stones were two of my favorites and I often tried to change the words in the songs to suit us. For example, "As the '*Years*' Go By" is how I sang the Rolling Stones' song. I also sang "Green, Green Grass of Home," which had the name of Walt's wife, Mary, in it. The song Walt liked more for the tune than the lyrics, "Someone's in the Kitchen with Dinah," was because the tune was used for "The Eyes of Texas," the alma mater for the University of Texas since 1903.

Walt was a proud Texan and a graduate of the University of Texas ROTC program. He told me about struggling at the Air Force's Command and Staff School with the public speaking course. Where he was raised in South Texas, a true man didn't use his hands to speak and stood tall. And above all, a true Texan never raised his voice. His speech course instructor encouraged him many times to "shake a leg and add some vitality to his speaking." On his final speech project, Walt choose to speak about why the air force should hire chiropractors to help align aircrew spines, especially for fighter pilots who pulled too many G's while twisting in their seats trying to watch a MIG behind them. And they could also heal many other ailments. Walt's father had been a chiropractor in West Texas, and Walt was a firm believer in their ability to heal. So when he started his speech with the instructor in the front row, he began by saying, "Most of you believe a chiropractor is a person who just jumps on your back." As he finished this statement, he moved to his left and took a huge jump to land right in front of the instructor, who jumped up and dropped all his notes on the floor. Then Walt returned to the lecture to stand tall (almost at attention) and read his speech for the next twenty minutes. The instructor admitted that the only reason he passed Walt was because of his flying leap of faith at the opening of his speech. However, when it came to briefing a group of officers or giving a recap of a mission, Walt was very professional in every sense of the word.

One day in late February Walt taught me the words to "The Eyes of Texas," which I sang frequently:

> The Eyes of Texas are upon you,
>
> All the live-long day.
>
> The Eyes of Texas are upon you,
>
> You cannot get away.
>
> Do not think you can escape them
>
> At night or early in the morn—
>
> The Eyes of Texas are upon you,
>
> 'Till Gabriel blows his horn.

The song is usually ended with the cheer of "Hook 'em Horns!" Now this I could relate to as it had spirit and put value in the moral right. It reminded me of a priest at Saint Peter's School who said being a righteous man means doing the right thing when no one is watching. I was quick to add this to my evening sound track that I broadcast to the other LULUs, and put it right before my Union College alma mater, "Ode to Old Union." Ernie liked to joke that although the Commies gave him a "radio" — his reference to me — at Christmas 1969 and he was "still searching to find the darn off switch."

One night as I was finishing my Buddy Holly medley, Peppy Le Pew entered the compound, which was late for him. He came to my window and asked, "What songs were you just singing?" I told him it was a few songs from 1956 and 1957 from Buddy Holly and the Crickets. He smiled and asked, "Who this Bud Holly?" I told him a Texan from Lubbock with a few of his high school friends who liked making music in their garage and became very successful. When I told him Holly died during a big 1958 snowstorm in a plane crash, Peppy Le Pew smiled all-knowing and said, "Maybe you need to fly more." He left laughing to himself and I got the impression that he may have been imbibing some type of alcohol and listening to everything we said and what I had sung that night.

On March 8, 1971, near the end of day, the guards with Peppy Le Pew entered and went straight to Ernie's room. They told him he was moving and I almost went into shock thinking that I would be separated from this man who had taught me so much and whom I really admired and respected. But he wasn't going far. They brought a double bed frame into the compound and placed it in Steve Long's cell where Ernie was then placed. In near darkness, with Peppy carrying a lantern again, another American POW entered the gate and went around to the rear to occupy Ernie's old cell. My first thought was that Ernie's escape tools and extra supplies for the escape were buried in the dirt patch in the floor.

Ernie tried tapping his name and questioned "Who you?" to the new man. There was no response to the "shave-and-a-haircut" call and response or to Ernie's message. Walt tried to whisper to him, but no reply was returned. Then Steve grew a little impatient and simply said in fairly loud voice; "New POW say your name!" We barely heard someone trying to talk, but it was mumbled and impossible to decipher. Walt asked, "Do you know the tap code?" It sounded like a "no" from where I was, but Steve thought he had said, "I don't know." Walt finally gave the order to go to bed, and he advised us, "We'll contact him in the morning."

The next day we found out the new prisoner was a shoot-down from the February attack on Vietnamese Army camps in Laos. Major Norbert "Norm" Gotner, USAF, was flying as navigator in an F-4 Phantom and his pilot, once on the ground, was shot and killed. We were excited to hear more of the details of the attacks on Laos and previous attacks on Cambodia that had succeeded in denying the North Vietnamese Army places to hide. Ernie said, "President Nixon sounds like he means business, Norm. Any chance he'll start bombing the North again." It was then that Norm told us that President Nixon announced a plan to remove all American troops in six months and "negotiate in Paris from a position of strength." We were elated; however, Norm said that no one at air force command thinks that the U.S. can meet the timetable that had been originally set and it might take a year. To Ernie, this was only good news. The Commies had told me and others many times, "We can never defeat the U.S. in the Tonkin Gulf, but we will beat you in the streets of San Francisco and New York City." It didn't sound like that was about to happen this year.

Norm was not allowed out of his room for two or three days, so when I was taken out to wash, I simply walked up to his window and shook his hand. We all did, and that made Norm feel like he was one of us, which of course he was. Norm had served in several missile commands and was deathly afraid that if the North Vietnamese ever discovered his ballistic missile background, they would ship him to the Soviet Union to get all his knowledge about our strategic programs. We tried to assure him that he was safe now, but he was a bit nervous and, just as Ernie never found a glass half-empty, Norm never met a glass half-full. Perhaps Ernie would be good medicine for this new POW.

Norm had a lot of detailed knowledge from NASA about the Apollo program and the Apollo XIII mission when an oxygen tank exploded and crippled the spaceship. The crew and the land team had to scramble to jury rig several solutions to life-threatening problems such as the damage to their carbon dioxide removal system. Norm said it was a miracle we didn't lose the spacecraft and the entire crew. We were on the edge of our seats for three days listening to his recounting of the mission. Norm actually drew from memory schematics of both the command module and the lunar landing vehicle so we could all appreciate the complexity and engineering feats achieved by the Apollo XIII team. Ernie and Walt told Norm to hide the pictures really well, because the North Vietnamese might think they were something else. As it turned out two weeks later in a room inspection, they found the pictures and accused him of making a map for an escape plan. Norm was flabbergasted and denied very strongly such a thing. He actually told them they could see these pictures in *Popular Mechanics* that was sold on any newsstand in America. What Norm didn't realize was that the soldiers and the North Vietnamese people had not yet been told the news that Americans had landed on the moon and walked its surface in 1969. The guards made a lot of threats and kept the pictures for higher command to analyze. That was the end of our space and NASA updates, we thought.

Norm redrew several schematic pictures of the Apollo XIII command module and the lunar landing module, which was ten times more detailed than I had seen from 1969. He was delighted that we all had such a keen interest in the space program. But most of all, he told us more details about the Nixon Plan to end the war, which thrilled the four of us. He also had a way of finishing by planting a "Yes, but" type of detail. He said the Paris Peace talks were a joke and that the Commies were making the U.S. look bad to the entire world. He also told us how the peace movement was growing by leaps and bounds after the Kent State shooting by the National Guard that resulted in four students being killed in May 1970. Of course the North Vietnamese had been quick to tell us this news on the camp radio.

Ernie and I were still of the mind that there were many who supported our role in the world and that the protesters were sore losers of the 1968 election. It was hard from a jail cell in North Vietnam to understand how helping an ally from being invaded was now so unpopular. We had seen a few films in the Little Vegas Camp that showed large groups of rioting protesters and saw them being hosed by water cannons and bombarded with tear gas. It reminded me of the racial unrest of 1968 when major cities across the U.S. had black smoke clouds for days because of all the fires. And when I saw the films with students waving the Vietcong and the Communist North Vietnamese flags, I knew in my heart that things had changed quickly. And it saddened me to see so much division at home.

As April approached, Ernie told me he didn't want to worry Norm about the escape tools that he had buried in Norm's cell, and it looked like the Nixon plan may be working. "Heck, by the end of this year we might be on a plane home," he would often say to me. For Ernie, hope always restored his spirit and lifted him up. And he never failed to remind me, "Semper Fi! Do or Die!" Ernie had a number of long conversations with Norm so he would stay positive and, for the most part, he did. Yet Norm always kept reminding us that he had held one of the two keys in a ballistic missile silo and was deathly afraid that the North Vietnamese would find out. The North Vietnamese never did and never had a reason to suspect Norm had that type of background. And that was a good thing for all of us.

One of the major health issues for us at the LULUs Hideaway was the discovery of a tiny blood-sucking type of bedbug. Ernie noticed one day when Steve was doing sit-ups that his back had a number of red bug bites. They were living in the only double bed setup and were both getting bitten at night. They found a few of the creatures and squashed them to find a droplet of blood exude from the corpses. Walt proclaimed that given the number of bugs, the new standard to become an ace would be much higher, because both Steve and Ernie at five kills would become aces so quickly and so often that we would lose count. So the number of fifty dead bugs was set as the initial standard. By sunset of the second day, both Ernie and Steve were aces.

Walt thought the medic might help, so he raised the issue and Peppy allowed the medic to visit us in the compound. He looked closely and then looked under their bamboo rack. He found a nest and scurried out of the cell as fast as he could. Ernie charged in and started doing his version of the "Bristol Stomp," and the floor started to turn red. Later that night when it was time to do a medley of rock and roll tunes just before dusk, I changed the words to one of those new dance tunes from the 1960s to say, "Ernie's as sharp as a whistle, when he starts to do the Bedbug Stomp." We had a good laugh, because humor seemed to help. The only thing the medic was able to do was bring iodine. We joked that if it was external, the medic had iodine; if it was internal, the medic brought aspirin. Prison lore had it that those two treatments were all that was available in North Vietnam, but we found out later that was not necessarily so.

None of the other rooms had these creatures, but we still suffered by seeing how Ernie and Steve were being bitten. Finally Ernie brought a pail of cistern water and soap solution into the room and saturated the bed board and the walls, where they had found the bugs living in the natural crevices of the stucco-like finish. Even a little improvement helped.

About this time, Ernie discovered a fairly large toad near the tank that was filled each day with washing water. We were told repeatedly not to drink it. I needed no further encouragement and only drank the boiled water brought to us in our teapots. We discussed the idea of catching the toad and taking it into Steve and Ernie's cell to feed on the bedbugs, but Walt said, "It's better to leave the toads to witches and get Peppy to clean the cell." Now this option had not worked in the past, so the next day Ernie made it his mission to catch the toad. It was a huge one with a very blotched and well-camouflaged exterior. The fat toad was hard to see and Ernie enlisted Steve and me to help. Finally Steve saw the toad and we started jumping and scaring it toward Ernie who, as quick as I ever saw him move, swooped down and picked up the toad.

The toad was at least three or four pounds and, if laid out horizontally, would have reached at least twelve inches in length. However, we never had the chance to measure him. Ernie had done the natural thing of picking it up and then showing it to us, so the toad's head was looking forward at us and Ernie had the legs facing him. *Big mistake!* The toad did an explosive voiding of its bladder and Ernie's legs were covered with urine. Steve and I started laughing while Ernie threw the toad down and ran for the water tank. He poured water all over his bottom half, and Walt and Norm came to see what we had done now. Ernie then took off his pants and started rubbing water on everything because the urine was strong and probably poisonous to most animals. It was so corrosive that large blisters started to rise up on Ernie's legs that turned a bright pink and he said that his legs were on fire. Ernie had discovered in the most difficult way that most toads in Southeast Asia use their urine as a defense mechanism and the acidity of their urine is greater than most lab acids. Again, the only medicine offered by our captors was iodine, which Ernie gladly accepted, but never applied. Instead, he used the iodine as an ink to draw a picture of his toad. He kept it hidden in a section of two bamboo mats and planned to take it home so he could learn what kind of toad it was.

In early May, we had our evening interrupted by a group of soldiers and Peppy, who took us one-by-one out of our cells. We were blindfolded and our hands tied by wire. Then they placed chains around our waists and through our hand bindings, and started to lead us out of the compound. Norm started saying out loud the prayer "Hail Mary, Full of Grace," And Peppy said in a very loud and angry voice, "No talk!" We were led to the side of the compound where the guard tower was, and I suspected we were in full view of the tower when we were stopped. Our blindfolds were removed, and we were shown an opening in the ground with a ladder. I was closest to the opening and first in this Congo-line dance, so I led the way down.

It was now very dark outside and only one light, a smelly kerosene lantern, was at the foot of the ladder, about eight feet below ground. Then another soldier pointed to go down a small passageway to the next ladder, which went at least seven feet down. At this point I heard Norm telling Ernie that he didn't want to die by being buried alive and we would now have to fight for our lives. I hadn't sensed that type of immediate danger, perhaps because I had already been in one of this type of an underground fort on my first day of captivity. In any case, I went down the next ladder with a little more fear in my heart and a hope that Norm was overreacting. The soldier at the top told me to crawl into a small tunnel that was at best four feet high and had no support beams. It appeared to be dark at the end of this tunnel, but I kept moving, because the man behind me was being pushed and kept hitting his head into my butt. It was a most unusual and uncoordinated move.

Once I crawled into the next area, I found it so dark that I couldn't see the hand in front of my face. But I felt around and thought that from the way our voices echoed, we were in a larger room. Ernie told Steve, "I hope there is one soldier with a light that stays with us." Walt was telling Norm that we were *not* going to be buried alive in the hole, but none of us knew for sure at this point. I noticed someone crawling with a lantern down the tunnel towards us and was relieved to see a solder had been assigned to stay with us. We were kept underground for about an hour and I lost count of how many times Norm said the Lord's Prayer and Hail Mary. I did join him with whispering the Lord's Prayer aloud and that seemed to help him. And it helped me, too. It reminded me that I was not alone in this journey.

Another soldier came down the tunnel and gave instructions in English to follow him and the ever-popular command of "No talk!" When once again on the surface, we were blindfolded and led to what proved to be our cells. We each got back under our mosquito nets and started to wonder what the heck this exercise was all about? Norm thought it was a drill for how they were going to kill us. Ernie suggested that it just might be an air raid exercise, because we were no longer close to the city. Then Walt said he thought it was an exercise to hide us if a force of helicopters crossed the North Vietnam border and headed to rescue us like in the Song Tay raid a year before. I was sure Walt was as close to the truth as we could get and so I asked, "If Walt's right, what can we do to foil their attempt to hide us?"

That one question was on all our minds and we started on a plan the next morning. Norm had already been caught with drawings of the U.S. space capsules that the soldiers thought were maps for an escape plan, so having something on paper was probably not a safe option. Walt said as SRO he would take the task himself of drawing a map on toilet paper that the guards rarely if ever touched in a prison cell. Ernie contributed some excess iodine that could be brought back to ink by adding a few drops of tea. Walt had collected lots of toilet paper for notes, so we were set. Within a few weeks, we were surprised by a team of soldiers who inspected and rifled through every moveable object in our cells. I could tell they were experienced and thorough. I was worried about Walt not having enough time to hide his maps in a room inspection and how he could leave them in case we were going to go underground again so the guards wouldn't see them, but a U.S. Special Forces team could find the map and then find us.

Through all the inspections Ernie's escape tools and supplies buried in the small dirt patch in what was now Norm's cell were not found. But Walt had thrown the note on top of the fluid in his stinky bucket and figured no guard would reach into it to retrieve a floating piece of used toilet paper. We all figured incorrectly; the note was brought out into the sunlight between two sticks used as tweezers and proudly displayed to all of us. Walt claimed complete ignorance about it, but I noticed Ernie watching the corner of Walt's eye that had begun to twitch. Walt had a heart condition, and we were all worried about putting too much stress on him. Someone had to do something, but what could we do?

Finally to the rescue was the quick thinking Ernie Brace. He did a double take and said, "Oh! I see you found my new house plans that I intend to build when I go home. I was showing Walt the plans." Walt played along and admitted he didn't recognize it, because he must have used it as toilet paper by mistake. I couldn't resist and added, "They must have been pretty shitty house plans." Only the English speaking soldier and Peppy understood all the dialogue and they both started to laugh. Then, the stoical Peppy Le Pew took out his notebook, tore off a page, and gave it with a pen to Ernie to recreate his house. Ernie knew he could come close but maybe not be exact. He drew it quickly and had the approximate size and lines right. Peppy looked at it in surprise and then showed several others who had to discuss among themselves what should be done. Finally, Peppy said in a very solemn voice said that we are no longer allowed to draw, write, or put anything on paper without the direct permission of camp authorities. We all breathed a little more easily until they left, and Walt asked who wanted to draw the next map and be the keeper of it. Then in his dry Texas humor voice said, "Just kidding, I'm starting the next map and instructions now and I'll find a better place to hide it this time."

The next day our entire conversations were on how to draw signs and symbols that pointed in the general direction of the underground fort. We all agreed that if it was in plain sight, the guards would get used to it and not understand it was a secret way to communicate to our own forces if they should ever land here.

At least twice a month we heard a supersonic boom followed by the faint roar of jet engines. Ernie and Norm knew all about these SR-71 Blackbird overflights. It was the highest and fastest intelligence aircraft we had and the camera resolution was continually improving. The idea sprung up that we could hang long and short clothes in sequence on our drying line to send a message through Morse code. I never knew if we ever got the laundry on the line properly, but both Ernie and Norm were sure that the aircraft's photos would see and decipher our message. The paper map became a backup and could be hid in a drawstring, perhaps. The key was it had to be something we could drop or find, and leave in plain sight very quickly.

As we were resolving all this, we experienced a new issue that terrified me. No soldiers had done any maintenance inside our compound. With the monsoon rains, the grass and weeds started to grow. Walt had asked on several occasions that the grass be cut as it would be a hiding place for rats and snakes. Even Peppy laughed at this. In early June, I was standing at my window serenading our LULUs with a patriotic medley when a movement caught my eye. I stopped and turned toward the door. Then I saw the head of what was clearly some type of cobra snake. I screeched the only word I knew to alert Vietnamese soldiers that we had a visitor that no one wanted: *"Gunzun! Gunzun!"* Ernie had taught me that meant something like big snake. I thought it would get someone to look into it. Instead, the guard in the tower said something that I interpreted to mean, "No talk!"

As quickly as I could, I told everyone what I had seen. Steve said, "Snake Charmer is already an air force call sign." The iron bars in our windows were spaced about four to five inches apart, so even a large snake could easily pass through and enter our cells. I was trying to see where the snake was when its head popped up about twenty feet directly in front of my cell's window. I must have screamed louder this time, and Ernie advised me to get my bucket lid and get ready to violently swat it if it stuck its head through the bars. If bitten just once by this monster, I would be checking out permanently in less than thirty minutes. I therefore armed myself with the bucked lid and started to bang it against the bars. I was later to learn that the vibrations from this noise may have traveled through the ground and caused the cobra to go elsewhere.

When Peppy arrived in about half an hour, I described in some detail the head and length of what I thought to be about eight feet long. I told him that once the cobra was in the grass, all I could see was his head popping up and swaying back and forth occasionally; it was definitely a cobra. Before Peppy could respond, Walt was yelling "Bao cao!" This was the only Vietnamese we were permitted to speak and was to be used to summon an officer. Walt said later that he knew Peppy was enlisted and Walt wanted an officer to see our horrible living conditions. Of course, when he told Peppy words to this effect, Peppy grew quite angry, but stayed in control. He left saying he would try to get tools for the next day. Ernie had reported seeing a work crew cutting weeks outside our camp where the soldiers ate and went about their daily training. Walt then told us that under no circumstance were we to cut weeds for this lazy Commie who allowed this condition to grow. I saw the truth in Walt's thinking. And on the other hand, I understood the practical suggestion that Ernie made and how it would protect us from more snake invasions. After all, no one wanted to meet one of these snakes in his mosquito net at night, which was exactly what Ernie had faced when he was kept near Dien Bien Phu.

In the summer of 1967, Ernie was moved to spot near a truck repair facility on the edge of the jungle by Dien Bien Phu. At night his feet were put into stocks and his hands were tied to a pole beyond his feet. While flat on his back, his neck was tied to a pole in the opposite direction of the other ropes. In the daytime, he was allowed to sit up and soon found slivers of bamboo from the recent and rough construction of his bamboo cage. The smaller pieces of bamboo became tools to help him untie the ropes at night, so he might turn in his sleep and get real rest. Plus it was the start to his next escape plan.

One night while still completely tied down, rats started to run back and forth and soon he saw what had spooked them. A large rock python slowly made its way to his feet and then up his side and over his chest. Without much thought, he had yelled *"Gunzun!"* and raised his arms. The snake panicked and became twisted in his makeshift mosquito net. The guards came running and saw how big this python was and started to back away. The snake escaped and Ernie was more certain than ever that he had to escape. The snake returned a few nights later and caught a mother rat that was just giving birth to a new litter between Ernie's legs and just below the bamboo rack that Ernie's back rested against. The snake came from a different angle and Ernie saw what looked like a huge fist slowly poking into his mosquito net and moving its head side-to-side as if sniffing the air. This time one of the guards tried to shoot the snake, but he badly missed. Ernie reasoned that the next time they were more likely to shoot him than the snake.

At LULUs Hideaway our situation was a bit different; there was more than one of us. We were not on the edge of a jungle and we had cultivated fields and army ranges surrounding us. The thing that made our situation dangerous was the tall, wild vegetation. Walt told Ernie that he was a civilian and could cut the weeds if he wished, but he was not going to touch that job. It was beneath our rank and place as POWs. We all tried to convince Walt that both WWII and Korean War POWs who had been commissioned officers all did menial work to provide for the common POW welfare. The next morning when the tools showed up, Walt relented and let Ernie and Steve cut weeds. Norm, Walt, and I were to sit it out. I wanted to help in the worse way, because both Ernie and Steve were getting over the infestation of bedbugs and had to get their strength back. Finally, Walt let Norm and me assist in the cleanup of the tall weeds in our compound. It was slow, hard work for us because we were not accustomed to working all day and we were neither getting the quantity nor the protein in our daily diet that the soldiers were normally getting. We were getting much more than what had been provided in Hanoi, but it still was less than what the guards received each day. After about an hour, my hands ached and one of the new blisters started to bleed. We were almost done, so I continued. Then the smallest guard, who always talked to us and given us extra things to eat like an occasional banana, saw the blood and said something to the others. He put me back in my cell and went outside to call for another soldier. Soon the medic arrived and shortly after Peppy, who explained to me that this was a dangerous time of year for infections and that I would have to put iodine on it no matter how much it might sting. We all thought this was unusual.

★

The next week we saw a group of soldiers coming into our compound with what seemed like three officers from Hanoi being escorted with them. They were here probably to check on our condition and attitude, but also to gather more information about us. For example, in the past when asked what nationality I was, I had always replied American. They were clear that this was not acceptable, because everyone in America came from other countries. After the family tree on my father's side didn't produce what they wanted—because they thought that 1737 was too long ago for me to be counted as German—they began on my mother's side. My grandparents were born in the United Kingdom, but that too seemed to be unacceptable. They wanted a country, so I finally told them Wales, which was factual for my Grandfather Edwards. Some of these questions were so detailed that I could not answer them. I said, "I don't know and I honestly mean I don't know."

Walt was not buying any of this and finally told both the officer-in-charge of this group and Peppy that all this information had been taken and recorded in Hanoi. "You're wasting your time here and you're wasting our time," he told them again and again. The three visitors were getting upset with Peppy, so Ernie and Steve named this inspection team the Three Stooges. Everything they wanted seemed like it was a repeated effort, such as location of capture and by whom. The answer for me never changed: "North Vietnamese Regular Army about twenty-five kilometers north of Kham Chai, Laos." Soon Walt told me he wanted to order us not to answer any more questions. We had been put together several times in the same room for guards to check Walt's room. Plus on other days, we were allowed to "'visit" in my room during the rest hour after lunch. I told him that Ernie had taught me how to say no with a smile and to turn any written task into broken pen nibs, spilled ink, and a complete mess. It didn't take long for the guards to stop asking us for anything. So they relented some here, and we were all thankful that we could resist in a style and fashion that we found more comfortable and increased our odds of not angering the enemy.

The Three Stooges stayed for about two weeks. The last day they came by and were actually cordial to Steve, Ernie, and Norm. But then they brought Walt into my room and told him that he had a "bad attitude" and their assessment was that he was corrupting and making the young Bep (me) have a bad attitude, too. We were surprised when they told us they had checked some of my answers and that they had verified the location of my capture with army records. But many of my answers had not checked out, and it was clear that we were trying to stop them from getting accurate information about us. We might have to be punished in the future (they resorted to implied threats a lot and we had grown immune to most of them), and we should think more clearly about being more truthful. Then, they left with no chance for us to even cough one good "horse-ship."

Walt said that we needed to lie low and not give the guards any reason to start worse treatment. He also reasoned that the weeds were cut and there were no more visits from the cobra to his snake charmer. I said my singing was not that good, and Walt said the cobra thought differently.

Our food had turned to cabbage, which always produced some flatus when more than several leaves were in the soup bowl. We were getting more and different types of vegetables, too. Shortly after the Three Stooges left, on a day that the siesta hour had lasted longer than usual, Peppy entered the compound after our evening meal was finished. First he went to Norm's room on the other side. We could hear some talking and Norm asking questions. Walt was still in my cell from the evening meal and visit. Then we heard Peppy telling Ernie and Steve that we had failed the inspection and would not be allowed out together and were no longer allowed to talk to each other. Ernie was a bit baffled and asked Peppy if we were the cause of the trouble or was it the cobra sighting in our compound that had caused the stir. There was no answer.

Then Peppy came up to my window with both Walt and I sitting on my bed with our legs propped up a little. He started out with the new rules by the "camp authority." We would no longer be allowed to visit one another. Only one POW was allowed to wash at a time. No talking ever was allowed from now on between the five POWs. Walt took one look at him and simply said, "That's bullshit." Peppy pointed his finger at Walt and said he was not allowed to talk back. Peppy became so incensed that his finger and arm were now coming through the cell bars of my window. Then Walt replied by raising his leg and emitting the loudest flatus I'd ever heard him let go. I was amazed at both the duration and the volume. Peppy's eyes got even narrower and his lips turned purple in rage. That is the first and only time I had seen this type of Vietnamese reaction to an American POW. Peppy abruptly turned and left.

All the LULUs started talking to ask if it was Walt or me who had told off Peppy. I think Ernie was the most amazed besides me, for this type of response to the Commies was not what we had seen before from Walt. He had advocated in the Little Vegas for us to avoid confrontation and his preferred style was to lie low. However, he was not the senior man there, while here he was. He told us if they ever removed him from the LULUs, Norm would be senior and no matter what was said or done, he advised us to keep communicating at all costs. He told Norm to buck up and don't let the enemy dictate to the LULUs. About a half-hour later, I heard chains at our gate and then keys rattling. Peppy led a group of three larger than normal Vietnamese soldiers into the compound carrying bamboo poles, a pair of leg irons, handcuffs, an armful of rags, and some rope. They walked directly to Walt's side of the compound.

I heard Peppy saying several times, "No talk! No talk!" and, "Now I do the talking." More keys rattled as they opened the door to Walt's cell. Then I heard the sound of blows being struck and Walt asking or saying so we could hear, "What the hell?" I heard the metal leg irons bouncing off the floor once or twice, and the sound of muffled resistance. Then we all heard the Peppy say, "Now you get it, Stischer!" We heard the sounds of a leather strap hitting and then what sounded like a rubber hose repeatedly hitting something. Of course, that something was our SRO, Walt Stischer. We all started yelling at the top of our lungs, *"Bao cao! Bao cao!"* Even Norm started yelling, "We need an officer here." I think it must have helped them to shorten whatever length of beating they had planned. It was hard to tell.

The three soldiers took the tools of their trade away with them and leave the compound as if another day at the office had just been finished. However, Peppy didn't leave right away. He first went to Norm and told him, "Keep quiet! No talk or you get it!" Then he marched to Ernie and Steve and said to them that Stischer was very rude and disrespectful and had to be punished. "No talk!" I had heard every word and was bracing myself for the bad attitude and all the fixings. Instead Peppy looked me straight in the eye and said, "Bep, you must understand that Stischer show great disrespect to me and my people. We cannot stand and will not stand that kind of rudeness."

My only concern at this point was Walt's medical condition. And so I asked if Maj Stischer was all right. "You know he has a bad heart." Peppy nodded and said, "Man with bad heart should never blow wind in the face of the man who feeds him." With that he added, "No talk and no sing. Mosquito net now and stay there until morning." And then he was gone and locking up the compound for the night.

Walt did not respond to tapping from Norm or from Ernie and Steve. I was afraid he was dying on the floor of his cell. I whispered out my door that was the closest door to his window, "Walt! Can you hear me? Cough twice." There was no response. Finally, Ernie practically yelled "Walt! Cough twice if you can hear." I thought I heard a muffled groan. Ernie then said to me, "Jim, sing Walt his favorite song." So I softly began singing "The Eyes of Texas." I sang the words, more clearly understanding their meaning as never before. Steve, Ernie, and Norm were listening intently, and when I finished the last line, I could not resist yelling in a very clear voice: "Hook 'em Horns!" And then we heard what sounded like a gurgling volcano explode, followed by what was two definite coughs.

Walt was back. It took him over an hour to talk and when he did it was with short painful breaths. He tapped on the floor that he was still in leg irons. They had left him with his mouth full of rags and a longer rag tied around his head to muffle him. The acid from his blood had finally broken the gag and he had vomited the rags in his mouth, which had moved half-way down his throat out. I went to sleep thinking that Gabriel had almost blown his horn that night, but Walt still had work to do on this earth. Thank goodness that God still moves the stone and hears our prayers.

The next day Walt was not allowed out of his cell and had reduced rations. That meant we organized a way to save some of our food and have Steve or Ernie deliver it to Walt when they were let out to wash. They reported that Walt didn't look good and was now missing one tooth and had two rather large black eyes. Walt probably was always on the slender side, but now he really looked decimated. We were all concerned; he sensed this and was quick to respond to us in several ways. Like me, he didn't want to see any more cobras, so he said from now on we take any and every opportunity to cut the grass. And of course, I was encouraged to produce an evening song fest with a special mind to the upcoming Fourth of July holiday. I joked that "99 Bottles of Beer" would only make the air force officers homesick and thirsty. It was strange that corny comments from me often received big laughs. I really think we found it refreshing and rehabilitative to laugh. As the *Reader's Digest* folks would say, "Laughter is the best medicine."

Near the end of June, Peppy came around and told us that we needed to write something along the lines of why the Fourth of July was important to us. Walt was back to normal and instructed us to mess up the paper and resist in any way we could to ensure Peppy never received anything that was relevant or useable for the Communist propaganda effort. We wrote about fast sports cars, the NASCAR races, baseball, and Ballantine beer (my input), and in the end we all came up with one general theme: it was a vision of a Communist Grinch who stole our Independence Day. Peppy never said a word about our obvious failure to obey what he had directed. Something was definitely up.

On the actual Fourth of July, Peppy helped to deliver some of our food, which was above and beyond normal for any holiday in North Vietnam. We had chicken that had been barbecued over an open fire along with corn on the cob. And we had other types of food I never did identify, but it was all very good, to my amazement. Ernie's application of "gastro-politics" said this meant the peace talks were going so well that we would soon be on the road back to Hanoi and freedom. It was a beautiful thought.

Ernie got half of it right. Several days later after our mid-day meal we were told to pack our things and be prepared to move. I could hear a truck maneuvering to get close to our gate. They were going to take us away from here, but Norm started saying we were doomed and were probably going back to Laos. This was a constant fear we lived with, but I didn't worry like some of the others. I knew that "the Lord is my Shepard; I shall not want." Ernie also was optimistic as we loaded up into a heavy duty truck with tarp sides and started off. We were headed east and not west, so that was one good thing.

Ernie was first to knock his blind fold off and could see we were in the suburbs of Hanoi again. He told us he recognized some of the landmarks from his first trip to Hanoi in 1968. This calmed Norm down, and we all became excited that we probably would be kept near other Americans and could communicate with them. When we arrived, the truck slowly went through a gate and backed around to the east end of a large compound. Ernie immediately recognized it as the Plantation, the first prison he had been kept at and where he was housed in the back side of the Warehouse building and where CDR John McCain had been the first American POW who had talked to Ernie and explained the tap code. They had talked through the wall about the American POW organization with tin cups muffled by T-shirts.

We were taken out and lined up and an officer I didn't know spoke in Vietnamese for at least ten minutes. Then Peppy said that we would be told exactly which cell we would be kept in. The building in front of us was a low one-story building that looked like it had four or five cells opening out to a porch. Ernie and I were taken to the cell to the east, right next to what looked like an electrical generator room with one door removed and the other open. Norm was placed in the cell next to us, and then Walt and Steve were placed in the third cell on the other side of Norm. We would have good communications with this arrangement.

After things quieted down some, my first songs that evening were a few tunes from Steven Foster with "My Old Kentucky Home," a favorite of the two prisoners we didn't know on the other side of Walt and Steve. A new phase of negotiation was starting in Paris and Ernie was still hopeful that the Nixon plan would work. All our troops were leaving Vietnam and we would soon be on our way home, too. That had to be the plan, because we were in a camp with many other POWs who must have seen the truck bring us into the compound's main and rather large courtyard.

Ernie also gave Norm a primer on how this camp was used in 1968 and 1969 as a show camp. It was here that some of the early-release POWs were kept before they met with peace delegations and went to the airport. It was here that Ernie talked to Seaman Douglas Hegdahl for over three hours one day. It was here that Dick Stratton had helped Doug learn the names of more than three hundred twenty-five POWs to take home when he was released. Ernie was upbeat in the best of ways and his optimism was contagious, not just to me, but to all the LULUs. Walt was busy tapping and trying to talk to the two POWs on the other side of them—we were getting into the loop. I went to bed that night with a lot of hope springing from various assessments and, as Ernie used to say, "Hope springs eternal."

CHAPTER 11

RETURN TO THE PLANTATION

The next day started early as Walt and Steve quickly made contact with POWs on the other side of their cell and were able to use their cups to talk through the wall. Soon Norm was on the wall passing information to Ernie and me. First, we learned that Col Ted Guy, USAF, was with MAJ Artice "Art" Elliot, U.S. Army. Col Guy had been the senior ranking officer of other camps before here, including the Little Vegas prison. He had actually been captured about one mile into Laos and was first listed by our military as a North Vietnam and then as a South Vietnam captive. After the song fest in February at Hoa Lo, Col Guy told us he had been moved well south of Hanoi and kept with a group of POWs captured in the 1968 Tet offensive and recently brought back to Hanoi. His cellmate, Art, was captured in 1970 near Pleiku, South Vietnam, and was harshly treated at the outset of his captivity. He had an interesting view of the army's lack of training for POW survival and code of conduct. Both men had tried to communicate with some army enlisted men and were immediately reported to the Commies. Art was acting as the deputy SRO to Col Guy.

Col Guy had been at the Plantation in 1968-1969 and knew of Ernie Brace in some detail. The cellblock we were in was called the Gunshed. It was known to be one of the hottest cellblocks in the prison. Nearby, the Warehouse was a long two story building with a high tiled roof that was previously used as a truck repair facility and then converted into cells for POWs. We could hear a guard walk back and forth on the roof. Col Guy said that the commies had built some type of anti-aircraft and watch tower on the roof about two months prior to our arrival.

To the southwest end of camp at one corner was the common water tanks and washing area, and next to that area was the Corn Crib cellblock. Both Art and Ted had tried to raise the warrant officers who they had been told were placed there, but they had had no success yet. One thing was for certain: the guards watched the senior officers much more closely than they watched the LULUs. Ernie said that we would get in touch with them and report back to Col Guy. It was then that Col Guy accepted a new call sign of "Hawk." He preferred Hawk because he was sure that other call signs for him had been compromised in the various crackdowns on communications.

After half a loaf of a small French bread and hot tea refill of our teapots, the LULUs were taken to the southwest end to wash. The cisterns were about five feet in height and eight to ten feet wide. There was little space between the tank and the wall and it was clear that Ernie was going to have to hop into the tank if he was going to raise the POWs in the adjacent Corn Crib. I jumped up to see if I could get a better view of where the guard was and discovered that I could look through the eaves and get a very good view of what was going on outside our compound. The guard was leaning right against our wash stall, so we had to abort trying to communicate that day. We tried hacking and coughing our initials to the Corn Crib, but they didn't respond. Ernie told me he didn't think they had been taught that yet; we would have to wait for another day.

There was a long screen made from bamboo poles and tar paper that was raised between the warehouse and the Big House, which was the main building used by the guards. This obstructed our view of the Corn Crib from the Gunshed, but there was one corner closest to the Big House that allowed us to see what was going on, and to see the area where the food was cooked and where the soldiers ate. Shortly after we were back, a group of about six guards arrived with a new officer I had not seen before. All the LULUs were told to step out onto our long porch, and the guards went to work tearing up our rooms. When finished, the only item expropriated by one sour-faced guard was Ernie's rather old and shabby self-made jacket. When he was out in the jungle, he had sewn together several old blankets and a piece of a ragged quilt with a bamboo needle. It kept Ernie warm in body and spirit. In all the inspections from 1968 to 1970, plus in 1971 at Hoa Lo and the LULUs Hideaway, no guard had even taken a second look at this article of clothing. It was like they dared not to touch it for fear of getting some dreaded disease from the jungle. We all thought that there had to be some misunderstanding about it this time.

Ernie intervened with a smile and put his hand around the sleeve of the coat. He told the guard that this coat had been with him from Dien Bien Phu and officers told him he could keep it. The guard, obviously not a graduate of the Hanoi Hilton training courses, said in a loud angry voice, "No! No! No!" The guard held onto the main part of the jacket and Ernie suddenly blurted out, "You son of a bitch! Give me back my jacket!" The soldier's eyes got very small and beady and he shouted, "No regulation!" Walt tried to intervene and that only brought two more guards into the fray. I had never seen Ernie react in such a way; I knew he always wore the coat at night and to all interviews in the winter time, but I had not truly appreciated how much this coat meant to him: it was an outward and visible sign that he had survived Laos and the jungle camps.

The officer returned and told Ernie that only regulation items were now allowed because some "war criminals" had received contraband and were using it to communicate. We learned later that microfiche file with a reader had been hidden in a Christmas package and sent to Hoa Lo prison. And the new military pay scales had been on the file by years of service and rank. Some of the men selected for promotion were giddy with the amount of pay they had accrued and would return home to find in their accounts. Unfortunately, few understood the impact of inflation and how expensive everything was getting. I remember trying to convince Steve Long that a new Ford Mustang would cost more than eight thousand dollars and he assured me he would get them down to four thousand and not a penny more. When we finally returned in 1973, even I was surprised at the cost of everything.

When we were being returned to our cells, we heard a voice from the Closet, a small cell to the south of Col Guy. He said very clearly, "Balls! Balls! Balls!" It was Capt Edward Watson Leonard, USAF, and a 1960 graduate of the Air Force Academy. He never liked either his given names of Ed and/or Watson, so he went by J.R. He was flying a Skyraider (A-1H) on a rescue mission over Laos in May of 1968 and was hit by heavy anti-aircraft fire. He evaded capture for two days and finally went to sleep in a tree. Later a North Vietnamese Army unit set up camp nearby and one of the soldiers hung a hammock under his tree. When this soldier finally laid down and looked up, he saw J.R. and quickly pointed his AK-47 and Leonard became a POW. He was kept in punishment for trying to get some army POWs to stop making tapes and propaganda for the enemy. J.R. reasoned well that it was one thing to oppose the way the war was being run or what we could eventually accomplish here, but it was quite another thing to turn on your countrymen, report forbidden communications among POWs to the enemy, and single out POW leaders who were encouraging others to resist. In addition, a group of collaborators was rewarded with being allowed outside most of the day, and received special rations of extra cigarettes, bananas, and other foods not provided to the other POWs—and they never offered to share these things with other less fortunate Americans.

Ernie and I were livid when we found out about this. Ernie wondered aloud if J.R. had been too strict or demanding of this group of turncoats; he wanted to make connections with others at the other end of this prison. Col Guy said that Captains James DiBernardo and Paul Montague, and Maj Bruce Archer (USMC) were all superb marines who could be trusted with anything. There were also three warrant officers, two army and one air force, who were solid resisters and good communicators. Col Guy had spent enough time in the same prison with these men to know them well, so the plan was to get Ernie back into that washroom, make a solid contact, and set up a note-drop mailbox that the enemy would never find.

In several days Ernie and I were placed in the wash area next to the Corn Crib. I was able to see the guard go off to get another pair of POWs to wash and told Ernie it was all clear. As I watched, Ernie jumped into the cistern and, with water up to his neck, began the sequence to get those on the other side of the wall to reply. It didn't take too long and then Ernie was talking with his cup muffled to get more information. Warrant Officer Frank Anton told Ernie that the camp had fairly good communication in their end, but with the Peace Committee in Warehouse Cell 1 and inclined to report any attempt to talk with the POWs in the Gunshed, it was almost impossible to tell Col Guy where the mail drops were in the wash rooms. We exchanged a lot of information in a relatively short time and were given a position to look for future notes from them. They were particularly glad to hear that Col Guy was well and as feisty as ever. He was clearly a respected and beloved SRO to this group captured in South Vietnam.

One of the first notes we had to write to this group in the Corn Crib was Col Guy's policy, which was a shortened version of what I had learned in Little Vegas from 1969. There were four simple points:

1. Communicate at all costs with your fellow POWs.

2. Don't say anything negative about the United States, our allies, and/or our leaders.

3. Resist the enemy to the utmost of your ability.

4. Don't tape, write, or help in any propaganda effort including visiting peace delegations.

Ernie once again took on the job of writing and passing the notes onto POW cells at the other end of the camp. The response was so positive and fast that Ernie told me it had to have been welcomed news to most of the POWs in the Plantation that Col Guy was back in touch and taking command to resolve any new issues that might come up. Steve and Walt were delighted to have an SRO like Col Guy leading us again. I soon learned that the Corn Crib had ordained Ernie with the call sign "Moses." I thought it very appropriate and told Ernie that he had fitted the commandants into four rather than ten items; after all, one would not want to tax the average army soldier with too much in these circumstances. Ernie passed that along to Art Elliot who laughed out loud at us. Walt was proud and glad to see Ernie so involved because, as he said to all of us, "Ernie is a natural at these types of clandestine operations." Or, as Ernie always was proud to say: "Once a Marine, always a Marine. Do or die."

——————————— ★ ———————————

The following month we had some disturbance at the siesta hour and then the all-too-familiar jangle of keys. We peeked through our door to see a new American being led to the Gunshed and Norm's door being opened. The new prisoner was Lt1 Jack M. Butcher, a USAF forward air controller who was shot down in Laos while flying an orientation hop solo in an OV-10 Bronco. He had escaped for three days while on the way to North Vietnam, but unlike Ernie, he had not received any harsh punishment. He was in an area with sensors and the air force launched several attempts to rescue him, but there was too much enemy activity around him. He shared news about the Nixon plan and the Paris peace talks. It seemed the North Vietnamese kept moving the bar as soon as the U.S. and South Vietnam tried to place a compromise position on the table to be considered. The good news from Jack was that the South Vietnamese forces seemed to be performing better and were operationally more independent, with the caution that they still needed American close-air support. When we returned home in 1973, Jack was awarded the Silver Star for his bravery and courageous attempts to evade and avoid being captured. He was a graduate of the University of Michigan who had proudly performed four years in their high-stepping marching band.

The normal time for communicating in the Gunshed was after the noon meal was finished, the dishes taken away, and most of the soldiers at the other end of the Plantation for their lunch and siesta. Col Guy had a few questions for Jack, which was our first order of business. The most common questions were on how soon Jack thought the war would end and when could we all go home. I could tell that he didn't want to dash our hopes, but he didn't want to be overly optimistic either. He finally admitted that he wasn't sure and perhaps it would take another year. The ever-optimistic Ernie told us if we had made it this far, we certainly could last until next summer—Ernie was already packing his imaginary bags to go home.

Jack also brought us a whole new group of stories that were delightful. I remember one hot day when he told us about playing in an intramural ice hockey league in Michigan. He was the team goal tender, so he didn't get too hot skating back and forth. They played on an outdoor rink with a cover that seemed to funnel any small breeze into a gale force wind that rushed through the rink and the games usually ran from 1:00 a.m. to 4:00 a.m.—the coldest time of the night with the chill factor often at minus twenty below zero. Just hearing how it went made me feel a bit cooler and helped me contend with the return of my ongoing summer heat rash. I was adapting some as the rash was less prevalent and didn't return to my scalp and armpits like it had the first summer. But our cell was just as hot or hotter as the summer heat came on full force. Our ceilings were a solid slab of concrete that radiated the heat of the day all night long. My fan was constantly beating the air all the time until I would pass out, which is how we described falling to sleep.

Jack's description of a typical Big Ten football weekend was terrific. Just the large crowds of fans and all the pageantry kept me entranced for days. I shared some of my memories from Union College with a small ragtag group that played their own instruments and followed every Union College touchdown with our own fight song. It was a real kick teaching Jack the tune and all the words and, of course, he taught me both the Michigan fight song, ("Hail to the Victors"), and their Alma Mater ("Sing to the Colors that Float on the Breeze, Hurrah for the Yellow and Blue"). It was a beautiful tune with meaningful words that seemed to capture the spirit of Michigan—and I can still sing the first verse to this day. I am often amazed to meet alumni from the University of Michigan who didn't even know that this was their alma mater, for they only knew the "Hail to the Victors" fight song. Obviously, even back then Michigan scored a lot more touchdowns than Union College, so the average Michigan student heard their alma mater a lot more times in the fall months than the Union students heard any songs from their ad hoc band. I should also mention that back then, the drinking age in New York State was eighteen, and the Union College band never hit all their notes by the fourth quarter, but they were always fun to be around in the stands. There was never a shortage of something warm to drink when you were near them. We all had a good laugh over the comparison and Steve said, "No wonder you became a navy fighter RIO!"

I also taught Jack the words to "The Eyes of Texas." Walt's birthday was in September and we were planning to have a special birthday surprise for him. When the day came, Jack and I (pointing our voices under our doors in the Gunshed), sang first the traditional "Happy Birthday" song and then, as a special for all, "The Eyes of Texas." Steve reported that it brought tears to Walt's eyes, but just a few that only took a single swipe to clear. Fighter pilots had to keep their reputations intact, even in the Hanoi Hilton.

Jack had some very specific stories of physical fitness training for the band, such as running wind sprints with their instruments on a hot August day to qualify to be in Michigan's high-stepping marching band. Steve and I both chuckled over the band running wind sprints, while on the next field the football team was hitting blocking dummies and running full hundred-yard sprints. So our idle chat started to question, "What was the best single physical exercise one could do to get into shape?" Even Walt wondered what would be prescribed for us when we got back home so we could get back into flying shape and resume our normal duties if we wished. It was from this discussion that the idea grew that we could do an experiment by limiting all activity to a single type of exercise. Both Col Guy and MAJ Elliot wanted to be judges and would help us determine after one month which LULU had developed the most visible muscle.

The great experiment started with Col Guy, Art Elliot, and Ed Leonard peeking out at the LULUs as we went and returned from the wash routine. We all made it a point to wear just our boxer shorts so that most of our bodies could be seen. We also had to select one exercise. Ernie's exercise was to touch his toes, Steve's was to run in place, and, with Walt's heart condition, he just had to walk as much as he felt comfortable doing. Jack was going to do sit-ups, which he found particularly hard, and mine was push-ups. The test was on.

In the first week I got up to doing fifty push-ups in one set and tried to do a set every half hour. I was straining by the end of the day. Ernie kept telling me; "No strain, no gain," so I kept pushing myself every day to do more. By the second week, I was doing over a hundred push-ups in one set; however, the more I tried to do, the faster I did them. Ernie told Steve that I was literally bouncing off the floor and shaking our cell when I was doing push-ups. We all got a laugh from the number of reports coming from each cell. Walt even got up to walking about ten miles in one day for approximately ten feet at a time before he had to turn around and walk the other way. One has to remember that we had nothing else to do, and so we were not only keeping busy with a short-term task, but also were having fun and experiencing some anticipation over which exercise would show the most physical fitness and growth of muscle.

As the month was coming to an end, I had made it to slightly over two hundred push-ups in one set and was doing more than two sets per hour. I was a veritable push-up machine, according to Ernie. Of course, all the others were doing a great deal more than when we started. Col Guy and Art Elliot were laughing every day when they could look out to see us. When the final day came for judging, we were supposed to go closer to Col Guy's cell as we picked up our noon meal and linger at the end of the porch. At this point, Ed Leonard could see us from his Closet cell at the very end of the building. Each group heard a distinct two coughs from the judges, so we knew they had seen us all.

The voting took a little longer, because they had to coordinate with Ed and that required no guards being around. By that evening the three judges had determined that the "push-up machine" was the clear winner. Not only did they see muscles on my chest and arms, but also on my back and legs that were either new or much more visible. I have always said that our group was small and I was never able to win any contest, but one day near the end of our captivity Steve told me I won the exercise contest and he pretended to be a little jealous that I had beaten him. I told him it had nothing to do with me; instead, it was solely a matter of which exercise we had done for a month. The push-up was the clear winner.

As the summer progressed, the North Vietnamese became increasingly concerned about communications between various groups. Not just at the Plantation, but at many of the other prisons in North Vietnam it had become more and more difficult to find new American voices to tape record anti-war news for the camp radio. Even worse for the Communists, writing war protest pieces was becoming a lost art. Col Guy's policy was working everywhere at the Plantation except with the Peace Committee in the first cell of the Warehouse. This group had been given new chances to join the other American POWs and each time they had replied with anti-war slogans and chants such as, "Hey, Hey, LBJ! How many kids did you kill today?" They also had learned what one guard had told them was the national anthem of Vietnam and were singing it more regularly now. They were getting powdered milk, what looked like instant hot chocolate, and other luxury items never given to other POWs. To most other POWs, this preferential treatment seemed to clearly be a reward for their behavior at protesting the war and reporting American POWs

who violated camp regulations. We would, unfortunately, see more from this group before we wore out our stay at the Plantation.

Several weeks later we heard a heavy truck maneuvering back and forth. Soon a group of guards were moving rolls of tar paper, several spools of wire, and bamboo poles into the area just to the side of the Gunshed. Pigpens had been in that area originally, but there was some room toward the other side of the prison that we couldn't see and we were all curious about what they were building. Ed Leonard quipped that it was a new pigpen for the Peace Committee. Other ideas equally funny were floated back and forth, but it didn't take long to discover that a new wash area next to the latrine dumping area was being built for us. Ernie thought aloud that the Commies might have guessed that we were using the wash basin area in the other end of the camp to pass notes to the POWs down there and, by having this new wash area, they could prevent any possibility of passing a note from one end of the camp to the other end. In this way, Col Guy would be isolated from other prisoners.

Once we "baptized" the new wash area, Ernie was first to notice that after dumping a number of buckets, the POWs from the south end would enter the new wash area and wash off their feet before carrying clean buckets back to their end of the camp. The most difficult challenge would be in reaching members at the other end of the camp without anyone from the Peace Committee in Warehouse 1 finding out. Jack and I thought about how the early Christians used the sign of a fish to pass secret prayers to one another. So Ernie decided it was worth a try; with a piece of chalk he had found, he etched the fish on a brick. The next day a smile was drawn onto the face of the fish. So, a general note, not identifying the author or our SRO, was written, wrapped in a piece of plastic, and stuck under the brick with only a small piece of twine showing. Instructions in the note told them to wrap the notes tightly in plastic so they didn't leak, and we mentioned the need to bury them at least three to four inches in the muck that always was wet beneath the brick. The following day the note was gone and we hoped it was a good sign.

Two days later, per instructions in the first note, we found a detailed note of who was in the other end of camp and who was being pressured to make tape recordings, and a question on how much torture should be endured before making any tapes. This issue was something that kept arising, and the answer often varied on the timeframe, the current conditions in the specific location, and who was the SRO. But we had now established what we thought was the safest mailbox in all of Vietnam. The Peace Committee never found it and the Commies were clueless without getting specifics from those POWs. This particular mailbox went undetected until the wash shed was dismantled during the height of the B-52 bombings and the shed's materials were used to make more bomb shelters for the soldiers.

A few weeks after the new washing area was finished the Plantation was organized under Col Guy as the SRO. The enlisted troops enjoyed his Hawk call sign and at times expended an extraordinary amount of effort into surreptitiously saluting his room. We all saw this behavior and were amazed. Occasionally, these same enlisted men shouted encouragement to Ed Leonard in the Closet. The North Vietnamese also felt the increasing resistance as more and more prisoners became quiet or downright sullen in their interrogation sessions. Everyone but the prisoners of the Peace Committee refused to say anything to a tape recorder. Whenever I was called for an attitude check I tried to take a deep breath and realized that whenever I wanted to cut the discussion short, all I had to do was to mention the lack of access to the Holy Bible. This was a sore point for some of the North Vietnamese with an education, because they knew Bibles were commonly found in every hotel and prison in the United States. It was not a bad thing for me to ask, and I always felt that some of the officers were uncomfortable defending the communist line on this point.

Around this time, we had a special lunch meal. Ernie got excited as he had been fed Vietnamese shrimp before. He was confident that the shrimp boats had a great catch and the POWs were getting some of the largess. To me, these transparent crusty things were tasteless and had no meat inside. Ernie had just finished his meal—he always was a fast eater—and I was only half way through the soup and bread when we heard some shouting from the Warehouse. Until then we had heard or seen nothing. But the word was finally reaching our end of the camp. "Don't eat the soup." One of the nastier guards, "Dumb-Eumb," had thrown several large containers of dead cockroaches into the POW soup pot." Ernie looked at me and asked sheepishly if he could finish my soup; after all, "protein is protein." We never had any repercussions from the soup and speculated that the big pot was boiling when the "addition" was added and so the germs were all killed. That was the only time I ever remember that Ernie finished my meal because he always wanted me to eat everything to keep my strength up and he urged me to try to maintain my shoot-down weight. I had estimated that by this point in time my weight was around one hundred thirty-five pounds, down from one seventy, so I was still close (depending on the meaning of close) to my flying weight. My biggest discomfort was getting headaches that progressed into convulsive vomiting. Ernie and I tracked the repetition of these bouts and it seemed to be related to incoming weather fronts. Just before a big monsoon storm hit Hanoi, I had an attack like this on a bright sunny day. By the next day, the wind was screeching and the sky was crying buckets of tears. It had to be pressure related.

As Christmas grew closer, the propaganda efforts increased. The Peace Committee had helped construct a new basketball court that had two baskets instead of one, and sidelines marked in limestone. There was even a slightly elevated platform at one end for cameras to be set up. The trick was going to be to find another group that would play a game with them and allow it to be filmed. The number of this group had recently been increased by two new members, so there were at least seven of them. It didn't take long for four of the newest prisoners to be introduced to the Peace Committee and start playing basketball with them. Col Guy had seen this all before in 1968, and he told us it would be next to impossible to stop the new men from helping, given the time limits. Our goal was to be sure they didn't cross over and start willingly giving the Communists some propaganda BS like Schweitzer, Miller, and Wilbur had done in 1969 to 1970 at the Little Vegas.

Both Ernie and Steve noticed that the group would take breaks and rest on a set of parallel bars in front of the Gunshed. The trick would be to wait until only the new guys were in this area with none of the other group. That opportunity soon arose, and while I once again climbed on a bucket to use the wide-angle peephole to look out, Ernie used the loose flap on the door itself to speak to the men. I had a perfect view of both the Peace Committee and the two guards at this end of the compound and Steve Long was watching from his cell. Ernie was not shy about telling them about who we were, how the Peace Committee had turned us over to the prison command, and how we had to be careful not to be seen communicating by anyone in their main group. They all shook their heads in understanding, and then one spoke up and said, "I can't believe they would turn in their own countrymen for just communicating, but they all seem pretty tight with the guards." Ernie told them the general four principles and said that they might mess up a filming by acting sick or just goofy. One of the youngest of these POWs then smiled knowingly and said, "My sister has always told me I was born goofy. Please give Hawk our best and tell him we'll do our best for him and our country. Merry Christmas!"

I think that was the first time I had heard that phrase in over a year and a half. Col Guy had heard every word and gave us a soft double cough. Ernie and I were coming up on our two year anniversary, so perhaps this year we would be taken to the Christmas room and given some type of package from home. Ernie and I discussed this subject often, and we both came to agreement that the first package was probably given to us by mistake and that we would not see another package or even a letter from home. We had been captured in Laos and the North Vietnamese were selling the lie that they had no troops or forces in Laos;

they only supported their Communist neighbors with supplies and "always recognized the territorial sovereignty of their neighbors." We LULUs were the living proof of their deception, and the Communists knew we had to stay hidden at all costs. That's why we were at the extreme end of the camp with the two most senior officers—they didn't want us talking to any of the other POWs and, therefore, our mission was to make every effort to continue communicating with them. And we did just that.

It was at least a month before Christmas when MAJ Walt Stischer, our LULU SRO, came up with the idea that we should have a mystery Santa Claus. Counting Ed Leonard, who was allowed to visit with us on occasion, and Jack Butcher, there were seven of us. So on one of these visits, names were thrown into an emptied tea caddy, and we drew to see for whom each one would make a gift. Ernie drew Norm's name and I drew Ernie's name. I tapped the next day with Steve Long to see if he could help make the pieces to a chess set for Ernie. Ernie was learning the game quickly and was always wishing he actually had something that looked like a knight or a rook. Steve was on it and the game was afoot. I also knew I had to do something else for my first cellmate and mentor.

For some reason the guards let Ernie go into Walt's cell one day and he tapped very softly to me, "Home is where you hang your hat. Stay safe and enjoy Steve's stories of college days." Steve worked on those papier mâché chess pieces while I continued to stand look-out duty and exchange college stories with him. The thought struck me that Ernie was having his seventh Christmas without his family. He had to miss the little things that make a house a home. I was going to write a poem just for him that would capture what he might be feeling, but would never want to burden others with this longing. After all, we were all reminiscing about past Christmases and being home for the holidays. Sometimes sad and sometimes basking in the warm glow of some past Christmases, we all had stories to tell. In fact, I was already singing some of the Christmas songs that I liked the most at my evensong.

Every day I kept thinking of another item to add to Ernie's poem. I didn't want it to be too long or too mucky, but it should express something strongly valued and something that told others he was loved, even though many miles once again separated him from home and his loved ones—they would be thinking of him. Christmas Day came and a big meal was served to us in the middle of the day. The LULUs were allowed to eat together and it was good food and even better company. Near the end of our meal, Walt opened the gift exchange. Most of us were surprised by the ingenuity and thoughtfulness of the little gifts. Ernie loved his chess set, but Walt knew that it was made by Steve who had drawn another name. So at the end he asked who had drawn Ernie's name. I raised my hand a little embarrassed. He asked me where my gift was and all I could think of was, "Between my ears, it's a poem just for Ernie."

Walt and the others would not hear of it. I was ordered front and center to recite my poem. As I looked at the motley crew in front of me, I was suddenly nervous as I liked them all and thought the poem might hit too close to home for most of them. Norm helped me get started when he asked me, "Does this poem have a name?" And I said, "Yes, it's called 'Home is Where.'"

> "Home is where you hang your hat."
>
> Why, I don't' know who said that,
>
> But home is much more to me.
>
> It's as precious as my liberty.
>
> It may be big and it may be small,
>
> But it's filled with love from wall to wall.
>
> You can hear the children laugh and play,
>
> And at the very close of day,

You can smell the smoke in the air

Telling you there's warmth in there.

"Home is where you hang your hat."

Well, I just don't know about that.

When I finished, I looked up to see a few teary eyes and Ernie awash in tears of joy. He didn't hesitate to say, "That's the best Christmas present I've ever gotten. Thanks Jim." And that made me feel something I had not felt in a long time and reminded me of the saying from the Bible, "It is more blessed to give than to receive." And that to me was the real meaning of Christmas anyway, anywhere, and at any time.

Ernie was able to keep his chess set; the guards never took it away from him. Just before our release, Ernie hid the pieces under the bottom of the little vinyl bag they gave us that had a cardboard interior bottom. It was easy to lift that up and place the pieces wrapped in a shirt there. And Ernie brought it home on the plane with him when we were released in 1973. He also had a poem he had inspired, and Ernie was forever remembered as our Civilian POW who lived by the code of conduct and by the old saying, "Once a Marine, always a Marine."

Late on Christmas Day, Col Guy and MAJ Art Elliot were taken from their cell and led up to the Big House. Ernie was sure this was a good sign, because that used to be where the North Vietnamese had the Christmas room each year. Soon they reappeared and were led back to their cell. Then our doors were opened and the original six LULUs, minus the ever-unrepentant and feisty CAPT Ed Leonard, were led to the Christmas room. It was not much this year, and it was obvious that many of the good things had already been given away, such as the oranges, bananas, and some of the chocolates. We got two pieces of hard candy each and were told that we had received "humane and lenient treatment thanks to the kind and generous Vietnamese people and the Democratic People's Republic of Vietnam."

Not a single word or cough sounded from the LULUs. Instead, we stood in silent contempt and disbelief that anyone would buy this line of tripe.

Once back in our cells, Walt tapped to Col Guy and learned that he and Art had gotten the exact same message from the prison commander, with a little different ending. Col Guy was told that any communication to other prisoners would result in severe punishment for him. They so much as told him that they knew he was the SRO and was giving orders not to cooperate. Hence, one last warning of the ever-popular command order: "No talk, No Tap." Col Guy had a way of making up fairly unique and very profane names for all the officers and main guards who kept us confused on occasion, but always amused. Tonight was no exception, and once again, the LULUs marveled at this true American patriot making the best of a bad situation.

CHAPTER 12

DEALING WITH QUITTERS

A few weeks later we received a note from the middle of the Warehouse cellblock that Army PFC Nathan Henry had some real health issues and needed medication. The North Vietnamese were attaching a price for treating him, and he was not sure what to do. His roommates were afraid he might die because he had been captured in 1967 in South Vietnam and kept in "tiger cages"[20] for over two years. His condition was complicated by fever and symptoms of malaria from what we were told. Ernie and Walt handled the communications usually and this was no exception. The word went to Col Guy and in less than a modest minute, Col Guy said, "Do whatever is necessary to get the medical treatment he needs."

Now the chore was getting this important message back to the middle cells in the Warehouse. We sent a note to the South end and knew it was a long shot, because the Commies had done a fairly effective job of isolating the officers there from the enlisted men in the Warehouse. Our best bet was to watch in front of the Gunshed and get the word to one of the enlisted men not connected with the LtCol Edison Miller's Peace Committee. The trouble was that a member or two of the Peace Committee was always hanging out there. Ernie and I both thought they had been asked to keep a close eye on us.

---

20 A tiger cage was approximately two feet high, four feet wide, six feet long, and constructed of bamboo or metal. Up to six men would be confined at once. Nathan Henry was permanently disabled as a result of his imprisonment.

When the message was said by Ernie, the response was a question of "Who says?" Ernie didn't want to implicate Col Guy, so I heard Ernie respond clearly, "Moses sends this word from most high." I smiled at that one, but I don't think the other side got the humor in it. We all had a very bad feeling about the exchange, and when we returned to our cells Walt was quick to tell Col Guy that we may have erred in trying to talk through the new screen.

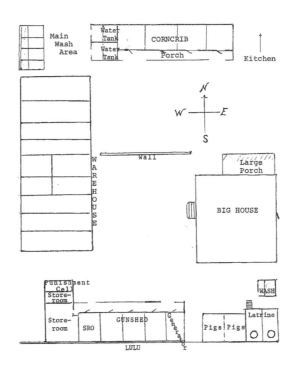

Map of the Plantation

The next day our fears were realized when several guards came to take Col Guy to the Big House. We were not sure at this time if they would get physical with the SRO, or just force some kind of apology from him and send him back. When Col Guy didn't come back the second day, we became increasingly concerned about him. Then Ed Leonard was removed from the Closet punishment cell and moved to Walt and Steve's cell in the Gunshed. Soon thereafter, PFC Henry was marched up from the Warehouse to the Closet, put in leg irons, and literally thrown into the cell. About a week later, the camp radio had a program announcing that there was a special announcement about a new policy on communicating. The voice proudly said, "Now we shall hear the confession of the War Criminal and leader of resistance, Theodore Guy." Then we heard the very weak and strained voice of Col Guy confessing his crimes of communicating and trying in vain to lead the POWs to resist. It was obvious no American had written this apology and Col Guy was being forced to read the script that told us all attempts at communications must stop immediately.

The program then shifted into some country and western music with a few war protest songs like, "Where Have All the Flowers Gone?" and "When Johnny Comes Marching Home." When the program ended, I was lookout and saw guards head our way. I pounded on the wall to warn the others and no one was caught communicating. Later it was established with MAJ Art Elliott that Col Guy needed to return to his cell before we could determine our next course of action. His instruction was to hold off on all communications until Col Guy returned. Walt modified that and told Ernie that as a civilian he could try to get notes to the south end of the camp. A few days later, a broken and very slow moving Col Guy was moved back into his cell. He had been held in leg irons for ten days and beaten with rubber hoses until he passed out. He was made to kneel for almost two days when he finally collapsed and had to be revived with a bucket of cold water.

Col Guy was in obvious pain and moved ever so carefully and slowly to wash the next day. As he passed our cell I noticed he was missing a few teeth. Later we learned that he had sustained three broken ribs in addition to losing three teeth. Col Guy wanted to stop communication between cell blocks because the risk was now too great for everyone. Ernie was able to get a compromise from Walt that we could maintain a very sparse number of notes and that all secret notes would be on resistance policy and better communication methods to avoid the Peace Committee. From this time on, one of the things we had to be very careful about was having any contact with the Peace Committee—they were not going to change and they were now our enemy. And as harsh as this assessment may sound today, it became even more ingrained from what I and others observed in the next several months.

──────────── ★ ────────────

In the early March, a truck backed up to the Gunshed Porch and stopped with its tailgate just a foot from being under the roof. As I watched no farther than fifteen feet away through our wide-angle peephole, the body of the truck started to raise and dump its load. A guard watched very closely and advised the driver to move forward before the rising body hit the Gunshed's roof. The load looked like fresh russet potatoes; we were not sure about the exact type, but we were about to enter potato season and that meant potato soup. We were all looking out when the guard called to the Peace Committee, who eagerly grabbed shovels and started moving the load to be more fully under the porch's roof. They were very conscientious and went out of their way to do an excellent job. We heard JR Leonard loudly yell, "Traitors!" They paid no attention or pretended that they hadn't heard him and Col Guy asked that we ignore them and not create a scene. JR's accusation was rewarded with a return trip to the Closet and reduced rations.

We watched for the next six weeks as a gal who worked in the kitchen pushed a small wheelbarrow to our porch and loaded the one-wheeled wonder with potatoes for the day's menu and push the length of the compound to the camp's kitchen. No man ever offered to help her. I thought that strange, but I had also observed the chow line being formed on a number of days. Inevitably the first two or three in the line were the women soldiers with uniforms as they were. When the men started to arrive, one by one the women stepped back, and before long all the men were at the front of the line and the women were always last in the line. They seemed very patient and very happy to have a place—any place—in the food line.

We got to thinking that we could augment our meals by obtaining a few of the taters on our porch and sanitizing them in our hot tea. No matter how long I kept a little potato in the hot tea and then added it to the lukewarm soup of the day, it seemed very hard. Ernie told me to stop whining or I was going to give the navy a bad name. It didn't take long for the effects of these few additions to our soup to have an effect on me. I remember the day well.

I was sitting on the bed playing Ernie in a game of gin rummy. I rarely won, but I loved trying, and Ernie just had a knack for discerning what I was doing and never played in a way to help me. On this day I started to scratch my behind a little. The more I moved and tried to scratch, the more it felt like something was tickling my rear. Ernie thought it might be a hemorrhoid. On several occasions I helped him push a hemorrhoid back into his rectum, so Ernie offered to return the favor. I thought it was worth a look-see. Ernie quickly said, "Don't move! This thing's alive!" All I could think of was a segmented parasitic worm like a tapeworm, and Ernie was in a tug of war with the thing. Out it would come, two inches or four inches, and back it would crawl in two inches. Ernie reinforced his grip on it with some toilet paper and the real tug of war started. I kept yelling, "Don't break it! *Don't break it!*" And Ernie kept saying; "I got it! I got it! Relax!" The whole Gunshed heard all this and were perplexed at what in the world we up to now.

Finally, Ernie's patience, strength, and determination won the war. He proudly held up a brown roundworm about eighteen inches in length. It was a wiggly critter and very much alive. This was a new ailment others had not reported on and we had no knowledge of. I was more than alarmed because, if there was one, there was sure to be more. Ernie also was so alarmed that he started calling "Bao cao." Unfortunately, Marvin, one of the more sadistic guards who spoke every vulgar word I knew with ease, was on duty. He did not open the latch to look in right away, and so Ernie started telling him through the closed and locked door that I needed the medic right away. Curiosity is a curious thing, and Marvin opened the latch and said, "What the matter?" Ernie held up the wiggling, warm worm so he could see it, and Marvin blew a gasket. He kicked the door and keep yelling; "Shut up! Shut up!" He slammed the latch so hard that it kept bouncing open again, which made Marvin even madder. Finally, he just stomped off.

The next day after washing we noticed Marvin hanging around in front of the Gunshed. When the medic came toward our building, a now normal part of the morning routine, Marvin told him to stop and that all was okay. Ernie was infuriated, but he, too, recognized that Marvin's sadistic character was hard to understand at times. Just a month before we had watched him trap a rat in one of the drainage gutters. He then took a pair of pliers and broke two of its legs and put the disabled and obviously terrified creature back in the drainage gutter. He wasn't done quite yet. He then took out a sling shot with ball bearing ammo and took target practice on the rat. Several times he hit it, and I could clearly see what looked like a bullet hole in the rat. This torture went on for almost an hour with other guards watching and laughing. Marvin was not an ordinary soldier or guard, and now we really had to be careful. The next day Marvin was on the porch when we came out to wash, and he told both Ernie and me that no one waves such a filthy thing as the worm just inches from his face. Ernie said he was really concerned that I might die. Marvin started laughing and said, "Everyone in Vietnam has worms. They no hurt you. Stop worrying and obey camp rules."

Col Guy still had health issues from his "interrogation" session and also needed to get more aspirin. The medic was good about treating his still-weeping wounds and putting on a new dressage every two or three days. Walt told us he was going to make a stink if we didn't get the medic the next day. Fortunately, Marvin was not in sight the next day, and the medic came by as usual. Ernie explained the length of the worm and wanted to show him a new one I had passed that was now swimming around in our bucket. This got the medic's curiosity and he looked like, "I gotta see this." The door was opened and he looked in the bucket while the worm did a high speed pass and tried to get out. The medic's eyes were like silver dollars and all he could say was, "Oiyssa!" (I think this means "wow!" in Vietnamese.) He said in broken English that he would come back a little later with special medicine. Steve overheard this and said, "Get any aspirin you can for Col Guy." At least we could help someone, even if all he was giving us was aspirin.

The medic did not leave the porch and then saw Col Guy, changed the last dressing the colonel needed, and gave him several aspirin for a broken tooth that was aching. He disappeared behind the screen that divided the compound and I thought to myself that it might be the end of it. About thirty minutes later, true to his word, the medic came to our cell. He gave me two yellow pills and watched me take them with a little tea. Then, he gave me two more pills neatly folded in a piece of paper. He stressed to take both after I ate our noon meal. Ernie was listening and trying to convert to English for me. It didn't take long for some side effects to hit me. My vision turned yellow like the pills and I felt a little dizzy, so I sat down and took it easy with Lt1 Jack Butcher next door serving as a lookout so we could talk to each other.

Col Guy had never heard of a POW getting any kind medicine other than iodine or aspirin, and he asked me if it tasted a little like iodine. Fortunately, it had no taste that I could detect when I was swallowing the pills. After the lunch, I opened the small packet to find two small pills that were very red. I quipped to Ernie, "Better red than dead; here goes again," and swallowed both before retiring for a little rest. However, after thirty minutes my vision turned pink. I had no other side effects and I didn't feel like I had to use the bucket yet. Finally, I did for a short relief of the bladder. Walt, Norm Gotner, and Col Guy were all concerned about what they had given to me and told Ernie to keep a close eye on me and, of course, no one had to tell Ernie such a thing after my sleep-deprived head-butting, wall-banging incident while at Hoa Lao prison.

The next morning I awoke feeling like I really needed to sit on the bucket. And I started to defecate in some rather loud and large amounts. Just when I thought I was done, here came some more. Finally, I was ready to finish the job with the paperwork. I had definitely had a loose one and needed more than my normal allotment of the course brown paper to clean myself off. Then when I looked into the bucket, I nearly fainted. It looked like a mini snake pit with at least nine to ten worms swimming for their lives. Ernie was even amazed and told the others that the navy had launched a new fleet of ships in the bucket. Steve Long congratulated me on being the youngest fleet commander in the navy, which got everyone laughing. And I never had the need for more medicine. I passed a few more roundworms, and that was the end of it.

In this same timeframe of 1972, Hanoi had a fairly famous visitor from the United States: musician Pete Seeger. I admired several of his civil rights songs and liked how he got audiences to sing along. But I also knew he was not here to help us—he was there to support the North Vietnamese people. He composed a song for the occasion that was about how "Vietnam was a nation of many different peoples and many different colors. There were brown ones, and tan ones and tall ones and short ones, but each voice seems to sing so clearly: 'we love our country so dearly.'" As much as I admired his singing for the cause of civil rights in the early Sixties, I had to wonder at his current effort. But I saw a chance for some humor here, so that night I sang the same tune as Pete was singing on the radio, but the words were slightly different:

"Vietnam is a nation of many worms. There are big ones and there are small ones. And there are red ones and there are brown ones. And each worm seems to sing so clearly: 'we love our host so dearly.'"

It was the show-stopper hit of the night. Col Guy told us the next day that he had not laughed so hard in all his years of captivity and was glad we were adjusting to life at the Plantation. "Some life" I thought, and then I began to appreciate the wisdom of Col Guy. I was indeed blessed to be with this group called the LULUs and to be alive—in several meanings of that word.

★

In early April we heard reports on the camp radio of a major Easter offensive that had the South Vietnamese forces in retreat. On March 30, 1972 we were told that over fourteen divisions of North Vietnamese regular army and one hundred thousand troops launched massive attacks across the Demilitarized Zone on the 17th Parallel and were already south of Da Nang. This sounded worse than the Tet Offensive of 1968. According to the radio, the attacks were all across the width and breath of South Vietnam. On April 6th and 7th we heard bombs in the distance and around two o'clock in the afternoon, a section of F-4 Phantoms flying at least at six hundred fifty knots flew over the Plantation prison to drop bombs just down the road, probably at the elevated main railroad line that ran right along one entire side of the Plantation. As the pair of F-4s pulled off the target, air raid sirens starting to blare and were obviously sounding off way too late. Then a very loud boom sounded and a nearby surface to air missile (SAM) site launched an SA-2 at the retiring pair of F-4s. Col Guy and Maj Walt Stischer were cheering and others joined in. The missile clearly missed the jets and then headed into the streets of Hanoi.

We heard more air attacks in the month and were hopeful it meant that the war would finally be coming to an end. But the recalcitrant North Vietnamese leadership was digging in, both militarily and politically. The camp radio program was now resorting to frantic histrionics and calling the American air pirates the worse war criminals in the history of mankind. Activist actress Jane Fonda was soon in town to record shows for Hanoi Hanna and our camp radio.

Fonda told us over the radio that, "Flying in just one mission over North Vietnam was a blacker and more hideous war crime than any WWII Nazi crimes." I have a number of Jewish friends who might beg to differ with her and to set her straight on this issue if the opportunity ever were to arise.

Soon after the F-4 Phantom flight over the Plantation, we heard the Peace Committee gathering in front of the Gunshed. They were measuring poles to be exactly twenty-five feet, with five feet underground, making the top of each pole twenty feet high. The leader in the calculations seemed to be Army Sergeant Robert Chenoweth, who was using an old trigonometry textbook to compute how large the F-4 models that they were constructing had to be the same size as a real F-4 at fifteen hundred feet, the effective range of most Vietnamese small arms. Ernie, Walt, and Norm were beyond themselves that any American would help an enemy like this. When they finished the next day, each pole was placed in spots where soldiers could look up and see if the passing F-4 Phantom was in range for them to shoot. I also remember Corporal Alfonso Riate (USMC) instructing one of the Vietnamese soldiers how to use the models to determine when to shoot. Col Guy had good reason to charge these men under the Uniform Code of Military Justice (UCMJ) on a number of charges with numerous specifications. He made sure we knew that these men would face some kind of court martial when we returned to the States.

When the LULUs were allowed to get together again, these activities sparked a discussion about the Code of Conduct. Capt JR Leonard was an early graduate of the Air Force Academy and was adamant that a military person could and should be tried for any Code of Conduct violation. He accurately stated that it was established by executive order under President Dwight Eisenhower and, like any executive order, it had the full force of law. I had learned in the Navy's SERE school that the Code of Conduct was a moral code; a standard to which every war fighter should strive to achieve. In short, it was a guide and set certain goals, which we were to try to follow. The phrase "to the utmost of my ability" was added to the article pertaining to the goal to evade answering questions that went beyond name, rank, service number, and date of birth. I used LCDR Dick Stratton as an example. He had all the fingernails on his left hand pulled out by a pair of pliers while three large guards held him down, and he still refused to cooperate. However, when they were starting on his right hand, he said, "I submit." A lot of men would have said that after one fingernail, but that doesn't mean they violated a moral code. They tried to resist to the best of their ability under the circumstances they were being held. We were not the only group having this type of discussion. I thought the key point was that Col Guy was cataloging violations to the Uniform Code of Military Justice and was asking us to search our memories on the various 134 Articles in the UMCJ and identify which ones the Peace Committee members had violated.

The most flagrant violation of the UCMJ that I observed from my lookout perch in our Gunshed cell was against another POW by one of the Peace Committee. Army Specialist William Baird had been captured on May 6, 1968 in the northern part of South Vietnam. When his unit was being overrun, he had the misfortune to meet up with a Claymore mine. This is the type of mine that pops up in the air and explodes a large grenade-type of warhead. This particular mine had bounced off Bill and damaged one foot badly, both legs, and some of his outdoor/indoor plumbing; the North Vietnamese had operated on him to correct some of the damage. For example, he had a tube connected to his bladder so he could void his urine. He walked with the use of two crutches. He was a determined and brave American who, when he returned home in 1973, was awarded the Silver Star for "distinguished gallantry and intrepidity" while a POW in North Vietnam. One day for reasons unknown, the North Vietnamese thought a roommate with a "good attitude" would help Bill to appreciate the "humane and lenient treatment" he and others had been afforded.

When Alfonso Riate was put into Bill's cell, Ernie said he didn't like the looks of this one. We had sent messages to Bill to encourage him and to thank him for being such a good soldier. On the other hand, Riate had the run of the camp and had been seen many times arguing with some others on the Peace Committee that didn't agree with his proactive war protesting mode. Although all of the five original members of the Peace Committee shared an intense dislike for the war, they all had differences of opinion on a number of topics and especially on how much they should help their North Vietnamese captors. Not one of them objected to turning in POWs who had tried to communicate with them into the Commies, but when they saw things that were violations, not all agreed that they had to report them. Riate was not like this; he reported anything and anyone to the Commies.

On the second day of this new cell arrangement, the men in the cell next to Bill Baird heard loud voices and knew a very intense argument was underway. They thought it was about cigarettes and bananas. The Commies were trying to give Bill an extra piece of fruit and sometimes a plate of powdered milk heated and mixed with chocolate powder and sugar. Apparently, Riate didn't think Bill rated these extra goodies and was taking all the cigarettes and had eaten both bananas that morning. Bill was a determined American war fighter who had a sense of honor and value for integrity.

The next day after lunch I was standing lookout and watching all the activity in the courtyard. Because of recent air raids, the Peace Committee now had to return to their cells and be locked up during siesta time. However, they roamed about the camp almost at will for the rest of the daylight hours. When Bill was getting off a chair in the front of his cell, the Maggot, an officer from the Ho Loa prison in 1970, asked him how he liked his new roommate with such a "good attitude." Bill was truthful and told the Maggot that Riate was a thief and for two days had taken all the bananas and cigarettes. Maggot pretended to be concerned and asked, "What else? What else?" Bill stood in the door way and calmly stated that Riate was threatening him every day. Maggot asked, "What you mean?" And Bill, now getting a bit exasperated, said, "He's going to beat the shit out of me!" Maggot just ignored this and motioned Bill into the cell; then Riate approached to go in and Maggot turned to him and said, "You must work on this man to have a good attitude."

In keeping with the daily routine, the soldiers filed to the kitchen for their meals and the officers disappeared into the Big House and points beyond. Normally there were only two guards on duty, one to the south end and one at our end. This day was normal. About fifteen minutes passed and I heard from Bill's cell a very loud, "Fuck you!" Then the door bounced about half a foot outwards, as if someone had hit it. Then it bounced again, and then again. The prisoners in the adjoining cells started yelling as loud as they could, "Bao cao!" The sole guard went running up to the door to open the latch to peek into the cell. Just as he opened the flap to look in the cell, the door was slammed again and then again very quickly. The guard was beside himself and ran off screaming to the Big House. There were more sounds and door movements before the officer with the keys was finally found in the Big House. Several of the larger guards came with him to the Thunderbird cell.

As soon as the officer with the key opened the door to Bill's and Alphonso's cell, Alphonso came out smiling and laughing, saying that Bill Baird was crazy. He kept his finger pointed at his head and circling it. The soldiers all started laughing, except for the officer. He had a stern look and told Bill in a very loud voice to put on his long shirt to go to the Big House. This made little sense to me.

When Bill emerged from the cell, it was all I could do to keep myself under control. His head had been beaten against the door. Both eyes were swollen, his nose was bleeding and looked broken, and one or two of his teeth were sticking through his cheek with bright red blood flowing out and down his side. Jack Butcher had to verify this in the next cell, because it was beyond our belief that any American would do this to a wounded fellow soldier. Bill's march across the courtyard was very slow, because now he had only one crutch. The other one lay broken in his cell and had been used by Riate to start his attack. I also noticed that the tube from Bill's midsection was hanging out much farther and had blood surrounding the opening. One step, Bill moved a foot. One more step, Bill moved another foot. I have never witnessed such a painful and tortured walk in my life. And on the other side was Riate with a group of soldiers still laughing and making crazy signs.

Col Guy saw Bill and was shocked. He said when Riate's court martial convened, he wanted me to promise that I would be a witness for this charge. I said by the grace of God and the U.S. Navy, I would be there. When the word of the attack went around the Plantation, there were some very strong feelings expressed against the Peace Committee. Apparently, several of the senior enlisted who had earned battlefield promotions had been identified by members of the Peace Committee group as "war criminals." One sergeant was kept in stocks or leg irons for eighteen months because of a lie reported about him to his Communist captors by one of the Peace Committee members. I had no knowledge of what they had done before, but I had seen enough in the last nine months to know I didn't want to be around them or have anything to do with them. Apparently many others had the same view or worse.

We were all shocked by what we had seen. What made it worse was seeing Bill, in about two weeks, returned to the exact same cell in the warehouse. At least this time there was no roommate and he had two new crutches; and if anyone needed a little extra help and kindness, I thought it was this man.

Riate was back in Warehouse 1 with the Peace Committee getting warm beer, extra rations, and fruit every day. One day he paused by Bill's cell and started yelling at him that he was going to get it the minute they let him out in the courtyard. "Everyone in Cell 1 wants to kick your ass." It was loud enough that many others heard it and commented on it in notes. One group wanted to know if Col Guy would approve an effort to poison Riate and his "peacenik buddies." Col Guy said "No!" and extracted promises from them not to retaliate. In return he said, "When we get back, I promise you to get these men before a court martial, even if I have to go to the White House." In the end that is exactly what Col

Guy did to get the Secretary of Defense and the Secretary of the Air Force to move on this action in the spring of 1973 after all POWs were returned to U.S. custody.

This was a dark time on many levels. We learned on the camp radio that President Nixon had authorized the use of B-52 bombers over North Vietnam, and shortly after May 8th we learned that our navy and air force joined assets to mine Haiphong Harbor; it was now closed for business. The first sign that we saw this was true was the increase of rail traffic passing alongside the Plantation. The railroad tracks were elevated about fifteen feet, so we could see the cars and often the cargo they were carrying. We not only saw more traffic, but we saw boxcars with Chinese markings and heavy equipment that was all moving south to the war front. Ernie had studied some of the railroad structure of North Vietnam and told us there were three primary rail lines from China to North Vietnam that all converged in the Hanoi area, and from there two rail lines proceeded south. One of these lines continued on the coast while the other one turned due west to the head of the Plain of Jars in Laos and the roadway that became known as the Ho Chi Minh Trail. In June we started to see troop trains with soldiers singing war songs and yelling cheers as their rickety trains moved south. They seemed to be well-outfitted and very happy to be heading to battle.

By late June the air attacks seemed to be decreasing and we were not sure if that had any big meaning or not. Both Norm and Walt felt it meant that the U.S. targeting command was running out of meaningful military targets short of main infrastructure. Norm also felt that nothing short of B-52s or tactical nukes would stop the rail system. He reasoned that the North Vietnamese Army had so many people that they would carry whatever was needed to the damaged portion of tracks and make all the repairs by the next day. Massive air power was what was needed, but we doubted the United States would go that far. What we didn't know was how the peace talks were breaking down in Paris and how the North Vietnamese seemed so close at one point to agreeing on a peace structure and then suddenly had moved away from that position. Later, when two new POWs joined LULU, we learned that the North Vietnamese launched a large offensive in Laos, which reached the Mekong River in southern Laos, and had exchanged artillery fire with Thailand's armed forces. We heard increasing strident name calling and accusations on the camp radio, and Ernie once again analyzed this change in tone as a futile attempt to hide the failure of this new offensive from their own people and armed forces. The food for the POWs by the end of October was also back to prison gruel with little to no fresh vegetable or fruits added to the normal fare. We were all convinced by this time that the mining of Haiphong Harbor in May of 1972 was starting to have an impact on imports to North Vietnam.

★

Another incident sticks in my mind. Around October 11, 1972, we awoke to a gray and very foggy day. After our morning half-loaf of bread and time to wash up, we remained outside to exercise. The fog was persistent and thick. Then we heard the rumble of bombs going off, quite close. I felt a slight tremor in the ground and heard the distinct sound of a single jet aircraft fading into the distance. I instantly thought it was a Navy A-6 Intruder and one of the navy sailors in the Warehouse shouted; "God Bless the Intruders." Then air raid sirens sounded and guards started running everywhere. We were immediately taken to our cells and locked away. Soldiers manned the walls with AK-47s at the ready. But all anyone could see was the opaque fog cover. The next day we learned that the French embassy had taken a direct hit and the French Delegate General (Ambassador) had been killed. I took no joy in the news and wondered how close the French embassy was to the river with the bridge nearby, or even next door to it. I never did learn the official story, but I suspect that it was an honest mistake with iron bombs and radar mapping.

The week after the bombing of the French Embassy we were taken on a tour of "American bombing atrocities" and a museum in downtown Hanoi that was not too far from the Plantation. We were given civilian shirts and loose trousers to fit in more with the civilian population. We were driven past the French Embassy that had been bombed and now was under emergency repairs. This was a new experience for all of us, and all eyes were focused on the streets and especially cross streets, which afforded longer views of both sides of a boulevard or major street. When we arrived at the museum, we saw directly across the street the remains of a church and the interpreter told us this was proof of Nixon's war crimes against the Vietnamese people. Norm whispered something to Ernie, who then asked the question of why there were large Fan Song radar antenna remains in the middle of the wreckage. To anyone with some military training, this site had been obviously used as a control center for a SA-2 SAM launching site with mobile launchers located in the surrounding areas. The interpreter told Ernie; "Do not show bad attitude on this trip and do not spread lies about our government or courageous people."

We also noted several rats that were huge—about the size of a large well-fed house cat back home. Jack Burcher asked if there were rats in all the city or just here, and he was told to keep silent. We were never taken on another tour into the city as I recall, and that was a good thing.

The impact on the Americans was almost immediate as the North Vietnamese went on a search for any American who wanted to criticize this attack. Around this same time, Ernie and I had been given the daily chore of washing out the pigpen and throwing some water over the mother sow and two piglets. This was one of the best jobs Ernie and I were ever given, because the pigs liked to have their ears scratched and they looked at us like they understood we were helping them. The mother was finally named by Ernie as Agnes, after Saint Agnes, the patron saint of gardeners, farmers, girls, and, especially, all virgins. The guards heard us call her by name and thought we were calling her Agnew, after the vice president of the United States. The propaganda machine was so much on the upswing that we were called to the Big House and questioned on why we thought Agnew was a fat pig. It took us more than a few minutes to understand that the common soldiers were getting politically fed the Communist line on the upcoming U.S. presidential election and, of course, were looking for anything that might sell at home and abroad. When we told the officer that our name for the mother pig was Agnes, his face dropped like a ton of bricks had just been dumped on him. We were told again, "Go Back! Keep Shylent!" Ernie and I were delighted that all that came of this incident was to be sent back to our cell and told not to communicate. Of course the first thing we did when the guard left our porch was to contact Norm and Jack in the next cell and fill them on what transpired at the Big House. Jack said it was good to have us both back, and that once again made Ernie and I realize how close all our LULU group had become.

Another part of our treatment that had changed was being included in films that were shown at night to the entire group of POWs. In the past we had been left in our cells, except for the few short months at the Little Vegas section of Hoa Lo prison in 1970. In the summer of 1972, they started to include us again. We were brought out last and sat to the rear of all the other POWs, and after the film we were first to be taken back to our cells. However, others saw us and gave coughs and winks of encouragement to the LULUs.

Some of the movies were Russian and some were Chinese. One was a Russian version of *Othello,* which we all enjoyed. I think Ernie was our white-wash critic, because he liked everything they showed us and used every movie night as an opportunity to tell other POWs who we were and that we were not getting any mail or Christmas packages. The most important thing the LULUs were all concerned about was being left behind in Hanoi in a general peace treaty and release of POWs captured in North and South Vietnam. And although movie night had some very amateurish and obviously propaganda types of films, it also had some very well-produced propaganda films for export purposes. No matter what the film, we were able to communicate at these events with other POWs.

The camp radio was telling us more about the peace talks in Paris and how duplicitous and dishonest the South Vietnamese leaders were and how Nixon and "his running dogs" were helping to stall the talks in hopes of winning a small victory on the battlefield. According to the radio, the Americans and South Vietnamese forces were losing every battle and in retreat to Saigon. Our interpreters were also quick to remind us, "Vietnamese communist forces grow stronger every day. We cannot beat you in the Tonkin Gulf or in the skies of Vietnam, but we shall beat you in the streets of San Francisco and New York City."

The films from back home we were allowed to see kept showing larger and larger crowds marching and shouting protests over the Vietnam War. For me, it hurt to see American students carrying the Viet Cong and North Vietnamese flags and cheering their war efforts. I wondered aloud if we would ever be free from this war. I think an entire generation of Americans is still critical of American efforts to help preserve a free nation, and they clearly still give a free pass to the decades of atrocities committed by Communist forces. When I try to recount today to younger audiences some of the history I have learned about Ho Chi Minh's Vietnam, I am greeted by blank stares of disbelief and sympathetic smiles with side whispers of "PTSD."

For several weeks we kept hearing about the death of the French ambassador and his wife and how the United States was engaged in war crimes of the worst order. We heard statements from "world leaders" like Fidel Castro, Zhou Enlai, and Mao Zedong. The latter had just entertained President Nixon during his historic visit to Red China, but no mention was made or acknowledged in any official North Vietnamese media of this changing relationship. All the news we ever were given was the negative things that made our country look bad and the North Vietnamese look good.

By the end of October and early November we all noticed the volume and pitch of the radio had increased against "Nixon and his running dogs." Several of us reasoned the behavior of the North Vietnamese in Paris might not be wearing well with many other countries. Ernie was sure that something was up.

Around Thanksgiving we heard on the camp radio that the North Vietnamese plan for peace had changed; they now were not committing to any POW exchange. This was a major breaking news story for all the POWs, and the reasoned position of the Communists was that all American forces had to be withdrawn and then they all could sit down and discuss POW exchanges. President Nixon was quoted as being enraged and "obdurate." Hubert Humphrey was recorded as pleading for more diplomacy from the White House, and the Democrat presidential candidate, George McGovern, was recorded and played on the camp radio saying that he would "go to Hanoi and get on my knees to bring home all the POWs." Ernie would groan every time they played that tape, and we learned from a single page from a *Stars and Stripes* newspaper smuggled in that President Nixon was calling for "peace with honor" and McGovern's was labeled by some as the "peace at any price" candidate. We tried do a poll of all the POWs in the Plantation on the Election of 1972 and never could get notes or replies from half the camp. Those who did respond all stated that McGovern's plan to come to Hanoi and beg would be a death sentence for many Americans who had endured for so long and had resisted to the utmost of their capabilities. And the LULUs all knew that included us. It was with great joy that the LULUs heard President Nixon had been re-elected.

One day in early December, with no explanation and no fanfare, all the LULUs were ordered to remove everything from our cells and place them in neat stacks on the porch. This was not just another room inspection or search. The guards were looking for something special and they found nothing. So when they were done, most of the soldiers walked off in disgust and disappointment and we were told to put our things back. Ernie quickly saw their lack of specific instruction and moved his stuff into Walt Stischer's room, next to Col Guy. Steve Long smartly moved in with Ernie while Walt moved into the middle room with Norm Gotner, and Jack Butcher moved into the end cell with me. He really had no other place to go and I was delighted to have a new roommate just before Christmas. No one said anything, but the next day an officer stopped by and gathered us all together to tell us something. We thought he was going to chew us out, but he only wanted to rant about President Nixon and never even seemed to notice or comment that on our own initiative we had reshuffled our living arrangements. Later JR Leonard was brought from the Closet, along with two saw horses plus a bamboo rack, and put into the middle room with Norm and Walt.

Things were looking up and the Communist attitude—or better, their lack of concern—told us that we were no longer individuals but were now seen as a group from Laos.

CHAPTER 13

WELCOMING THE B-52

On the night of December 18, 1972, our life on the Plantation came to a sudden and complete end as we had known it. It started like any other night, getting our mosquito nets raised and taking one last wiz into the bucket for a long winter's nap. I was not as light a sleeper as some of my cellmates, and Jack was just like Ernie—quick to awaken if I got out of the rack at night. I remember Jack saying that it looked like a dark night and he could see a lot of stars. Just as I was falling asleep, the loudest sound I'd ever heard thumped our doors and continued to roar like rolling thunder. It reminded me of what I had heard in the distance in Laos one night when the B-52s lit up the sky and shook us as we passed on the edge of an Arc Light mission. But these bombs were much closer, and the first wave caused our doors to reverberate and rattle, and plaster fell from our ceiling in one spot. And the noise from the 130 mm KS-30 and 100 mm KS-19 Anti-Aircraft gun across the street from the Plantation was deafening; the recoil from every firing shook the ground like a minor earthquake tremor. We heard Norm saying, "B-52s! B-52s! God bless those BUFFs." Col Guy and Walt Stischer were looking out the peep holes now, too. Then we heard a SA-2 SAM being fired and soon the glow of its engine racing skyward told us the war had finally came home to Hanoi.

What was interesting about the first bombing wave that night was that most of the bombs seemed to be north of the Plantation. Col Guy said that is where the main MIG Airbase at Kep was located. Another area seemed to be just to the west of town where we could see a SA-2 SAM had found its mark—a B-52 flamed like a comet to earth. It was too far away and much too dark to see if there were ejections or parachutes. I just prayed hard for every American up in the sky; they were there to bring us home. Ernie was absolutely dancing with joy. On the other hand, Norm was very worried, because the B-52s were designed to be strategic bombers for nuclear war and they were not known to be useful in doing interdiction or specific target bombing. He said; "It's going to take a lot of luck for all those bombs to never land on a POW prison." I prayed even more for the accuracy and for our whole team up in the sky.

The guards were running around in a panic while the air raid sirens sounded and putting on flak jackets and helmets we had rarely seen before. Norm told me that B-52 Stratofortress was affectionately called a BUFF, which meant Big Ugly Fat Fellow. He said that they could be loaded with up to eighty-four Mark 82s (five hundred-pound bombs) internally, and twenty-four Mark 117s (seven hundred fifty-pound bombs) on the under-wing pylons—that meant one hundred eight bombs of some size and explosive power. Norm said that a typical Arc Light mission dropped in string pairs would create a bomb blast area over a mile long and at least a half-mile wide.

And this night was only just beginning.

Just as I had decided the show was over and had gotten under my mosquito net, the air raid sirens started again and everyone outside began yelling. This time the first string of bombs was much closer and the ground actually shook. The explosions of the bombs lasted a long time and kept illuminating the night as if it was day. The lonely anti-aircraft gun on our roof was small and rarely fired, yet the SA-2 SAM site nearby, which we had heard fire earlier, fired at least three more SAMs at this second wave and the large 100mm KS-19 across the street was firing continuously for more than seven minutes. I jokingly said to our LULUs, "If this keeps up, no one is going to get any sleep tonight." What was even more frightening about the second wave was that the strike was obviously on military targets close to downtown Hanoi, which was where the Communists were known to hide their reserve fuel and ammo supplies among the population. Norm seemed to be the only one who voiced concern, but it was on my mind and I was sure others were also concerned about a stray bomb or a failed SAM full of fuel crashing into the Plantation. In fact, given the number of SAMs fired that night which missed and came back to earth undetonated, they may have done the majority of the damage to the civilian population that first night.

After the second wave was finished, I went to readjusting my mosquito net so I could use the bamboo slat with blanket as a cover and sleep under the rack on the floor. I had extra rice mats and an extra blanket, so I was getting very comfortable. Just as I was settling in, the roar of tactical jets zoomed by and J.R. yelled out, "The Thuds (F-105 Thunderchiefs) have joined the party." The air force had developed an anti-radiation missile (ARM) that homed onto the frequencies associated with SAM sites launching and guiding missiles. The ARM missiles were called Wild Weasels because of the high screeching noise they made and the Thuds were modified in 1966 to execute such missions. Everyone started watching for SAMs rising and then going into corkscrew turns to finally crash into the city. Norm thought we were doomed. Ernie said the war was over and we'd be going home soon. Ernie made a lot of sense to me, and Col Guy was quick to agree with Ernie on this point. Not one guard seemed to be concerned about the POWs or even watching any POW cell. We were talking in normal voices and calling out things we were seeing in the sky. And the BUFFs just kept coming in what felt like an endless line. We learned later that they flew three BUFFS as a "cell" and worked as teams on specific military targets such as rail yards, fuel storage sites, military airfields, and weapon storage areas with both ammo and heavy duty weapons.

By midnight I was getting very tired and told Jack I was going to try and get a little shut eye. The next morning, Jack said that I was sound asleep in about five minutes. All the other LULUs were in and out of bed all night. In the morning we had counted at least eight major strikes. This became the main discussion point in the Gunshed for a while that day.

It's difficult to count exactly how many targets were hit because the air force's plan of attack was made at the Strategic Air Command (SAC) headquarters in Omaha, Nebraska. They had about three days to plan and train the crews,[21] so they stuck with the tactics used from WWII and divided the attacks into waves comprised of two or three cells of three planes each. On the first night there were actually one hundred twenty-nine B-52s used and sixty-eight SAMs were fired at them. Three B-52s were lost that night.[22],[23]

By noon I was quietly shaking my head and Jack asked me how many I had counted. I replied that I thought I had awakened four times during the night. Steve Long wanted to make an award for me as the sailor who slept through the most B-52 bombing raids on the first night. Walt said there would be more nights to follow, because "the North Vietnamese were not smart enough to know when they were beaten." However, we saw immediate reactions and signs that the soldiers here were digging in for the long haul.

Everywhere in the prison holes were being dug. Boards, tables, and any other pieces of flat wood, metal, or plastic were being collected to make roofs for these make-shift air raid shelters. Even the ping-pong table on our porch was taken apart and dragged to the center of the courtyard where the Peace Committee was helping a group of soldiers dig and build a large central air raid shelter. When they were finished, they were instructed to take the tools to their cells and start digging in there. That was the start of having all prisoners in the Warehouse dig shelters in the middle of their small cells to stay in during air raids. The Corn Crib got tools the next day, but there were no tools yet for the LULUs in the Gunshed—the LULUs would have to wait until all the other POWs had dug their shelters.

---

21 Earl H. Tilford Jr., *Setup: What the Air Force Did in Vietnam and Why* (Maxwell Air Force Base, AL: Air University Press, 1991), 253-54.

22 John Morocco, *Rain of Fire: Air War, 1969-1975* (Boston: Boston Publishing Co., 1985), 153-54.

23 Steven J. Zaloga, *Red SAM: The SA-2 Guideline Anti-Aircraft Missile* (Oxford: Osprey Publishing, 2007), 23.

In fact, a week later on Christmas day the guards finally brought us tools to dig holes in our cells. Digging through the concrete and tile floor was made a bit easier with a heavy crow bar, which was like a hand-impact drill. The work was really difficult, but we all took turns helping each other when the tools arrived. We were sure that the nights would bring more B-52s over Hanoi and being in some type of underground hole might help protect us.

The second night, December 19, found the B-52s dropping bombs much closer to the Plantation. It was much louder than the first night as the targets were all close to downtown Hanoi. We saw at least six SAMs fired by the SAM unit nearby; fortunately, we didn't see any B-52s streaming down to earth as we had seen on the first night. Later, the history written of these attacks stated that ninety-three B-52s were launched, twenty SAMs were launched and did damage, and no B-52s were lost that night.[24]

The Plantation was located one block from Vietnam's Ministry of Defense where the Alcatraz prison had been built for the toughest POW leaders, and we were about one-half-to-one-mile from the Paul Doumer Bridge (now called the Long Bien Bridge) and the main Hanoi power plant. The Gia Lam rail yard and main airport for Hanoi were across the river and extended several miles to the north and east.[25]

There was a growing fear on every Vietnamese face we saw. By the third day, the camp radio was going full bore with stories of how many B-52s were being shot down. They claimed the numbers for the two nights were already twenty-five to thirty planes shot down by the Vietnamese Army, and we knew instinctively that this count was not correct. The truth was more in the eyes and faces of the soldiers. They were terrified, and when we were taken out to wash the guards kept saying, "Quick! Quick! Quick!" We noticed the ground was well-covered with shrapnel from the anti-aircraft ordnance expended in the

---

24 Steven J. Zaloga, *Red SAM*, 23.
25 Wayne C. Thompson, *To Hanoi and Back: The U.S. Air Force and North Vietnam, 1969-1973* (Washington, D.C.: Smithsonian Press, 2002), 298.

night. Long after a wave of B-52s left the area we could hear the sound of metal rain falling on the concrete roof. Now we had to be very careful where we stepped because the edges of these metal chards were quite sharp and jagged and our thin sandals were made of aging tire tread.

It was on the third day, December 20 that a number of soldiers with two new officers struggled to get something onto the roof of the Gunshed. At first, Ernie was sure it was a 37mm anti-aircraft gun; I thought it looked more like a 14.5mm anti-aircraft machine gun with its own trailer and ammunition trays. The one thing we knew for sure was that it was lifted by ropes with a lot of young soldiers on our roof. They even fired several times to make sure the gun and its crew were ready for the night. When this gun fired, our rooms literally shook and bounced at the recoil from each round going off. And I thought the high firing rate seemed to confirm it was a 14.5mm heavy machine gun with perhaps a dual barrel that was developed by the Soviets after World War II and widely exported to their allies around the world. I told Steve and Ernie that I didn't think I would be sleeping through that night.

After the first two nights and days of attacks on Hanoi we saw a pattern of tactical strikes with precision bombs on railroads and key military targets during the day, and the wider-area B-52 bombing attacks at night. Between the Navy's Task Force 77 in the Tonkin Gulf and the 8th Air Force Tactical Aircraft, we estimated at least one hundred sorties were flown through the daylight hours and often resulted in bombs or air-to-ground missiles exploding before the air raid sirens even sounded. During the day, few SA-2 SAMs were being fired. Walt, our LULU SRO, said emphatically, "They're saving all the SAMs they have left for the BUFFs."

With nightfall quickly approaching, something new occurred; an English-speaking soldier made the rounds of the Plantation and told each cell to get under our bamboo bed racks and not to speak loudly during the night. In other words, they didn't want any more cheering for the B-52s up in the air. So in defiance, the LULUs, with the help of the aging

220

football players and one Michigan Marching Band member, came up with our cheers for that night: "Hit 'em again! Harder! Harder!" and "God bless those BUFFs! If they can't do it, nobody can!" Little did we know that the targets selected for the third night were the Yen Vien rail yards just north and east of the Paul Doumer Bridge, and targets very close and just north of the Plantation, such as the main Hanoi power plant.[26] We were sitting on the front row for the night show!

Just after dark the first wave hit and the skies were afire. SA-2 SAMs from at least three sites near the Plantation were fired as well as several larger anti-aircraft guns. The F-105 Thuds roared low and fast and we heard several Wild Weasels get launched. The doors on our cells reverberated and moved at times six inches in and then out. Jack found a high perch and looked out without the door hitting him. I moved to the floor and found a space on the hinge that afforded me a wide view of the night sky. And that night when I saw another B-52 get hit and stream down toward the streets of Hanoi, I mourned before it hit the ground. And yet more B-52s joined this attack and more SAMs were fired. This night we witnessed what was called "the most pronounced NVA defensive effort against the B-52s and the highest single-day losses of Operation Linebacker II."[27] It was a night to remember.

The LULUs were never able to do much cheering as the noise and proximity to the targets on this night gave us all pause to remember the Americans high above us who were putting their lives on the line to bring us home. And I knew we also thought of the North Vietnamese civilians who were too close to military targets and were being wounded and killed that night. The next day we were told that an amazing number of B-52s were shot down—more than twenty according to the North Vietnamese sources. Yet in reality it was seven direct hits over Hanoi and one badly damaged B-52 that crashed just short of the runway in U-Tapao, Thailand; so the real number was eight. The North Vietnamese

---

26 James R. McCarthy and Robert E. Allison, *Linebacker II: A View from the Rock* (Washington, DC: Office of the USAF History, 1985), 81-89.

27 McCarthy and Allison, *Linebacker II*, 83.

also claimed that many civilians were killed near the downtown rail yards and these were the "most vicious of war crimes." We knew instinctively that the North Vietnamese were getting seriously frustrated and that the soldiers who were guarding us at the Plantation believed their eyes more than any state radio pronouncement. What we didn't know was that the B-52 losses of that night reverberated back to SAC headquarters and the White House, which forced changes in how the war would be conducted in the future. Wayne Thompson, U.S. Air Force Historian, Gen James McCarthy (USAF), and Col John Allison's (USAF) histories recount the changes well.

The original plan was to bomb for only three days, but the North Vietnamese hadn't seemed to change their stance in Paris. President Nixon decided to extend the bombing period, but made no public announcement about how long the bombing would continue. Retired Air Force Intelligence Officer Earl Telford also told of how the ingress and egress points were varied and how the post-target turns (standard B-52 tactic up to this time) were modified. The newer B-52s needed older jammers that were more capable against the SA-2 SAM radars, so they did not fly for a few days while the modifications were made to the B-52Gs at Guam. Tilford said that, "Poor tactics and a good dose of overconfidence combined to make the first few nights of Linebacker II nightmarish for B-52 crews."[28]

---- ★ ----

On the morning of December 21 the LULUs were gathered onto the porch of the Gunshed and stood there waiting until a small troop led by the camp commander, Dead Eye, came up. He didn't appear to be happy at all. We just stared at him and he stared back. Then, he proceeded to speak to us in Vietnamese with the Maggot translating. It was a typical propaganda tirade about American war crimes against the heroic and glorious Vietnamese people.

---

28 Tilford Jr., *Setup,* 256.

"Nixon and his running dogs only care about killing Asians, but he can never win."
And then the old line was brought up of "we will beat you in the streets of San Francisco
and New York City."

It was too much for Ernie Brace. He stood at attention and politely raised his hand.
Maggot shook his head, but Dead Eye pointed at him and nodded. Ernie said words to the
effect "that the war was coming to an end and that Hanoi was defeated. There would be a
peace treaty, and we soon would be all going home." Dead Eye was furious and told the
guards to take Ernie immediately to the Big House and off he went. I was alarmed that they
would start punishment for a "bad attitude" so quickly.

We were sent back to our individual cells and locked up. We were all concerned that
Ernie might be made an example of to all the other POWs. However, Ernie was a civilian
and usually the examples were our senior officers. That rule held true. Within fifteen to
twenty minutes a soldier brought Ernie back to his cell and locked him up with the old-time
instruction, "Keep shylent!" We soon learned that Dead Eye scolded Ernie and told him that
now was a time to keep quiet. Dead Eye also admitted to Ernie that the Army was "very
busy in their preparations to shoot down more Yankee air pirates." Ernie's assessment was
similar to both Walt Stischer's and Col Guy's: the war was over and we would all know that
soon.

The next few days and nights before Christmas were stressful. We had no protection
and the B-52s keep coming. However, they seemed to be bombing either south of the
Plantation or in the northeast area where Kep Airfield and several large railroad terminals
and storage yards were located. We also heard parts of Haiphong Harbor had been hit hard,
and a foreign cargo ship had been damaged at a pier and would be there for some time to
come. Moreover, the camp radio announced that a hospital at Bac Mai was hit, and "twenty-
eight innocent civilians were killed." We learned later that all the patients had been moved
the day before because the hospital was less than a half-mile off the end of a runway at the

Bac Mai Airfield. The NVA, with a group of doctors and nurses, were left to use the facility as an emergency triage facility. One B-52 had been hit just at the bomb release point on the raid, and many suspect the errant bombs that hit the hospital were a result of that B-52's bomb loss and not a target.[29]

The new tactics of approaching a target with cells coming from different directions seemed to be working well. On the December 21, thirty B-52Ds with the best-suited electronic packages, hit storage areas and an airfield in heavily defended downtown Hanoi and lost two B-52Ds to SA-2 SAMs. The SAMs were very active. One B-52 co-pilot, Capt Dave Drummond remarked, "it looks like we'll walk on SAMs tonight."[30] From the ground it once again looked like a July 4th fireworks show with the addition of the ground shaking and new pieces of old plaster falling on our heads as we darted to and from our lookout positions.

The next day we heard more tactical aircraft, but were unable to see any of them. The night of December 22 saw action farther from Hanoi, with some centered on the Port of Haiphong again. We heard and saw SAM firings; and we were relieved to learn that not one B-52 had been shot down. By comparing notes with POWs from other parts of the Plantation, we had at least a three hundred-degree field of view and most of the action was all in that field of view.

On the sixth day of the B-22 bombing, December 23, the attack consisted of thirty more B-52Ds from U-Tapao, Thailand. They struck at SAM sites north of Haiphong and other sites near the border with China. The cells planned to split apart at the initial point (IP)

---

29 Thompson, p.262-263. (This part also has notes of Telford Taylor, Columbia University professor, who was visiting Hanoi at the time and had WWII experience prosecuting Nazi war crimes at Nuremberg. Although he was not in favor of the war, he found no evidence of counter-value bombing or war crimes in Hanoi by American forces. He also protested North Vietnamese behavior towards captured B-52 crews.)

30 McCarthy and Allison, *Linebacker II*, 93.

and the first plane would fly directly over the SAM site. The plan lulled the ground crews into thinking the B-52 was going to another target and didn't realize their mistake until more than one hundred heavy bombs started impacting their site. These tactics worked better than had been expected, and again all thirty B-52s returned to Thailand.[31]

When the order for a Christmas stand down came through to the Americans of the Guam and Thailand B-52 forces, it was decided that only the Thailand B-52s would conduct the December 24 attacks. The targets were going to be far to the north of Hanoi again, and the ingress tract would take the B-52s over northern Laos and through the northwest quadrant of North Vietnam to attack the rail yards at Thai Nguyen and Kep. These targets had been hit before. However, aerial reconnaissance revealed areas undamaged and a more concentrated attack was needed. This again was a total success with no B-52s shot down and all cells delivering bombs on target. The post-photography described in accounts by McCarthy and Allison showed a concentration and precision in the results that far exceeded pre-mission forecasts.[32] What made this last mission of the Linebacker II phase operation revealing is that two waves of B-52s transited over the entire northern tier of North Vietnam, then exited south to the Gulf of Tonkin, and finally headed at high altitude east to Thailand. There was no lack of North Vietnamese effort to stop this attack with multiple SAM launches and several flights of MIGs that took off to intercept and shoot them down—those efforts all failed.

We guessed things were not going well for the North Vietnamese because the camp radio never played any Christmas songs, but continued to harangue us about war crimes. They also continued to report unbelievable numbers of B-52s as shot down. We knew that there had been a number of losses in the first week of attacks, but the number was not in the

---

31 McCarthy and Allison, *Linebacker II*, 107-11.

32 McCarthy and Allison, *Linebacker II*, 117. Photos on this page show one of bombs impacting and then an after-mission photo of the damage. "Simply spectacular!" was my comment when I first saw these photos.

seventies or eighties for sure. Norm told us we only had a total of just over two hundred B-52s in the USAF inventory, so we naturally figured with less action around Hanoi and no visible B-52s shot down close to downtown Hanoi in the past three days, that the action was happening at more distant points and tactics were being adjusted to keep the enemy confused and wasting their SA-2 SAM inventory.

The North Vietnamese were expecting the U.S. Air Force to keep attacking until their leaders would agree to return to the peace talks. We also suspected that there would be some new plan and new tactics designed to handle the next phase of bombing military targets around Hanoi. Both Walt and Norm surmised that much had already been accomplished, and more to the point, our intelligence analysts would find places that would discourage the North Vietnamese leadership even more. Around noon we were served a roast chicken dinner with fresh vegetables and white rice. It was quite good, compared to our normal fare. However, even Ernie noted that it was not as special as some of the past Christmas meals. We thought all Vietnamese focus was now on shooting down as many American airplanes as possible.

December 26, our last night at the Plantation, turned out to be a pivotal moment in history. The North Vietnamese forces in Hanoi had not been hit since December 20, so they had that time before Christmas to reload, adjust, and set up new SA-2 SAM sites. Other areas of North Vietnam had been attacked right up to midnight of December 24, and the U.S. forces planned accordingly. The USAF had shifted specific planning from SAC headquarters in Omaha, Nebraska, to the "Rock" at Andersen AFB, Guam. The plan was to launch a very large and very well-coordinated B-52 attack on targets close to Hanoi. The thinking was that the U.S. wanted the leadership in Hanoi to know that there were no safe places in Hanoi to hide. Targets of any type of military nature at Thai Nguyen rail yards north of the downtown, Van Dien Storage just north of the Doumer Bridge in downtown Hanoi, and any railroad portions left undamaged were designated for total destruction.

Additional jammers in B-52Gs were added as well as tactical aircraft with an array of electronic warfare active devices; these were major improvements for jamming the SA-2 SAM radars. One hundred twenty-nine B-52s launched on Dec. 26, 1972 and has now been called "the largest single launch of B-52 Stratofortresses on a combat mission in the history of the Strategic Air Command."[33]

And once again the LULUs would be sitting in the middle of the action.

Our thinking was proved correct on the evening of the 26th. A large number of B-52s arrived one hour after dark and kept coming all night in different parts of the city. Instead of attacking in a stream, we clearly noticed the B-52s seemed to be coming at targets on three or four different tracks. We had noticed that not one train had come south along the rails to the west side of the Plantation after December 23, and we correctly guessed that the North Vietnamese would revert to truck transportation. We heard street noise and several POWs closer to the east side reported increased traffic on the road. However, no one had any visual information and strangely, the North Vietnamese reported the next day that many SAMs had hit more than a dozen B-52s over the Van Dien truck depot. The folks who could see south reported seeing only one B-52 go down. As it turned out, there were two B-52s lost the night after Christmas and one of the crews were reportedly captured and kept at the prison dubbed the Zoo. This capture of six B-22 crewmen was hailed as "a glorious victory for the brave Vietnamese Army," but given the huge number of B-52s in the air, two losses were a vast improvement over the night of December 21. Norm was first to say that the new tactics and changes were making a big difference. We all were starting to think that we were, indeed, getting to the end of the road. Yet, we had no idea what was going on or not going on with the diplomatic side.

On December 27, around noon, we were told to pack up everything and get ready to be moved. One of the soldiers, who was considerate and not like the other guards, told

---

33 McCarthy and Allison, *Linebacker II*, 128.

Steve Long that we were going to Hoa Lo where we would be safer. How were we to know? Norm was sure we were going to be taken back to Laos. When we loaded onto a big army truck we saw there were a few members of the Peace Committee already there. This was not a wise move on the part of the Vietnamese. When Air Force Capt J.R. Leonard (promoted in absence to Major and later to Lt Col) saw one of the clowns who reported him to the Commies, he made a beeline to him and said out loud, "I've been waiting for this moment for a long time." Walt was quick to intervene and Ernie reasoned with J.R. that they were not worth getting further punishment from the Commies. "Their day will come when we are back at home, J.R.," Ernie assured him.

Our ride was not long, and we were surprised by the open back of the truck and no blindfolds. Even more surprising was the lack of any significant bomb damage that we could see from our viewpoint. I tried looking at the city behind us and how crowded the traffic was on the streets, and Ernie spotted a new SA-2 SAM site being finished about five blocks away from the Plantation.

When we arrived outside the Ho Loa prison, I recognized the wall, the glass shards, and concertina wire on the top of the wall. The gates were opened and still needed a good dose of WD-40. We were taken into the main courtyard that we referred to as the Heartbreak Hotel. We were led into a passageway to what we used to call Little Vegas. It was completely reconfigured now for cells with more POWs and the wash stalls had been-replaced with two open air cisterns. We were led to the Golden Nugget and found that there was a passageway cut into the back wall of one of the cells that led to a different small compound. It had four 2-man cells, an open area in front, and to the outside, a small courtyard to hang wet clothes and get a little sunshine. The wall to the east was a little higher and was the back-side of the Golden Nugget. Before long, we had found a way to climb up to a second story window and peek over the wall. And sure enough, the entire prison population of the Plantation was being moved into this area of the Little Vegas. Ernie and Steve were already planning a way to make contact through notes to the other prisoners, but first we had to get prepared for the night and the arrival of more B-52s.

Before dinner time we were all set in the rooms. Ernie was telling Walt that as soon as we finished our air shelters in the Plantation, they moved us here where there were no signs of digging or air raid shelters. Walt heard it from J.R. and Norm too, so he turned and told us, "This is not a snake pit, so stop trying to bite at everything and anything." So the die was cast: we named our new quarters the Snake Pit. When counting all the pros and cons, the consensus was our move was a good thing because we were being kept near those captured in South Vietnam and might be released with them.

Our first night back in the Hoa Lo was also a night when B-52s were in the area, farther to the north and south. There were fewer SA-2 SAMs launched this night. We learned later that they had fired around sixty-eight SAMs on December 26, so the next night they had less inventory and were trying to conserve their supply of missiles.

We had made contact with some of our old neighbors and communication friends from the Plantation. The courtyards in Hoa Loa had tall conifer trees with hard, green fruit pods about the size of a golf ball. At Camp Unity we used to mark or scratch an X into the nut and throw it over the wall. If there were no guards in sight, the POWs on the other side would throw it right back. Then we would throw our note inside an old nut shell and sometimes inside an old discarded toothpaste tube back to the waiting POWs. This was a simple and reliable system for exchanging information. We learned that day that the other POWs had seen at least one B-52 shot down and they had heard that the North Vietnamese were moving all the newly captured B-52 crews to the Plantation. That explained why they moved us all over to the Hoa Loa. The Vietnamese were going to try to make the Plantation into a showplace from which they could release new POWs and spin their fiction about the "humane and lenient treatment" Americans were being given despite "their war crimes against the Vietnamese people." No matter how many times they said this, it never sunk into me that it was believable.

We were not able to count the number of B-52s flying over that night and had to guess that it was about half the number used on December 26. That trend continued, and we found out later that the total number of B-52s had been reduced to sixty planes per night until the scheduled end of the bombing. We also noticed a decrease in the number of day attacks by naval fighter/light attack and air force tactical aircraft.

On the nights of December 28 and 29 we heard more bombing, but most of it seemed farther away from downtown. We learned later from other sources that no B-52s were lost on the last two days in December and that the number of available targets had been greatly reduced. The SA-2A SAM storage yards and several very dangerous SAM launch sites were attacked at the end, and again with no losses. New tactics, more chaff, and better active jamming all helped to reduce American losses and defeat the strong and persistent attacks by North Vietnamese forces. The LULUs noticed there were smaller numbers of tactical aircraft flying at the end of December. It was not until around the January 8, 1973, that we learned the North Vietnamese had agreed to return to the peace table to find common points that would define an acceptable peace treaty. But for now, the routine at Hoa Loa seemed to be on stand-by.

On January 1 we were served another better-than-normal meal of braised pork ribs and what we thought was a local Tonkin Gulf fish. The POWs over the wall from our former Plantation group had this special food, too. Ernie kept telling us the signing was on. Finally, we heard from Col Guy that the peace treaty terms had been agreed to and all POWs would be going home. We learned a bit later that Dr. Henry Kissinger had initially met with Le

Doc Tho in Paris on January 8 and on January 13 they "brought the draft agreement to completed form, with all supporting protocols and understandings attached."[34]

Ernie didn't feel confident in this and wanted to get his hands on the actual words of the peace treaty. He kept asking the guard who kept shrugging his shoulders. Both of them knew the other knew the war was over, but the soldier had his orders. A few days later, Dead Eye entered our little compound with the Maggot. This time he wanted us to stand in two lines. It was like we were falling into a military formation, and this indeed was a first. Then the explanation started. An agreement had been reached and POWs would be returned. Ernie asked if that meant us, too. Dead Eye spoke only Vietnamese, and he and Maggot proceeded to have a long conversation with the Maggot making some points very emphatically. Then Maggot said bluntly with Dead Eye nodding his head, as if he understood what we were being told, "No apply to Laos. No Truce in Laos. You must wait for peace in Laos." We were all crestfallen. That night, Ernie started a note for Col Guy with Walt helping him. The next day it was over the wall. We didn't expect an answer right away, but to our surprise within a few hours a nut came careening back over the wall with an X. We threw it back and the note was tossed over the wall.

Col Guy told us we would not be forgotten. The language was specific that all POWs would be returned; however, there was no mention of Laos in the language. Col Guy said that he would never forget the LULUs and, if by some chance we remained behind, he would go to war again and go to the White House, if necessary, to get our release. Although that made some of us feel appreciated and hopeful, it was still a bleak time. Even the weather that had already been damp and overcast turned to a windy, hard rain. All I could think of was Bob Dylan singing, "It's a hard rain's gonna' fall."

---

34 Vernon E. Davis, *The Long Road Home: U.S. POW Policy and Planning in Southeast Asia* (Washington, DC: Office of Secretary of Defense, Historical Office, 2000), 481.

On January 17 the door opened and two guards led a new POW into our area. He was Capt Charles ("Chuck") Riess, USAF, captured on Christmas Eve, 1972. He had not even been a POW for a month and was a wealth of new information. He was an A-7 light attack pilot who had ejected over the Plain of Jars in Laos. He told us that the war was virtually over and that Operation Linebacker II was very successful. He said that very few losses were incurred on the first two days, but on day three we had lost eight B-52s and his last mission was part of a coordinated attack on the truck traffic coming out of North Vietnam. The December losses for the Vietnamese were growing, and he was sure any peace agreement would include everyone held in Hanoi; but we still couldn't be sure. He was a quiet, thoughtful man and a welcome addition to the LULUs. We were now a total of eight and had his name over the wall to Col Guy in one day.

On February 6, two more, very young POWs were brought into the Snake Pit. We were starting to get crowded because there was only room for eight prisoners with racks in the eight small cells. The guards brought four saw horses and two bamboo racks. The two new beds were set up in the main area in front of our doors, and Ernie and J.R. jumped at the chance to sleep in the outer area. Lloyd Oppel, a twenty-one-year-old Canadian missionary, was very weak and very thin except for his extended stomach. He had fought malaria and disease on the way north for at least two months. He made it to Hanoi because fellow missionary Sam Mattix, twenty, had carried him when the soldiers wanted to shoot him—they had already assassinated Beatrice Kosin, another of the missionaries. Sam was from Centralia, Washington and had studied para-medical science in London and had even performed an emergency appendectomy on a native Laotian. They were spreading the Gospel as part of a nondenominational, fundamental Christian church and had settled just south of Savannakhet, Laos, located near the Thailand border; both spoke several dialects of Laotian. Ernie was very impressed with their language skills.

Lloyd and Sam had been captured during the North Vietnamese offensive drive toward Thailand in Laos. They were driving north in their Mazda pickup truck in an attempt to help two women missionaries working in Kengkok and were shot at, pulled over, and made prisoners before they could reach the young women.[35] They prayed every day for us and truly were a blessing to all of the LULUs.

It didn't take long before Jack Butcher told me that we would have a church service the next Sunday. And of all people, raised as an atheist and still a true believer in no God, Walt Stischer, our SRO, asked the next day for a Bible for the two men of religion. We had already received some remains of a Red Cross package with several books like *Three Who Made a Revolution* by Bertram D. Wolfe, a founder of the American Communist Party, and several older Russian novels. We all shared and devoured every book that they gave us; yet they had never given us a Bible. So Walt had a new program of incessant asking and demanding for this cause. One of Walt's most admirable traits was persistence in the face of adversity. He taught me a lot.

After a few days, Walt was called up for an "attitude check." His demands for a Bible were even unusual in the eyes of Maggot and the officer we called Bug, so they wanted to know what was up with him. He returned in about an hour and told us he had been forthright about freedom of religion in America and how all religions are honored, no matter what government officials thought. He was told, "Yes, we know, we know. We shall see." The very next day, Marvin, the guard who liked to trap and torture rats, stopped by our front door to check on us. As he left, he turned with a very sour face and threw a book onto the floor of the open space in front of the four cells. It was a *Gideon New Testament* with Psalms and Proverbs as addendums. It was beautiful.

The next Sunday Lloyd, Sam, Jack, and I met in one of the cells and conducted from memory our version of a Holy Communion service. Having been raised in the Episcopal

---

35 Marjorie Clark, *Captive on the Ho Chi Minh Trail* (Chicago: Moody Press, 1974), 52-53.

Church, I had to question if this would really count. After all, none of us were ordained priests. Sam asked me which of the disciples had been ordained ministers? Of course, I had to answer, none, because there was no official Christian Church with ministers and bishops at that time. Our conversation caused Ernie and Walt to roll their eyes, while J.R., Chuck, and Steve Long started some kind of card game. We did start a little choir and sang several hymns. My favorites were "What A Friend We Have in Jesus!" and "Rise Up, Oh Men of God."

Our little service was noticed by several of the guards. The next day Maggot stopped by and told us that we were getting a "special instrument, but you must play it softly." In a few minutes a surly guard brought an accordion into the Snake Pit. It was truly a gift from God. I had tried to play hymns on our piano when I was growing up, and I could figure out some of the tunes by ear. Jack and Sam encouraged me to play the accordion, but I could tell my practice would soon be getting on Ernie's nerves. I found a way by adjusting a knob to lower the volume and closed the door to my cell. I actually relearned at least five hymns and could play at least the melody with my right hand for Sunday services. The chords on the left hand would take longer to learn. It almost sounded like an organ, and there were other tunes I tried to learn as well. Walt's favorite was "The Eyes of Texas," and I became adequate on that tune; Ernie liked "The Battle Hymn of the Republic," and J.R. wanted to hear "God Bless America." We Americans are spoiled with so many options and preferences; yet that is exactly what "the pursuit of happiness" was and is all about.

Shortly after this we received two more books and they were another step toward home because they were still best sellers in the United States, according to Chuck Riess, who had already read both of them. They were *Love Story* and *The Godfather*. Ernie got to choose first and took *Love Story*, and in less than five hours he finished with wet eyes and tears running down his cheeks. This was only the third time I had seen him in such a state, so I was the most eager LULU who wanted to read this book. Chuck said it had already been made into a movie back home and had a very good song to go with it. He showed me the tune on our new accordion and I learned to play the melody to *Love Story* in one day and added a few chords to go with it the next day. When each person who read the book after me got to the sad part, I would wander by and play the tune, which always exercised the tear ducts, no matter how long or how short we were in captivity. Steve joked that only Bedinger on the accordion could drive a grown man to tears. Steve was born in the spirit of a tough air force fighter pilot and had a heart of gold beneath his exterior.

Mario Puzo's *Godfather* was much longer than any other book we had, but it was amazing to me how fast we all sped through it. When it was my turn, I was sure it would take me a week. I was wrong. It was such a fascinating story and so well-written that I sat for hours doing nothing but be buried in that book. On the third day I finished and was told that I was not going to win the Evelyn Woods' Speed Reading Award.

Competition was becoming a topic of conversation. We had several makeshift decks of cards and had just received an official Red Cross package with two real decks of cards. Pinochle, Hearts, Gin Rummy, and Dump on Your Neighbor (name changed slightly to please our two missionaries) were great group games, and we all proved to be fairly competitive. That's when the idea hit us to have a tournament of many different games and give different points by whether one placed first, second, or third. The horse racers had the majority, so there would be no points for a no-show. Chuck Reiss led the way in setting up the details and schedule of games.

Before we really got underway with the first LULU International Grand Master Tourney, Maggot and Marvin came into the Snake Pit to tell us to pack everything up. We were moving. Norm immediately thought we were getting trucked to Laos and said; "I'm not going to Laos." Both Maggot and Marvin spoke English and understood immediately his concern. They started laughing like hyenas and left the cell for a short while. When Maggot returned, he told Norm; "No worry, you not go far and stay here in Ho Loa."

We were taken to the southwest corner, which was on the other side of the Heartbreak courtyard where we had entered in December, and into a spacious yard with at least five large cells. This was what the POWs referred to as New Guy Village, because in the early days of the conflict (1965–1966), every new POW stayed there for a few months of "attitude adjustment." We were taken to a large cell near the end of a row of cells and they told us to take any bed we wanted and keep quiet. Ernie asked if this meant we were going to be released and Maggot said, "We shall discuss later." That was such a change that we all were ecstatic and still trying to not show any emotion to the Vietnamese guards.

We had heard on the camp radio that the first group of American POWs had been released on February 12. We had no details and found out later that there were other releases, and the reason we had been moved was to get the majority of the Plantation POWs such as Col Ted Guy, Dr. Hal Kushner, CPT Bruce Archer, and the Peace Committee ready to be released.

The second day after our move we heard noises like a new prisoner was being brought into a cell further down from us. We continued with the first-ever LULU international master competition and made much ado about the smallest things and it was great fun. The next day when it got quiet at siesta time in the early afternoon, it was time to get in touch with what was now very apparent to all of us—a new POW. Ernie had initially tried to contact him in the morning when it was still quiet, but not even a cough was returned. Maybe the new guy didn't speak English? Walt, being the senior officer, took over in the afternoon by stating very firmly and clearly, "This is Maj Walt Stischer, United States Air Force; say your name!" No reply was heard. Then he tried a less military approach; "Hey buddy! If you hear this and speak English, cough twice." Then we heard two very distinct coughs. But it was clear this new POW was afraid to talk to us or didn't know what to make of us. We were a wild and crazy bunch for sure. We had little or no luck in getting much out of him, especially his name. By a process of elimination and coughing once for no and twice for yes, we discovered the next morning that he was a naval aviator.

We had a team meeting at lunch on what our next move should be. Chuck Riess had discovered on the first day that by placing a bed board vertically, we could step on the back braces much like a ladder and climb up through the overhead ceiling and get into the attic. The only good that came of that is that we broke up some rat nests and sent them away by throwing stones and attacking them with long sticks. Chuck and I had been the main climbers, and Chuck reasoned that we should send the navy guy in our group to talk to the new sailor in town. So it was quickly decided I would go where no one had gone before and try to crawl and wiggle my way to the other end of the building through the attic; my mission was to get this new guy's name and give him the SRO guidelines. We were fortunate that there was only one guard assigned at this time to New Guy Village and he was very inactive during most afternoons when his fellow soldiers were enjoying naps and quiet time.

I was boosted and pushed into the attic through the bamboo screen overhead. I carefully started to the other end and had to climb over what were several brick dividers that ran to the tiles of the roof. The first divider was half in ruins, so that was easy. The next divider was less ruined; I had to use a loose brick to break some more bricks out in order to squeeze through. I weighed about one hundred thirty-five by this time; so my profile was well suited for getting through small spaces. I finally got to the last brick divider and found it was nearly solid. I removed about five bricks, which gave me enough room to stick my head through a small hole about six inches in diameter and look down into the cell below. I could see the new guy walking back and forth like a caged animal, talking to himself. I said softly, "Hey buddy, say your name." He stopped in his tracks and shook his head like he had something in his ear and started pacing again.

I remembered how Harry Jenkins had told Ernie and me to say our names almost three years ago and thought it was worth a try. So in a much louder voice heard by all the LULUs, I said to the new guy, "This is LTJG Jim Bedinger of the World Famous Puking Dogs, United States Navy. Say your name!" That stopped the new guy in his tracks and he looked up right at my smiling face.

"Howdy, is that you? I'm Canine from the Puking Dogs and I got to the squadron a few months after you went down." I said; "Roger, Canine! What is your full name and rank so I can pass it on to the rest of the POWs in this prison?" He eagerly replied, "Lieutenant Commander Phil Kientzler. I was flying in the back seat with the XO, CDR Harley Hall and former skipper of the Blue Angels. We went down just before midnight on January 27, but they told me I was captured after midnight and was the first to violate the peace treaty. They say I can't go home until I'm tried in the People's Court."

I told him that was nonsense and that we would pass his name to the other POWs. "You're going home with everyone else," I said.

I then explained to him who we were and how we were having a Grand Master Tournament to pass the time before we would be released. I also told him that Ernie had been captured in May of 1965 and survived three years in the jungles before he was brought to Hanoi. The rest of us were brought just after capture. Then Phil was busting to tell me some news. He told me the squadron had set sail for Yankee Station in early October and he had seen my wife at a squadron party just before they left on deployment. She was in graduate school at San Diego State University for a Masters in Computer Science and was working as a grant intern on some type of top-secret computer project at the Naval Electronics Laboratory at Point Loma. And he had seen the new car she had bought and was driving—a Porsche 914 in a deep British Racing Green. I had really liked Porsches since my fraternity days at Union College where one of my brothers, whose father owned two Porsche dealerships on Long Island, had given me a beautifully framed picture of the new Targa taken in the Black Forest of Germany. That picture had been the centerpiece of every place we lived and Laura knew how much I really liked all the Porsches. Phil told me Laura had sold our old VW bug to another Puking Dog officer whose son wanted to learn bodywork by fixing it all up. It was amazing news for me.

I was overcome with joy and told him that was the first news I had ever received about how she was doing. He bucked me up even more by saying, "We Puking Dogs are loyal. You are still on our squadron roles and Laura is invited to everything we do. She is one beautiful and neat gal. She keeps telling everyone who will listen that she knows you're alive and will be coming home."

That news meant more to me than words could ever describe; I was floating on air. I told Phil we could talk at the back windows later that evening when it got quiet. We would look out for him and thump on the wall if we saw a guard coming his way.

I had no idea how long I had been in the attic. The news was so uplifting and so encouraging. I always knew where I was—at least approximately—but Laura had no idea. And Phil had told me that all the POW wives had been told to expect some terrible things when we came home and to put everything into their own names, because there was no guarantee that we would be in shape to do any type of business. He also told me that there were not too many POWs from Laos known to be alive. He was truly surprised and relieved to see and meet me. Phil told me that the Commies had taken his POW bracelet with my name and shoot-down date on it from him, and he said he remembered and prayed for me every day.

This news reminded me of when Ernie and I had first arrived at the Plantation in 1971 and contacted the POWs in the Corn Crib. One day Ernie, standing in the water cistern with water up to his neck, had talked through the wall to George Archer. George told us that the League of Families had been started by the navy wives led by Sybil Stockdale, wife of CDR James Stockdale, and in 1970 they started a bracelet program that sold more than one hundred thousand bracelets in the first six months. There were chrome bracelets for two dollars and bronze ones were five dollars. George told us, "You are not forgotten. Thousands are wearing your names on a bracelet every day. No one will be left behind." College organizations were selling the bracelets all over the United States and now I knew that my name was out on those bracelets. That was very good news all over again. And it said something to me about being a Puking Dog. To this day, the "ODF" on my squadron coffee mug reminds me of "Old Dogs Forever!"

After we established a good time and routine for talking with our new neighbor, we had great news updates from him about how the North Vietnamese had tried to take back their October agreement to release all POWs and went back to demanding total U.S. withdrawal before discussing the terms of returning American POWs. He told us how soundly the Democrats had been defeated in November 1972 and that it was the largest landslide in electoral votes up to that time in history. We were all relieved in many different ways. But once we had great communication going with Phil, the Maggot arrived with news to pack up and move back to our old cellblock. This made little to no sense until we walked through the old Little Vegas to find it completely abandoned. There were no prisoners there. The next day some of us were asked to help collect clothes, buckets, and items left by the Americans who had been there.

Lloyd Oppel was still not in any shape to do any work and was left in the Snake Pit, and on that morning I had a massive headache and was vomiting, so we suspected another weather front was coming. As the day grew older, the skies darkened and became a stormy dark gray before night when the rains began. It was a hard downpour with lots of lightning and thunder. Some of the strikes were less than a mile away. I always started to feel better when a front had passed and the rains were almost done. This storm was no different, except we had extra things that Ernie and J.R. were able to sneak back from the old Little Vegas prison.

The chess tournament was scheduled, along with some other two-man contests of checkers and gin rummy. So Walt directed, "Let the games begin." It was a lot of fun with banter back and forth among all of us. At the end, Norm Gotner was chosen to tally all the results. It was very close; the clear winner was the only foreigner of our LULU group, Lloyd Oppel. It was time for the announcement and the crowning of the Grand Master of the first LULU international tournament.

Norm was very careful to have warm (but not hot) tea ready for toasting and he had made up a rough paper certificate to mimic a military certificate that accompanies the presentation of awards. He also had a primitive crown made out of some old cardboard. In this case, the air force wanted to keep up the tradition of a "wetting down," but no one shared this with Sam or Lloyd. We gathered in our little courtyard and Walt did a terrific tongue-in-cheek take-off of introductions and then passed the baton to Norm to make the announcement and presentation. The certificate looked great and had the fairly common statement that "this certificate entitles the recipient to all the rights, privileges, and benefits of a Grand Master." Then the teacups were passed around and everyone ready for the traditional toast. Norm made the toast and only Sam and Lloyd drank a little tea. The rest of the LULUs in unison threw their tea on Lloyd. The shock on his face was priceless, and then he threw his tea right back at us. Then a water bucket was thrown into the fray and we all enjoyed a mid-day bath. Our laughter was so loud that the little guard assigned to watch us was sneaking peeks at us through the door flap; he definitely didn't want us to see him and, most of all, he didn't want to come in and join our shower.

Ernie had also been able to explore around the area surrounding the Snake Pit and found another small corridor in which there were two prisoners being kept in solitary, but I was hoping that Phil was put in with some other recently captured new prisoners. When we got to this separate corridor a few days later, Ernie found his old Thai radioman, Sgt Chai Charn Harnavee. He had a Thai tank commander as a cellmate and they seemed in good spirits. Ernie had learned that the Vietnamese were in separate discussions with the Thai government and told Chai that we would keep him updated and, if we were to be released, we'd let him know. And if he was kept behind, we would tell U.S. authorities about him so that our government would exert a maximum effort to get him released.

We were counting down the days to March 28 for the sixty days that were mentioned for the period of releasing "all American prisoners to U.S. custody." This may seem like a small thing; however, we had seen in a number of early releases from 1967 in which a large and varying group of war protesters had accepted custody of American POWs. The U.S. government didn't want this for any of the American POWs who had been imprisoned for so long and were to be released by the treaty. The official agreement specified the exact time period, to whom POWs would be released to, and the order of the release. We knew from Ernie's early capture date that he should have gone first, but as usual, the LULUs were indeed different. So let me be clear at this point how different we were and how close we came to not being released.

One of the first issues we learned of after our release, which explained some of what happened to us up that point, was the omission of all our names from the documents signed on January 27, 1973, at the Grand Majestic Hotel in Paris, France.

My parents had finalized the divorce they started before my release and were living separately. My father was visited by the commanding officer of NAS Willow Grove and told, "We have bad news and good news. Jimmy's name is not on the list, but the good news is that none of the other POWs captured in Laos and detained for years in Hanoi are on the list."

My mother received a visit from her casualty assistance and claims officer (CACO), a navy chaplain, and a medical corpsman. She supposedly fainted before they could tell her the good news. Neither of my parents really thought that I was alive from all they had heard, but my wife felt I was alive all the time. It was difficult for her most of all. And she had also been baited and called some nasty names by anti-war activists when she publicly supported the League of Families.

On January 28, 1973, many families received the good news that their loved ones would be soon released and were officially on the list. None of the LULUs were on any list—we were simply listed as missing in action (MIA) again.

For the next four days, Dr. Henry Kissinger and Le Duc Tho met in Paris on the issue of the one Canadian and nine American prisoners held in Hanoi and not officially on the list of prisoners to be released. When the post-agreement summary was written, the following was specially added to the summary about the Laotian situation:

> The DRV has assured us that all U.S. military and civilian prisoners detained in Laos shall be released no later than 60 days following the signature of the Agreement. The DRV has also assured us that it would be responsible for making the necessary arrangements with the Pathet Lao.[36]

With this language clearly understood between both sides, the U.S. delegation in Paris was very concerned that the LULU names were missing. We were told many years later by Dr. Kissinger at the Nixon Library that he finally had told Le Duc Tho that with some American military and civilian names not on the official lists, there would be no release and that President Nixon was ready to resume bombing Hanoi unless all the names were released at the start of the process as called for in the summary of the agreement.

---

36 Davis, *The Long Road Home*, 484-85.

Late in the afternoon of February 1, 1973, the Hanoi delegation released to the American delegation the one Canadian name and the nine American names of prisoners to be included in the release. This resulted in both personal notifications to the families, and then notification by official telegram. My wife received the good news by telegram very early on the morning of February 2,1973. However, there was no specific date of release ever mentioned at this time.

Back in Hanoi, the LULUs were told nothing about the official release of our names. Yet there were indications of a different attitude in both officers and guards. As more groups left the Hanoi Hilton, we were getting more and more concerned about no date of release being told to us, as it had been told to other American POW groups. For example, Col Guy had been told on March 10 that his group would be released on March 16 and he had written a note telling us this date of release. Ernie was sure the Commies would wait to the last day. He had carefully computed that date as either the March 28 or 29, depending on what time zone was used to start a sixty-day calendar. Needless to say, we all were getting very edgy as the last week of March approached and there were no sounds of other POWs in the Hanoi Hilton. Never had the walls of Hoa Lo prison echoed in such a sound of silence since early 1965. No tapping on walls and no surly guards yelling "Keep Shylent" could be heard now.

On Friday, March 23, the barber arrived and began the slow process of cutting the hair of all the LULUs. The clippers were hand-powered just like the scissors, so this took almost half a day to get through all ten of us. Ernie was the first to voice what we were all thinking. We were getting our last haircuts in Hanoi and would be going home next week. It was fairly early on Monday morning that we were brought as a group to the Heartbreak courtyard and ushered into the camp commander's office. We were told to stand in ranks and Walt stood in front. He had briefed us very quickly as we got into long shirts that we would not show any emotion and we would not give this "bastard the pleasure of seeing us cheer." With little prelude, the NVA major went right to the matter by stating, "Due to the humane and lenient policy of the Vietnamese people, you will not have to be returned to Laos to be released. You shall be released from Hanoi." I sighed a silent thanksgiving and tried to look serious. Ernie asked if we would be fitted with clothes and he smiled and said, "Later today or tomorrow." Walt tried to ask the man what exact date we were being sent home and he simply said, "Later. Go back now!"

We were escorted back to the Snake Pit and gathered to discuss. Ernie was sure that the date would be Wednesday, and both Norm and J.R. asked then why they didn't tell us. Lloyd said, "It might because they still have to call the Canadian Embassy to clear my release." We were all guessing. Early the next day we were led to the New Guy Village and fitted for trousers and shoes. The shirts were to be long sleeve white shirts with open collars and crew neck sweaters were to worn over the shirts. They had a number of sizes and we selected the one that fit best and put it in our piles. When we completed selecting all the items to be put together for us, the guards bagged each pile and marked it with our name. Then they gave us some candy, as if to say, don't forget how well we treated you.

Later that Tuesday it became almost surreal as we were fed a special meal that included turkey legs, fresh-fried Fish, and vegetables. They even had beer and some peach wine for us to wash down the meal and several of the soldiers joined us. It was during this time of festivity that Ernie gave me a nod and told me to take some extra food for the Thais, so I did my best to go for seconds and hid food in my pockets. Plus, I grabbed a huge handful of candies, because I knew Chai really liked sweets. Ernie and I pretended to be going to use the bucket, took a quick turn down the corridor where the Thais were, and gave them our largesse. I could tell by Ernie's face and the tone of his voice that this farewell was very difficult. Each time Ernie had escaped (three times in all), the North Vietnamese also punished Sgt Harnavee and he never complained. He had the calm demeanor and acceptance of a true Buddhist monk. He smiled at both of us and said farewell and good luck. Ernie's last words were, "We're going to get you out of here and back with your

245

families." On the way back to our farewell dinner, Ernie told me he hoped that was the one promise he would be able to keep. Little did we know then that it would take another year to bring the two remaining Thai POWs back to Bangkok and their families.

CHAPTER 14

EMBRACING RELEASE

March 28, 1973 broke gray and overcast in Hanoi, but the light of freedom was shining in our eyes and beating in our hearts. We were up early before the traditional gong rang the start of each day because there were items we wanted to hide and try to smuggle out. For example, Lloyd really wanted to take home the now well-thumbed *Gideon New Testament*. Maggot, the day before, had told him we could not take that or any other books home. "They are property of the People of Vietnam." Lloyd was going to try anyway. We discovered the day before that the inexpensive overnight bags we were going to carry out with us were not well made and the bottom of the bag had a cardboard insert that could be easily lifted up and then, around the wooden frame, we could hide various things that were not listed as "approved" for us to take home. For example, my aluminum cup was okay, but my purple and red prison stripes were not okay. There were some contraband bricks that were not approved, but small enough to go into this spot. Once all my contraband was in place, Ernie was going to help me place the cardboard insert back inside the bag. The items had to be smuggled to where we were going to be outfitted, so each one of us helped out others and mixed the items so we could carry it all with us.

We were escorted with all our take-home items to the New Guy Village where our bags, clothes, and shoes were laid out on two long tables. There were fritters of some type, bananas, hot tea, and some hot French-type coffee—it was my first cup of "Joe" in over three years. The camp commander and Maggot had big grins and kept saying, "Eat! Eat all! All for you!" Cleverly positioned behind us were a film crew and several photographers. We kept our smiles to a minimum and Walt, in typical fashion, showed them all his appreciation with a particularly loud fart. Jack and I had a hard time not to laugh out loud at that point. Then we were told to get into our clothes and pack our one bag. We had to line up for an inspection in which all our bags were rummaged through. Maggot found the Bible in Lloyd's bag and said in a very angry voice, "What's this? I told you no can take!" Lloyd simply shrugged and said; "I wanted to show it to my mother." The Bible was placed on the table behind us. Much to our surprise, J.R. Leonard created a little fuss over something, and Walt slyly took two steps backward and reclaimed the Bible in the palm of his hand.

Shortly thereafter, Lloyd was separated from us and taken away. He had to go to the Canadian Embassy where he was to be turned over to their ranking diplomat and then taken to Gia Lam Airport. Meanwhile, we formed a single file and were marched out the front gate of Hoa Lo prison with Walt still cupping that Bible in his hand. The bottom treasures in our bags were not discovered and, to this day, I believe the soldiers just didn't care; we were going home.

We boarded a bus for the airport and as it started moving north, it was clear the nine American LULUS were going to cross the Paul Doumer Bridge that had been bombed so often. It was still badly damaged with only one lane open to cross. When we got to the other side, we noticed a very long line of trucks, bicycles, and a few buses waiting to cross south. Then there were the remains of the railroads, better described as twisted metal. When we were close to the Gia Lam rail switching yard, I could see a damaged locomotive engine upside down. Children were climbing up the sides and trying to get on top of it. Concrete rubble and twisted steel were everywhere. Clearly the B-52s had done some very concentrated and precise bombing to inflict so much lasting damage. Ernie leaned over to me and whispered, "Too bad LBJ didn't do this back in '65 and spare us and a lot of other Americans from such a long war." He had a point. I knew this; and I also knew we were all looking forward to restarting our lives with our loved ones in a land of freedom and many choices. I tried to say that, and Ernie looked me in the eye and patted me on the shoulder. Words were not needed.

We had a short stop to wash up and comb our hair if needed. It was like a roadside bathroom on the highway. As we were taking turns in the small accommodations, I heard the roar of a large plane. I looked up and saw directly overheard was a C-141 flying over us and turning to final approach. On the high vertical tail we all clearly saw the American flag. It was the most beautiful in detail and the most official American flag I had seen in over three years. And it reminded me of LT Mike Christian, who had sewn a small American flag and shared it with us at Camp Unity. I hoped that Mike and his cellmates were already home with their families and doing well.

It was still fairly early in the morning as we reloaded into the bus. I noticed a group of women along the road suddenly started piling what looked like wheat in the road. There were mounds of it before our bus. We went right over it, and Ernie explained that is how the poor farmers thrashed the wheat crop to get the seed. Everything was used and it kept the stalks intact for other uses.

It didn't take long from this point to get to the entrance of Gia Lam Airport. The minute we came to a stop a group of about twenty reporters came rushing out of the terminal to take photos and talk with us. The windows in the bus were all down and some reporters reached inside and shook hands. Steve Long was our unrepentant smoker and was asking within a few minutes if they had any American cigarettes. We had all been given both Truong Son and Dien Diem packs of Vietnamese cigarettes, which were strong and smelled more like pipe tobacco. Steve lucked out and traded one of his Truong Sons for an unopened pack of Camels. I had to laugh at this bartering in such a Communist setting. One of the reporters was from the well-known French newspaper, *Le Monde*, and spoke some

English. He wanted to know how we survived so long in Laos and was the bus trip tiring. We all laughed and Walt informed him that we had been kept at Hoa Lo for many years.

There were no follow-up questions because several officers came jogging up to our bus and told the driver to move away. Something was not going well inside, and we were not permitted to stay at the very front of Gia Lam terminal any longer. Instead, we were taken to the west end of the parking lot and the driver found a shady spot far from other traffic to park. He turned off the engine, and there we sat. Norm said words to the effect that we could not blame Brace and Bedinger for this one. Walt told Steve to check his camels to make sure they were not exploding cigarettes. J.R. Leonard was the serious one who suggested that Lloyd was probably enjoying some Canadian Club with the Canadian ambassador and was kept at the embassy longer than expected. Little did we know that Lloyd was in a jeep at the other end of the parking lot thinking we had been delayed.

The truth was that the senior American officer for this release was asked to sign the official release document that read, "I accept the *only* nine American and one Canadian prisoners of the Pathet Lao." Our small and motley crew hardly seemed like a full accounting for around five hundred missing in action over Laos. The colonel had steadfastly refused for an hour to sign the document. His aide told us later that he rose from the table and started to leave with the comment that he had missed his departure time and the B-52s would soon be airborne to resume bombing Hanoi. "Frenchy," a particularly well-educated, multi-lingual interpreter intervened. He quickly called it all a matter of language and that he could get the misunderstanding settled. The release paper was very short and so it was retyped to read in part, "I accept nine American and one Canadian prisoner held by the Pathet Lao." The indefinite reference resolved the impasse.

With the papers for release now agreed upon and ready for being signed, a soldier on a motorcycle rode out to retrieve us and Lloyd. We were quickly ushered inside the terminal. There were a few words said that went in one ear and out the other for me, then with our senior officer, now Lieutenant Colonel Walt Stischer, was called out. He walked up and saluted, shook hands, and was turned over to an escort who took him to the C-141 waiting outside. The same procedure was repeated for all of us. When I met the escort, his first words were, "We have to hurry before they change their minds." Then, when we walked up the ramp into the plane, there were hugs, back slapping, and lots of handshakes. I think Steve was the first to get a massage from one of the nurses. And Sam and Lloyd had a very meaningful reunion. We had all been worried about our LULU grand master, yet, here he was on the plane. A young major explained that the colonel would be flying back to Saigon because there was another release scheduled for later in the day; we were flying directly to Clark AFB in the Philippines.

Walt had packed away the *Gideon Bible* to return to Lloyd next time we saw him. Lloyd joined us on the plane and Walt made a short presentation of the gift in recognition of Lloyd's strong faith and being the grand master of the LULUs. An air force photographer heard Walt and asked if he could take a photo of us. We all gathered around Lloyd and then signed the Bible. Above Walt's signature were the words, "Complimentary Issue." Today Lloyd still has that Bible, and whenever I'm in a hotel, I always check out the *Gideon Bible* and pray for Lloyd, Sam, and all the Christian missionaries around the world. And I thank the Lord that I was able to survive with the other LULUs.

There was a temporary taxiway for a short distance, repairs were still ongoing, and then we were taxiing at a more standard speed. The plane was already cleared for takeoff. The crew took the runway and did a rolling engine check with transition to full power, switched the radio frequency, and rolled down the runway. The engines were loud; both Walt and J.R. knew what to listen for. The second all wheels were moving up and the landing gear was retracting, they raised their hands above their heads and starting screaming. We all were—those were the sounds of freedom, too.

We had not flown far when the flight engineer in the third seat of the cockpit, came out and asked for LTJG Henry J. Bedinger. Ernie immediately yelled, "He didn't do it!" The LULUs all started laughing, and I was a bit confused. Was this a joke on me they had set up before I entered the plane, or did they really want me up front? The C-141 has no windows in the passenger area, so it would be nice to look out and see the ocean below us. When I got to the cockpit, the crew had already checked into Red Crown, a navy guided missile cruiser that kept watch on the overall air picture around Yankee Station in the Tonkin Gulf. The *USS Long Beach* (CGN-9) had been the Red Crown in 1969 when I went down, and here it was on station again in 1973. The chief petty officer of the watch had been a first class petty officer in 1969 and had worked my search and rescue mission. He had prayed for me and worn my bracelet for three years. He knew my birthday was in two days and he had gathered a group for this occasion. The chief welcomed me home and said that they had "gotten up bright and early to say they had a song for me." Then they sang "Happy Birthday" in three-part harmony over the UHF radio. I was speechless—and that doesn't happen to me very often.

Before I returned to the cabin, I asked the pilot in command if the LULUs could come into the cabin one-by-one and check it out. I told him that it had been a long time since most of us had seen a cockpit and looked down on the ocean, which was such a dark blue that day. He agreed, so when I returned to the other LULUs, they moved up front to visit the pilot and co-pilot. The flight engineer told me this was their fourth Operation Homecoming mission and he thought it was the first time anyone had been in the cockpit to hear the U.S. Navy sing "Happy Birthday." Ernie heard that and told the officer that the navy was smart and didn't want to hear me sing. I told the young officer who looked like he was maybe twenty years old, that my singing days were now over, except for when in a hot shower. The LULUs all laughed.

The planning for Operation Homecoming was thorough, and the materials on the C-141 were well-thought out. There were even a few *Hustler* and *Playboy* magazines. None of us were very interested in them, but Ernie finally had to check one to verify that the models showed "everything." He just looked, nodded his head, and threw it back down.

There was one official photographer on the plane, and he was snapping pictures at every moment, it seemed. He was quick to notice Walt presenting the *Gideon Bible* to Lloyd and to get all the details. His interest in this and our signing of the small Bible caused several to say that the first thing we would do when we landed was to visit the chapel and thank God. Walt asked all of us, "Is that what you all want to do, because I seem to remember a small but nice chapel on the first floor at the hospital at Clark AFB." Steve asked; "Does it have an organ?" It did and I was appointed to try my hand in leading us in one song. Walt said that no matter what his beliefs were, he would never miss this one last thing we LULUs could do together. Walt went to someone up front who conveyed our wishes to the ground forces in the Philippines awaiting our return.

The flight didn't seem to take very long and when we landed, an air force colonel came in and briefed us on how we would depart the plane. The military were to go first by date of rank and the civilians would follow by age. I told Ernie that I didn't feel right getting off this plane ahead of him and he told me; "It's just for a minute and I'll be right behind you anyway. Just don't trip and hurt yourself."

What I remember most when I stepped off into the bright sunlight was the rows of children and civilians waving American flags. There was a crowd of at least two thousand. There were salutes and handshakes, and then a quick walk to a bus that took us to the hospital. As we drove down the first road and the second road to the hospital, it seemed that the entire route was populated by Americans and Filipinos waving flags and welcome home signs. Even in our wildest speculations before our release, no one imagined such a reception for our group.

When we entered the hospital there were public affairs officers ready to escort us directly to the chapel, just as Walt had requested. But a young navy doctor inserted himself to the front and asked for LTJG Henry Bedinger. "Here we go again," said Ernie. The hospital staff had organized all the prior releases to intercept any returning POW who had a death in the family or some other type of bad news. The purpose was to take the individual to a private exam room and break the news gently. For some reason, my mother had thought the news of my father's remarriage was bad news, and my name was put on the bad news board. However, I told the doctor he would have to wait a few minutes more, because we all needed to go to the chapel and thank God for our safe return. He looked me in the eyes and simply nodded with a smile.

My emotions were running so high that I have forgotten a lot about our LULU chapel service. I do remember that I played "Dear Lord and Father of Mankind" on the organ, and the LULUs had the Armed Forces Hymnals and sang along. Both Jack and Sam read passages from the Bible and Lloyd led us in reciting the 23rd Psalm. J.R. led us in the Lord's Prayer. It may not have been very long, but it was indeed heartfelt. And Walt was smiling with a peace that totally surpassed my understanding. As we were walking out, he told me very quietly, "The eyes of Texas are still upon us and now we have to make the most of everything."

My time walking with the LULUs was cut short by that navy doc waiting right outside the chapel. We went to an examination room that was quite close and he started asking me a number of medical questions. He asked me what my blood pressure was, and I told him I had no idea. So he started to get the cuff on my arm and began the process. Just before he finished, he asked me, "Did you know that your father remarried and that you now have a step-mother?" I think to this day he had thought I would break down sobbing or crying. Instead my reply was simply, "Thank goodness! Praise the Lord!" He seemed almost stunned. So I further explained that my mother was quite active in a number of community organizations and I was never very worried about her finding lots of support. On the other hand, my dad spent most of his time trying to make his tree and landscape business profitable. He had few hobbies and friends outside of work. I told the doctor that I was very concerned that the loss of my brother in 1969 and then my shoot-down and capture three months later would have had a great strain on my dad and so I was very relieved to know he had met some gal and was now happily remarried. The doc said, "That makes perfect sense. Let's get out of here."

The doctor led me to the elevator that took me up to where our LULU team was being kept. The next day there would be tests and preventive shots for most. Plus, Ernie was quick to tell me that we had been assigned an intelligence officer from our particular service to start our debriefings. Ernie handed me a business card of a LT Donald McClain, USN, who would meet with me later in the evening to introduce himself. I asked Ernie when we could call home and he said it was all being set up for us, and a young airman would take us to the telephone exchange when an overseas line was connected to our homes. I then asked if anyone had been to the cafeteria yet, because I was hoping I could get a chocolate malted milkshake, extra malt and extra rich. It was just the way my dad liked them and I wanted to drink one to celebrate his marriage. Ernie said, "No, but let's go find it and celebrate together." I had told Ernie about my past in some detail and about the Certificate of the Society of Cincinnati signed by George Washington that was still in my father's office. Ernie had told me that he was going to San Diego and was hoping he would meet my dad when we got there. I told him, "You can count on it."

Steve Long, Ernie Brace, and I shared a hospital room. Steve had just learned that his wife had divorced him and said, "I'm not surprised." Apparently he had expected it. Ernie and Steve compared "divorce experience" notes while I was setting up few things and getting into the approved hospital gown and robe. Then we three amigos went to find the cafeteria and three milkshakes to drown or celebrate our individual news. And as only

Ernie could say, "No matter what happens, we can make our own world again and won't have any guard to tell us we can't do that." That first chocolate malted milkshake was so good and so cold. I sipped it for at least twenty minutes.

As we were finishing up a young airman came up to us and said, "There you are. LTJG Bedinger. We have a line connected to your wife in San Diego." I think I shouted a bit too loudly, "California here I come!"—then I was off to the phone center. At that time overseas phone service was a one-way process. You had to press a button to talk and only one phone could transmit at a time; it was much like a UHF radio. Laura's voice sounded so soft and so beautiful. When I told her that Phil Kientzler had told me about the Porsche and her going to school for a Masters, she was a bit surprised. And then she asked me if he had told me about the new home and renting our old home to a nice family. No, I wasn't sure he knew about that, but it sounded terrific. When I asked about my parents, Laura's voice changed just a little, and she asked me to tell them to stay in Philadelphia for a week so that she and I could get adjusted some. I knew there had to be something else, so I asked if it had been harder to deal with my mother or my father who had remarried. She said that they both were very set in their ways and didn't listen to what she had to say very often. I got the picture and told her I would do my best to talk them into waiting a week before they came west to San Diego. Little did I know that both parents had the same casualty assistance and claims officer (CACO) and had their plane tickets in hand. There would be no changes for either of them.

Later that evening I met my naval intelligence officer, who was a very easy person to like. He explained the whole process that we'd start the next day. When I left for home, he would fly directly to San Diego and meet up with me there to continue from start to finish all the debriefing and pick up some extra photos and other things he had left in his office. The main point was that he was there to help me, answer any questions I might have, and to gather any useful intel from Laos.

The next day was a blur to me. First there were a lot of routine tests, including a real blood pressure and eye tests, nose/throat exam, dental exam, and new glasses ordered so I would have both a regular lens in aviator frames and prescription lenses in sunglasses, also with aviator frames. I was amazed that the air force could make the glasses up so quickly. These new glasses would help me see in the distance and bring everyone into focus.

We all had different schedules, so we had to eat at different times. LT McClain was waiting for me and suggested we go get some lunch and talk a little. That was perfect. He was an avid sports fan and started telling me about the Padres and the Chargers. He didn't live in San Diego, yet he followed both the football and baseball teams closely. He also told me he would be finishing up on another case and then could get started around 2 p.m. after my last medical appointment for the day. He also told me that in the evening the base Army/Air Force Exchange Store (AAFES) would be opened just for the returned POWs, who could shop for civilian clothes and gifts. I must have sounded very naive when I asked him how I would pay for any shopping. He smiled and said we all had accounts set up for us and we could take up to two thousand dollars with no special approvals necessary. I told him I didn't even have a credit card and was glad that my signature was good for a few shopping items. And I told him I didn't want to fly back to the United States in anything but a navy uniform. And that was the next thing on my schedule. The planning was so good that they already had service dress khaki, service dress blue, tropical khaki long, and tropical white uniforms ready. All I had to do was try them on and have some minor adjustments made. I was still a very trim and light naval aviator, exactly one hundred thirty-six pounds when first officially weighed.

That night we were driven to the main AAFES for Clark AFB. It was the largest exchange I had ever seen. It had everything one could imagine and then some. All the clothes were modern styles in bright colors and even the shoes came in two tones and very fancy toes. I was fairly conservative and was looking for sky blue oxford and pinpoint white all-cotton dress shirts. They had a few in my size and I was happy. Then I had the decision of buying a wristwatch. The selection was mind boggling. Finally, Ernie Brace came up to me with an excited look and saw instantly my dilemma. He grabbed a Seiko self-winding watch with a gold and silver watchband and told the smiling clerk, "He'll take this one if you can adjust it to fit his wrist." I still have that watch and don't have the heart to discard it. I wore it every day for the next forty years, and often thought of Ernie when I looked at the time.

There was a stereo section that had so many new types of tape decks and receivers that I was again most perplexed. Another returning POW who had been a Puking Dog and one of my instructors at Brunswick told me to get the overseas AAFES catalogue. He had the clerk explain to me that we could take this home and order for up to six months anything we liked. "Wow!" is all I thought to say. Then my former instructor, LCDR James Souder, also a Puking Dog, took me to the clothes section again and told me what shoes to buy and a few more wild and crazy slacks and shirts. He said, "We want no Puking Dogs looking like stiffs when we get home. Trust me." I did and found out he was right. That night I was so exhausted that I fell asleep in about two minutes and didn't wake up until Jack Butcher shook me and told me I had best hustle or I would miss breakfast. I was up and dressed in less than five minutes and once again started the day with eggs, bacon, sausage, orange juice, and a good cup of coffee. This day they also had freshly baked cinnamon rolls with pecans and lots of gooey syrup. Now that was a breakfast for champions.

My schedule on this day was to set down with the Intel officer and make some real progress in what data they needed to collect. LT McClain had found a small private room to discuss my capture and everything I had seen and experienced. However, the very first thing I had to read and understand was the disclosure that the info he would gather would remain classified and could never be used in a court of law and could not be opened even with a court-ordered subpoena. I thought at first, who would be that interested in getting my story, and then I realized there might be some ex-POWs who never would want their experiences revealed to anyone. After signing the form, I verified on a map the exact coordinates of where I thought my pilot and I had gone down; LT McClain's eyes lit up and he began sorting through a group of photos. He spotted the one he was looking and asked me if I had ever seen this man. I took a double-take, because I was looking at the pilot who had lived next to Laura and me in Brunswick, Georgia. I said; "That's Richard Deuter; he lived right next door to me. His wife was named Susie." LT McClain jumped out his chair in total joy and excitedly asked me, "Where and when did you last see him in Laos." I looked puzzled and asked him what he meant.

Then he told me that Dick was flying with VA-196 off the *USS Ranger* and had gone down over Savannakhet Province, Laos, on November 22, 1969, less than five miles from where our F-4 bought the jungle. I then realized how sad this must be for his beautiful blond wife who loved Simon and Garfunkel and played the sound track to *The Graduate* many times over. "The Sounds of Silence" was one of the lead songs in the movie soundtrack, and Laura and I heard it many times through the thin apartment walls with his wife singing along to the record. I explained it all to LT McClain and saw his immediate disappointment. I was suddenly very aware that the intelligence community was hoping we few who returned from Laos could bring back first-hand evidence and support for special operations in specific areas. In fact, I had seen a few groups of native hill tribespeople, but not one American.

There was also a photograph of a very young looking aviator with a flat top haircut. It was a picture of Barton Creed, a graduate of Saint Peter's School in Peekskill, NY, where I attended high school. When I was a freshman (ninth grade), my brother Bill was finishing his senior year. Bart was one of his classmates and had been shot down over Laos in Savannakhet Provence in 1968 with no further word of his whereabouts. When I was holding that picture in my hand, memories of my brother Bill and his passing flooded my mind. Without even realizing it, tears started flowing down my face. LT McClain quickly said, "We have many more photos to show you, but not today." He told me that there were over five hundred Americans officially missing in action in Laos and that the LULUs were the only ten released as part of Operation Homecoming. We LULUs, as motley and varied as possible, were the most fortunate of all. And I often would hear in the passing years that Laos was the "Black Hole for all MIAs."

I was reminded by CDR John McClain that the issue of our release date was not resolved with the addition of our ten names to the list of those held captive until the evening of February 1, 1973. The releases were organized to occur in batches about two weeks to fifteen days apart. The names of the next prisoners to be released were normally issued by the DRV officials about ten to twelve days before the release. This was the process that was followed until the last batch. The U.S. delegation in Paris was led by U.S. Army MG Gilbert H. Woodward and his deputy, BG John A. Wickham. On March 19, 1973, the U.S. delegation in Paris asked when the Laotian-captured prisoners would be added to the release schedule. The Hanoi delegation claimed that it "Has no authority to discuss the subject since it falls outside the Paris Agreement. The U.S. government would have to negotiate with the Pathet Lao for the men's release." This clear reversal came with time running short.[37]

On March 22 the U.S. was asked by the DVN delegates on which date our troop withdrawal would be completed and said the last batch of two hundred forty-six American prisoners would be released to coincide with that timetable. The U.S. realized the ten American prisoners captured in Laos were not part of this number and issued a strong a statement in regard to the remaining release of all the POWs:[38]

37 Davis, *The Long Road Home*, 509.

38 Davis, *The Long Road Home*, 508-18. (See "The Return of the Laotian POWs and the Rest of the Prisoners".)

"The United States would complete the withdrawal of its military forces from South Vietnam in accordance with the Agreement "and coincident with the release of all, repeat all, American prisoners held throughout Indochina."

Both the DVN (Democratic Republic of Vietnam) and the PRG (South Vietnamese communists) were indignant at this firm stand and responded that the agreement didn't formally specify the Laotian release and that withdrawal of American forces from South Vietnam "could only be linked to the return of persons captured in Vietnam, not all of Indochina." Then they suspended the provision for the release of all the remaining American prisoners previously agreed to. Several secret meetings were held by the most senior officials and, without any resolution, the last batch of prisoners would remain behind. On Saturday March 24, the PRG listed thirty-two Americans (twenty-seven military and five civilian), who would be released on March 27 from Gia Lam Airport in Hanoi. The Hanoi delegation returned on March 25, a Sunday, with a list of two hundred fourteen names for release on the March 27, 28, and 29, but still no LULUs were listed with a date of release. Early on Monday, March 26, the Hanoi delegation promised the Americans that much progress was made in their discussions with the Pathet Lao, and they were sure a date would be set in a few days. Having received instructions from Washington "to accept nothing on faith," MG Woodward said there would be no releases without the ten POWs captured in Laos. The North Vietnamese rose in unison and walked out.

Late on the evening of March 26, with the last-minute details of the release trying to be set for the very next day, the North Vietnamese delegation requested a second meeting with Maj Gen Woodward. When they arrived, they handed over the Pathet Lao agreement to release the one Canadian and nine American prisoners captured in Laos on the morning of March 28, 1973 at Gia Lam Airport. The final negotiations had become very tense, and it was clear to the Americans in Paris that getting the remaining six thousand five hundred U.S. military to leave South Vietnam was worth more than feeding two hundred forty-six

POWs for two more weeks. The LULUs were going to go home. It was something I never realized was that close until the Vernon E. Davis history, *The Long Road Home: U.S. Prisoner of War Policy and Planning in Southeast Asia* was published and released in 2000.

————— ★ —————

On March 30 at Clark AFB the LULUs met up to eat dinner together and get ready for a second round of shopping. First, we had to eat and the choices were even more than the day before. There was steak and baked potatoes, crispy fried chicken, roast beef, honey glazed ham, and much more. The desert section was a cornucopia of sweets including ice cream, pies, and cakes. Just as I was getting up for some dessert, J.R. Leonard put his hand on my shoulder and told me to stay seated. Out came about a dozen air force mess specialists with a birthday cake with candles ablaze and smiling from ear to ear. The whole room started singing "Happy Birthday" and then Walt ordered me to, "Make a wish and blow all those candles out before the fire sprinklers go off." When I started to cut very small pieces, so everyone could get some, Ernie said I didn't have to be so cheap anymore and showed me another, big sheet cake that was there, too. The cakes were inscribed, "Welcome home LTJG BEDINGER and Happy Birthday." There was plenty for everyone.

The main group of LULUs was told we would be flying back to the United States together on the same plane and we would go through Hawaii. The only LULU who needed to stay behind for some medical treatment for malaria was Lloyd. Sam wanted to stay with him and I think they tried to do that, but failed. I was so excited to have talked to both my mom and dad; then I was able to call Laura again and tell her all I knew. She was disappointed that the CACO for my parents had not delayed their travel to the West Coast. I was not able to get her to tell me much more, but I knew there was more to this story. It would become clear when I got home.

Laura was very excited to find out that I was happy about her purchase of a town home at La Jolla Vista in the area west of the then-NAS Miramar base and that I was so eager to drive the car that I wasn't going to wait for the California DMV to issue me a new driver's license. Of course, I told her I was even more excited to hold her in my arms and once again chase her around the living room and into the bedroom. That got her giggling and reminded me again of how much I had missed her and how her sweet support and love had helped me to endure the hardships and years of separation. Not all the returning POWs were so fortunate and, as I said my prayers that night, I thanked God for looking after Laura and asked Him to give those less fortunate the strength to continue on in the next phase of their lives.

The excitement was mounting that evening and the LULUs were talking about a number of things, but not all were positive. Sam Mattix and Lloyd Oppel were met by a leader of their missionary team who was now stationed in the Philippines. They were informed that Les and Emma Choppard, who were in charge of the effort in Laos, were able to escape before the North Vietnamese forces arrived that fateful day in the end of October of 1972. Two young women were not so lucky, but were able to hide in their house for several days. When they were discovered, their hands were tied behind their backs and they were walked across the road by a wall. Their bodies were found with one bullet to each of their heads the following week when friendly forces retook the town of Kengkok. Why did the Communists kill the two American women while Lloyd and Sam were walked almost five hundred miles and then driven to Hanoi? No one knows for sure. But as Sam was to later write, "Bea and Ev gave their lives in the service of our Lord Jesus. We take comfort in that fact that they are now with the Lord."[39]

Our flight to the United States was scheduled to leave late enough in the afternoon that we would arrive around midnight for refueling in Hawaii. I mentioned to Ernie several

---

39 Clark, *Captive on the Ho Chi Minh Trail*, 4.

times that my dad had told me my great-aunt Margery was still alive and living in Kaneohe, Oahu, Hawaii, but I didn't think that at eight-three years of age she would meet our airplane when we arrived. Ernie said, "From what you've told me about Margery, she will be there, one way or another."

I had more trouble this night getting to sleep than any night before. I was truly excited like a seven-year-old on Christmas Eve. It turned out that several other returned POWs also had the same problem and decided to take a back staircase to the first floor and discretely search for the nearest club serving alcoholic beverages. No sooner had they opened a door than the alarms sounded and they were surrounded by military police. The official concern was to keep the press and any gawkers away from the returnees, so they had set up special security to protect us. The only thing the security network caught were returnees in search of some pure malt whiskey or American bourbon. The escapees were returned to the top floor where we were all corralled and a very considerate sergeant found a bottle of Jack Daniels and brought it to us to toast the air force. That was the best Jack Daniels I had ever tasted.

The next day was a just another gorgeous day in the Philippines. The sun was bright and the sky had turned to a bright azure blue. The LULUs were all packed and ready to go hours before we needed to be. When the time came to go to the ground floor, Walt told us that we were still in the military and had to act like it. The last of the POWs had been released from Hanoi and the Department of Defense had announced that press conferences would begin the next day, April 1. I thought at first it was an April fool's joke; it wasn't. We all formed up in some type of rank order with all agreeing that after Walt Stischer, the SRO of LULUs, the next man in line by his side should be Ernie Brace. Walt had already talked to an air force personnel expert about pursuing the case of counting all of Ernie's captivity as active duty. If we could prevail in this, Ernie also would be a LtCol in the U.S. Marine Corps and the second highest ranking officer among us. He was honored and said so. I jokingly asked, "Doesn't a lieutenant colonel in the marine corps outrank a full-bird colonel in the air force?"

The bus arrived early and we all pilled in. The C-141 was waiting for us. We took off with little fanfare, but a very small and short ceremony was conducted to wish us all well in the rest of our lives. There were more magazines, newspapers, and at least the last two months of *Stars and Stripes* newspapers for us to read and catch up on much of the news we had missed. Before long we were served a typical boxed meal for dinner. Night seemed to arrive before I had expected it, mainly because we were flying high and going from west to east. Around 9:00 p.m. one of the cabin crew gathered us together and told us that on all these flights, the returning POWs choose one to sit in the cockpit for the in-flight descent, approach, and landing at Hickam AFB. When we finishing rolling out, the side window on the pilot's side would be opened and the returning POW would wave an American Flag out the window as we taxied up to the terminal.

All the LULUs volunteered to do this task. So Walt devised the proverbial straws, and whomever picked the shortest one would get the seat in the cockpit and wave the flag after we landed. I was already trying to tell myself how each of the others was more deserving of such an honor than me, but I still wanted to wave that flag. And sure enough, I drew the short straw and was chosen. The first thing I remember as I sat down into the flight engineer's middle seat was the view of the sky above and the tiny lights that appeared like a bundle of small stars on the horizon. Those lights were the entire island of Oahu.

As I watched the TACAN (tactical navigation system) and listened in on the radio chatter, a lot of memories flooded back. The crew was most professional. When we were one hundred fifty miles from Hickam AFB the air controller asked if the cargo on board was the Legendary Union of Laotian Unfortunates?

Every minute the plane descended and got closer, but the lights still looked small. Finally, the island's outline became visible. It was a clear night with unlimited visibility and the closer we approached, the more beautiful it looked. As we landed and took one of the exits, the window came open and I stuck out the small American flag. I wasn't sure if anyone would be up to see this little flag—after all, it was almost midnight and there were only about fifteen returning POWs. (Several of the last-captured POWs from late fall and early December were also with us.) As the plane turned toward the front of the terminal I saw a crowd of about two hundred people cheering and waving flags. The next day, national TV news programs carried our landing at Hawaii.

When we were safely parked I was quickly escorted to the cabin and rejoined the LULUs. We were scheduled to be here for at least an hour and they had suggested that we all get off and walk around some. As the ramp was opened, a very sharp air force major entered and asked in a loud voice, "Where is the LTJG Henry Bedinger?" The LULUs all looked at me quizzically and Ernie with a big smile, asked, "Now what have you done?" The major quickly explained that the commanding officer of the base had a special guest waiting to see me and I was to be escorted to a small tent that had been set up for this occasion. I immediately asked the officer if Ernie Brace could also accompany me. He looked a little upset but said, "I guess so." So off we went. It wasn't far and when we went inside we found my great-aunt Marge sitting alongside the colonel who was the commanding officer of Hickam AFB.

I immediately introduced Ernie to both my great-aunt and the CO, and then said in the firmest voice I had, "He's the reason I'm here tonight."

My great-aunt had already heard something from my father whom I had spoken to by telephone, and she nodded her head and gave Ernie the first really big hug and kiss he had had in more than seven years. "Thanks again for bringing Jimmy home safe and sound," she said.

I remember having a small cup of pure Kona coffee and remarking about how mellow and flavorful it was. I also remember some discussion about how my direct ancestor from the Revolutionary War had been a POW of the British and survived to fight again. Other than my wife, Laura, I believe Marge was the only one in my family who was certain I was alive and would return home. She would say often than she just "felt it in her bones."

Our plane was soon ready and we were off to get onboard. My great-aunt was still there when we taxied out of sight to take the active duty runway and take off. Although she died several years later, she shall always remain in my heart with her beautiful smile and loving hugs.

Our flight from Hawaii to Travis AFB, just east of Oakland, California, had gone very smoothly. This leg reminded me of how in 1969 I had flown into this same air force field and was taken to San Francisco International Airport to meet my wife at the USO and then fly east for my brother's funeral. After we landed, Ernie, being a civilian, was getting an earlier direct flight in a DC-9 to San Diego while the rest of us would be taking another military flight. I was routed to the group that would fly on what looked like a Boeing 707 and be routed first to March AFB in Riverside, California, and then continue south to NAS Miramar where I had been stationed with the VF-143 Puking Dogs, who were still on Yankee Station in the Gulf of Tonkin. It seemed that Walt and Steve had gone one way and Jack, Chuck, and Norm had gone on another Military Air Command flight, so I was the only LULU in this group. When we landed at March AFB, those of us going onto San Diego were asked to stay on the plane, but then a change was made and we got off the plane after all. The others, who had left before us, were now being officially welcomed home on the other side of the terminal. We had enough time to look around a little, go to the restroom, and get a cup of free coffee. I remember ordering the latte special and enjoying the cream and foam. I also had to go to the restroom and clean off my new white mustache.

We boarded a smaller plane that looked like a regular medium-sized passenger airliner. We had window seats and watched the land slip by for the whole flight. I remember marveling at the brightness of the snow covered mountains and how blue the little mountain lakes looked. It was truly "America the Beautiful."

Once we were all settled and headed for NAS Miramar, the senior officer among us, a navy commander, suggested that the longest-held POW should be first off the plane. The others all agreed but me. Being the only one who had been in captivity for more than a year, I suggested that the proper protocol was for the most senior to exit first, and so forth, to the most junior, which would be me. The others weren't buying this. When we landed I was seated in the front row on the right side, closest to the side door that swung outward and down to make a ladder. In this seat I could clearly look out the small window of the plane.

We had a straight-in approach from the east and I watched for old familiar landmarks. Some things had changed, but not the El Capitan and San Vicente reservoirs, the golf course to the east, and the eucalyptus trees of Scripps Ranch. As our plane was rolling out on runway 24-Right, I could see a large area of bleachers set in a U shape and at least twelve feet tall. There was a huge crowd there. I asked the senior air crew in the cabin if there was another special guest arriving. He bent down, looked out the window, and said, "No sir. They're here for all of you."

There is a certain protocol for the first one off and I wasn't very confident in my abilities to pull it off. Plus, there were new titles with new unpronounceable, alphabetic acronyms to recognize in prepared remarks. When the hatch was opened and the ladder folded down, a young looking navy captain, Owen Resweber, from Washington D.C. who served as the assistant chief of naval public affairs, came aboard and asked for the senior officer of the group. He then told CDR Theodore Triebel, USN, that the order for debarkation was set by navy regulations and would be in order of seniority. I let out an audible gasp of relief that drew looks and laughter. I was embarrassed, but relieved.

Everything went well. After each man shook hands with the line of dignitaries, he walked up to the array of microphones and spoke to both the crowd and media. When I was the only one left in the cabin I asked if there was a back door to the plane and the leading air crewman told me that even if there was, he would not let me take it. Of course, he was smiling ear-to-ear and told me, "This will be a day you will remember for the rest of your life." The man just before me was greeted by his squadron with some special well wishes such as, "Hey Taco! We got fresh fish tacos and tamales at my house for you tonight!"

Then it was my turn and as I stepped off the ladder, I immediately saw that one of the receiving dignities was the commanding officer of NAS Miramar, CAPT Billy D. Franklin. He had been the CO of our sister F-4 squadron on the *Constellation* in 1969. When I saluted him, he reached out and gave me a big hug that practically knocked off my cover and simply said, "Thank God we've got you home." That meant so much to me. Then I approached the microphones. The words were just the thoughts I had had in the last twenty minutes with no notes, not even an outline, but a picture from long ago when I was a small boy. This is what I said then:

> As a small boy growing up north of Philadelphia, I went on many trips to Independence Hall. Back then the Liberty Bell was right on the first floor hall and one could reach out and touch the bell.
>
> When I was about 8 years old, I was in front of that bell right where the crack was and wondered if it had really ever rung. In the eyes of a small child that was a very large crack. Today I know that it did ring, and it still rings 'life, liberty, and the pursuit of happiness,' and not just for us here at home, but for freedom-loving people all over the world. God Bless you for making this day possible and keeping that Spirit of '76 alive and well.
>
> *God bless America!*

I then turned to the right where an official navy vehicle was waiting and my wife was standing beside the open back door. She wore a black and white flower print dress and her hair was just the way I remembered it. I started walking in a fairly brisk pace and saw Laura begin running toward me. I think my heart skipped when she jumped into my arms. A local photographer for the *San Diego Union-Tribune* caught that moment and snapped a picture. About a month later, I received the photo in the mail with a note that simply said, "Welcome home from all of us." We placed that photo in an oiled teak frame and it's on the dresser where I put my wallet every night and put my things in my pockets every morning. It is a daily reminder of an outward and visible symbol of an inward and spiritual grace. Faith in God, faith in our nation, and faith in my family were the three values the enemy could never take away from me.

The ability to communicate with other American POWs and to be led by men of such extraordinary faith and courage like James Stockdale and Robbie Risner were inspirations to me. And to have a cellmate like Ernie Brace and a neighbor like John McCain were other great blessings that made a difference on every one of my one thousand one hundred eighty-four days of captivity. I am blessed to this day by so many people who helped me along this journey. Why did the gunners who shot at me in my parachute miss? Why did that Arc Light mission in Laos come close, but never near enough to harm our small group marching north and eastward?

In the end, I was the only naval officer returned from Laos who was released as part of Operation Homecoming in 1973. I was indeed a very fortunate LULU and thankful to be home at last.

Laura and I Reunite

CHAPTER 15

RETURN TO DUTY

The ride from NAS Miramar to the Balboa Hospital seemed like a very short time. Laura was eager to tell me about her news and what she was able to learn about how the navy was going to handle both the medical and intelligence debriefings. For tonight, we would stay at the hospital and she could stay with me in my room. She also told me that the other POWs were not allowed to have press conferences until all the POWs were back in U.S. custody. And that was to get started the next day, April 1.

She said there would be a lot of reporters gathered in front of the hospital, which was exactly what the captain from the U.S. Navy Public Affairs office had told us on the plane before we got off. The driver told us that he had driven several returnees to the hospital and when they arrived at the front of the main hospital entrance, the reporters were held back by a short cord on both sides of the sidewalk. Laura and I would only have to walk from the car door to the front door before we were away from the cameras and questions. Laura was also concerned about my mother and my father with his new wife. Apparently, the folks that got the airline tickets were not aware of the family issues and had booked all three on the same plane and in the same row of seats next to each other. My mother had to be moved to the first class section to settle everything down. Laura was tired of trying to talk to them because they wouldn't listen to her. And the differences that broke up my parents' marriage all came out again on my return.

Just two groups returned during this week and the national news services had sent their teams of reporters to cover the main places where the prisoners were being returned. For two months the media had been held back and were not even able to report much from the Philippines. James Stockdale, now an admiral, was scheduled to have his first major press conference the next day. Therefore, the San Diego location was a primary site to get the full story from the POWs. The young upcoming stars for CBS news, Dan Rather, for NBC, John Chancellor, and for ABC, Sam Donaldson, were all there. When our car arrived and drove up to the front doors of the Balboa Hospital, the TV reporters and about fifty to sixty people were crammed into a small space on each side of the walkway into the hospital. The driver told us to wait until navy personnel opened the door. A first class petty officer came out to open the door with a navy doctor who was a captain.

When we got out of the car, cameras started flashing and clicking like machine guns and people starting shouting a myriad of questions. Standing just before the door was the tall, well-tanned Sam Donaldson who asked in a loud, friendly voice, "What was it like in Laos?" I smiled and broke all procedures by simply replying, "I am just so happy to be home with my wife." The irrepressible and ever-questioning Sam looked at us and smiled.

Before I knew it we were inside and in the elevator on our way to the top floor. When the door opened there was some type of commotion down the hallway where we were headed and several corpsmen ran by us. I could see Ernie Brace, already in a hospital gown and robe, in the hallway talking to my father and a gray haired lady. As we got closer, I saw that just across the hall from his door was my room and in the doorway stood my mother, arms akimbo, saying that she was my mother and "not that woman over there." The issue of the two senior Mrs. Bedingers had only just begun, but it was a fitting start for the next half-year of my recovery, visits, and getting started back in the navy.

Once inside my room the door was closed for Laura, my mom, and myself, and a tearful, emotional reunion was begun. The corpsman put his head in the door to check and to tell us that we had fifteen minutes before the next visitors were brought in. Apparently the two Mrs. Bedingers got into a heated argument on who would get to see and talk to me first. That seems almost comical to me now. Yet, it was something that concerned the medical staff, my wife, and of course, me, and somehow Laura and I got through the rest of the day without too many flare-ups. Lunch was served in my room and was quite simple compared to the fare at Clark AFB, but it was still hot, delicious, and included the best chocolate pudding west of New Orleans. The naval hospital was serving every patient in the hospital from one kitchen and was doing it well.

Later that afternoon I saw my first doctor who explained the plan for medical screening and treatment. He had my schedule of appointments for the next two weeks, which included all general medical and specialists such as eyes, dental, ears, orthopedics, dermatology, and psychological evaluations. I also saw that LT McClain was on my schedule the next day for a two-hour time slot.

The key part of the debriefings was to gather as much information as possible about my experiences in Laos, no matter how short the period. We actually tried to trace a fairly detailed chart my march through the Truong Song Mountains and my route from the border to Hanoi. In all that travel I never met, never saw, and never heard anything about another American prisoner. Another part of this debrief had much to do with the types of questions initially asked us by our interrogators and the more political questioning and propaganda approaches used on us.

The next day I found the staff office for the handling issues concerning former POWs. Next door was a large conference room that had been converted for returned POWs to use for preparing correspondence, such as the many thank you letters to those who had worn bracelets with our names on it. One returnee was going through a stack of almost two hundred letters with many containing bracelets in them. He asked me, "What the heck am I supposed to do with all of these?" I thought that if given the chance, I would tell those kind people to keep the bracelets to remember those who gave all and were never recovered. I would also tell them to let my bracelet be a reminder that freedom isn't free and that our armed forces are stretched around the world, often serving in harsh conditions and under duress. I shared that with him and he asked me to type it out so he could use it, too. There were never enough words to use to thank all the Americans who prayed for us each day and wore those bracelets.

My medical exams were going well, except for the issue of recurring headaches, especially with weather changes, and the possibility of some remaining worm eggs in my intestines. The internal medicine experts prescribed some type of liquid medicine that would ensure no eggs would remain without cleaning everything else out of my system. When I finally saw the ear, nose, and throat doctors (ENT) I had even more X-rays taken of my head, especially different angles of my nose. The first doctor asked more about injuries caused by ejecting from my F-4 and surmised that the front visor and part of my helmet probably broke my nose. The head doctor said that a congenital deviated septum had made a clear passageway improbable after a broken nose, and that I would need surgery to correct it. I would be scheduled for that in less than a week, with no waiting. He told me he didn't want me to worry and that the operation would just require a local anesthetic.

LT McClain and I were spending at least two or three hours per day with a tape recorder that was later made into a transcript and I told Ernie that the "Legend of Ernie Brace" was finally getting typed up. He laughed and introduced me to Nancy, a cute blond nurse who was working with a major insurance company and personally running all his claims. Ernie had been a civilian contract pilot and the company he had worked for had been bought out by Continental Airlines. She was there to make sure he would get properly compensated. She was as sharp as anyone I had met, had a great sense of humor, and was obviously as taken with Ernie as he was with her. In one year, he would marry her at the Naval Hospital Chapel and have me as his best man. It was an honor second to none, and

I shall always cherish that I was there to be a part of that ceremony. Ernie lived in many places after the hospital and they seemed to move around the world. They were happily married until Ernie passed away on December 5, 2014. He is missed by many to this day.

★

Laura had to attend a graduate class and turn in a project at work and when she returned around the third or fourth day back, she parked in the large hospital parking lot and walked up to see me. Dressed in a pair of indoor slippers, a navy hospital gown, and a thin white hospital robe, we took the stairs to the first floor and quietly went outside and through a maze of walkways that eventually led to the parking lot. And there was the Porsche 914 in dark British green. It had a white Porsche stripe on the gunnels below the doors and a dark green tint bar across the top of the front window. We got into the car and she drove me around the parking lot to explain the gear shift. Then I jumped in and drove it for about five minutes. I was hooked. And forty-six years later, I still have that car and am still married to Laura. I am one lucky man.

My appointment for the ENT surgery came and as I sat waiting for the Novocaine to take effect, the head doctor with a team of six other doctors entered the small operating room. The primary doctor told me he was teaching a new class of young navy interns and that he would like for them to watch how this type of operation was performed. The technical name was "septoplasty with out-fracture of the subturbanate bones." This essentially removed the deviated cartilage dividing the left and right sides of the nasal passage and then trimmed the turbinate bones that grow out from the skull to expand and free the nasal passageways. When my nose was spread wide with a special tool, the doc inserted a scalpel and made a quick incision that freed the septum. He then inserted what looked like a brand new pair of chrome needle nose pliers into my nose and removed the deviated septum. He held it up to his students to make sure they could see both the congenital defect and the very slight trace of a line from a prior fracture that had healed. As he was showing this to his group, I reached out and tugged on his white smock. When he turned around, I asked him, "Hey Doc, can you save that in a bottle of formaldehyde so I can show it to the guys in my squadron." The group started laughing and the doctor told them, "Twenty years of pulling out noses and it would take a former POW to be the first one to ask for his nose back."

The first part of the operation was finished. Then the docs went back into my nose with another device that looked like a long-nosed wire cutter and started cutting the small bones that form the inside of the nasal passageway. Any small sound inside the head is magnified many times so this work, although not painful, was indeed uncomfortable. It reminded me of the advertisement for Rice Krispies with "Snap, Crackle, and Pop." So when the doc said, "All done. What do you think?" I told him, "I won't be having any Rice Krispies for a long time." We were all laughing now—so much so that several others in the other area were now looking into the operating room to see what on earth was going on.

Even though I was on out-patient status, I had to stay overnight until the cotton pack could be removed the next day. During the middle of the night, the acidity of my blood ate away the string holding the cotton packing which then traveled down the top of my throat and was hindering my airways and breathing. I rang the alarm and the nurse immediately called the emergency doctor on call. He was there in a few minutes and had me quickly taken to the ENT area where he removed all the cotton back through my nose. Because of the bleeding and the cotton packing that was now an obstruction, there was no way to anesthetize my nose. So I was in agony while the doc pulled foot after foot of the cotton packing out through my nostrils. Then he had to stop the bleeding by cauterizing the nasal passage. After we waited to make sure that was sufficient, the doc broke out another cotton packaging kit with some cocaine to lessen the pain and he repacked my nose. The next day they decided I might have some vitamin deficiencies and that I should stay another night at the hospital. Laura was now by my side and didn't want to leave me. I finally told Laura to go home and get a good night's sleep for driving me home the next day. They removed the cotton packing the next day and I once again felt the agony of not having Novocaine.

Laura arrived and home we went, which was on the edge of canyon with a view that went for miles. Every morning when the NAS Miramar flight schedule started at 6:30 a.m. we would hear the first section of F-4s flying by at 6:35. I shall always think of that as the "sound of freedom" and think of the section of F-4s that screamed by the Plantation in full-stage afterburner followed by a SA-2 SAM firing at them. It was just so good to be back with my wife and to continue to visit with family who had come west to see me. One of the most memorable visits was my brother's widow, Doris, who had a baby girl and was pregnant with their next child when my brother Bill had died. She now had a sweet six-year-old girl, Lisa, and a boy almost three, Andy. Her parents, now retired, had rented a camper RV and traveled across country to see us; it was a great family get-together.

Most of the Bedinger family had returned to their respective homes by the time I had the nose operation, so it was good to just relax in our condo unit and watch some television. And that's where the next hurdle was crossed. We were watching "The Odd Couple" several nights after my operation, and I got to laughing so hard that I burst a blood vessel in my nose. Ice and a cold towel pressed against my nose did little to stay the flow of rich red blood from those capillaries, so an ambulance was dispatched to take me to the hospital.

When the doorbell rang, I found a heavy-set, middle-aged Black gentleman who was a cab driver for the Balboa Hospital. The ambulances were all at a big accident, so they had sent him. I piled into his cab with a small towel and lots of ice on my nose. When we started south on the Interstate 5 freeway, the driver checked in with the on-base operator and told them that he really did have an emergency. Half way to the hospital, I noticed the driver was looking at me more than the road and then he asked me, "Sir, is that blood coming out of your eye." I told him it might be; the nose is connected through a duct to the corners of the eye or at least that's what I remembered from a human biology course at Union College. He was on the UHF radio for the base cabs and soon was talking to the ENT department. His voice was rising in pitch and he finished by saying, "This man is going to bleed to death through his eye balls and I want you all ready for him." I reached across with one hand and padded his shoulder. "Everything is going to be all right. I've been through this drill before and it's okay. Don't worry." I think we had sped up some and when he took his foot of the gas, we both realized the old taxi for short on-base trips was going more than seventy-five miles per hour.

Thanks to the driver's advance call and the front gate calling ahead, the ENT team was up and ready for me when we pulled in. I refused the wheelchair and walked into the first room from before and sat down in the chair. The same doc from the midnight wake-up call while I was in the hospital was on duty. He looked at me and said, "Not you again!" I told him I liked the way he packed my nose so well that I thought I might come back one more time. "And Doc, let's get it right this time, because we've got to stop meeting like this." Even the nurse was now laughing, and that just seemed to put everyone at ease. Humor is still the best medicine.

I was cauterized and repacked that night and sent up to the ward in a wheelchair. Laura arrived and we just bundled the night away. The next day I saw the head ENT doctor again and he was amazed that the repair had reopened so long after the original surgery. He ordered a special blood test and then had them give me shot of Vitamin K and another medicine to help the clotting process. That extra step helped hasten and complete the healing from the nasal nightmare. Once again, the third time was the charm.

I also had developed some type of skin rash on my back and chest. There was a division of opinion, but several creams and medicines were applied to see if it might lesson the discoloration and occasional discomfort of itching. Nothing seemed to work, including a technique of applying shampoo at night and leaving it on all night. Then I would wash and scrap it off in the morning shower. That only seemed to make the skin a brighter red, and so I told the skin doc, "I'd rather be dead than red." They finally told me to avoid hot and humid places and to wear natural cotton with no polyester uniforms or clothes that can't breathe. That was good advice and it helped some. It has mostly abated, but remains today in the middle of my back. When it flares up, I scratch myself on doorways and tell my wife that the bear in me is coming out.

We also had an aide called an aviation detailer visit us at the hospital and advise us personally on what our best options were. He had my academic record and told me I was a really good student and could go to any graduate school in the country and study any field, and that the navy had a special program for all the returning POWs to further their education. In addition, there were fewer seats available to F-4 radar intercept officers (RIOs) at this point in time because of the end of the war, and it would take two or three years before the new F-14 Tomcat program would open up. We discussed a plan for me to be stationed for one year at a base to test operational improvements and then get orders for two years to attend graduate school.

On one of our trips to visit old friends on the East Coast, we stopped in at Doctors Wesley and Otta Reynolds' house for dinner. Wesley, a Harvard Business School graduate, was the head economic adviser to AT&T at that time. Otta had also earned her Ph.D. from Harvard and was head of the speech department at Hunter College in New York City. I learned from them that San Diego State University had an excellent business program and its master's degree program was one of the best. AT&T had done a recent study to determine what could best predict success for those who entered the AT&T junior executive program. The analysis said military officers from either West Point or Annapolis followed by MBAs from San Diego State University—so that became my goal.

---- ★ ----

LT McClain was almost finished with the intelligence debriefing. We had gone over about a hundred more photographs and he said there were some official inquiries about possible misconduct by some POWs and that I had been officially listed as a witness for the prosecution. Apparently COL Ted Guy had made some waves and the process of a Uniform Code of Military Justice Article 15 hearing was starting. LT McClain asked me how I felt about testifying. I told him that I had a clear and close view of both the construction and use of the F-4 models on poles twenty feet high and of the assault and battery by Cpl Alfonso Riate on army specialist Bill Baird. When he heard my description and saw the look in my eyes completely change, he told me it would be difficult for him to convey in his report the conviction he saw in my face. I was later interviewed at a classified site in San Diego to record my deposition for potential use in the case against the Peace Committee.

The Peace Committee had very professional *pro bono* legal counsel planning a vigorous defense and stated that they would get evidence from the North Vietnamese about all the prisoners. Many newspaper accounts at the time misstated the actual charges being pursued under the UCMJ and instead portrayed the case against the Peace Committee as violations of the Code of Conduct. There were reports that their legal counsel was already in contact with the North Vietnamese to get damaging statements that senior Americans had been tortured to sign. However, all talk of legal action was halted when SGT Abel Kavanaugh committed suicide on June 27, 1973, in the outskirts of Denver, Colorado. LT McClain may have been in communication with those on the legal side, but I think he was asking these questions from a personal interest and the need to document something in his report on why I might be called as a witness.

After the first and second waves of returned POWs had been set up in press conferences, it was time for those of us who were released later in the cycle to have our day before the cameras. I was chosen to go with a group of prisoners with whom I had flown into San Diego. One had been a POW for less than one hundred days and another had been there for about four to five months. I was the longest held POW as a part of this panel and was the only one not captured in North Vietnam.

Most of the reporters who remained in San Diego to cover these events were the younger reporters and many of the press that day were from local San Diego media sources. Our public affairs naval officer gave us the seating chart and covered the format of the press conference. Then the senior officer among the POWs asked if there was anything we should not discuss at this time. The officer simply said; "You're free to discuss any unclassified matters you wish to share with the public. Admiral Stockdale has advised all to speak for yourselves and avoid speculating or trying to explain what happened to another group of prisoners." That sounded like good advice and it was not even close to what many in the media were saying, including Jane Fonda, who had stated that we were all given a script to recite and were protecting the Nixon administration. She was as wrong about her assessment of President Richard Nixon as she was about the good intentions and honesty of the Communists in North Vietnam.

After several general questions we were asked to respond to, the focus clearly shifted to me and the conditions in Laos. I always started my answers to Laos' questions that my sum total experience in Laos was limited to the first five days of my captivity in November 1969. I told them I had no idea what the conditions in Laos were like today. There were some questions about the treatment we received in Hanoi and what impact the visits from American war protesters had on us. When my turn came, I talked in terms of how I felt when I heard familiar American voices make derogatory remarks about our country and our leaders. I also said that I suspected some were told in general terms to say things about war crimes against the Vietnamese people, which they would not have had much, if any, first-hand knowledge about. The part that got the most attention was when I told them how I started passing rather long roundworms a year ago and the guard told us everyone had worms in Vietnam. That guard prevented the camp medic from coming into our cell block, because he was so angry at Ernie Brace for showing him one of the eighteen-inch-long worms that was still alive. The eyes in the room widened and several started leaning forward in their seats. I also shared how we changed the words of Pete Seeger's song to include "the worms that loved their hosts so dearly." Several of the doctors the next day said our interview was one of the best they had heard because it clearly put to rest the myth of good treatment for American POWs.

LT Henry J. Bedinger explains his case of round worms at the
press conference at Naval Balboa Hospital in April 1973

The next day I was again rescheduled to see the psychology department. A message was posted on the board in a special POW office so the other POWs all nodded knowingly. Several kidded me and told me that the docs had to double-check my test results and I should watch out for any electric probes. In fact, the head of that department had heard several accounts about the LULUs. The senior doctor was curious and wanted to ask me about the day I knocked the screens down, my case of worms, and several other incidents in which other POWs reported that our LULU antics had made their day and encouraged them. He also told me he had heard from the hospital staff that I was a joy to work with and had a great attitude toward life. He was active in the Greek Orthodox Church in San Diego and wanted me to know that Laura and I would always be welcome to worship with them. He then told me the senior chaplain at the hospital wished to speak to me. The doc told me where the chaplain's office was located and I went to see him.

Easter Sunday was quickly approaching on April 22. The chaplain had heard several others talking about me and thought that my youth and my story might resonate with younger navy recruits in training at Naval Training Center San Diego. When I spoke with him, he immediately put me at ease and told me that the recruits would be eager to hear how my faith in God helped me to survive. He also said that he had already received funding and permission to bus the recruits to the parking lot of the hospital where a large assembly of bleachers would allow everyone to have a seat and a stage was being assembled as we spoke to hold an altar and have a speaking area. He wanted me to be the keynote speaker on Easter morning,

The average recruit in 1973 was around nineteen years old and was away from home for the first time in their life. The challenges physically, mentally, and emotionally were great, and the drill instructors were a tough lot. I really didn't have a choice, given how God had made his spirit known to me on a number of occasions in a land so far away. When the day came, Laura's sister, her two children, and their Aunt Beatrice drove down from the Los Angeles area to be in San Diego before dawn. We drove together in the dark to the hospital where there were two parking spaces set up for us by the side of the chapel. What I had not realized was the expected size of the audience—it was well over two thousand people and, when I walked up the stairs to give my witness for Jesus Christ, I was awe struck and suddenly very nervous. My knees felt like they were shaking and I could feel the sweat in the palms of my hands turning cold. I told my story in about twenty minutes and my wife lovingly saved my notes all these years in a photo album. My speech ended as follows:

> You don't have to become a POW or eject from a speeding jet fighter to meet with Jesus or to feel the spirit of the Holy Ghost. Jesus dwells among us every day and all we have to do is accept him.

> We need to look past the water buffaloes and crowds on the roads in front of us. Look pass the clutter of our everyday lives and behold the hill. Remember the empty tomb we celebrate this Easter. Remember Jesus began his ministry by proclaiming liberty to all captives and recovery of sight to the blind.

> Through Jesus Christ, our Lord and Savior, comes Good News of a new and everlasting life in the world to come. Praise the Lord! And May God continue to bless America.

The audience response was immediate and heartfelt — a spontaneous standing ovation. One section of recruits starting chanting a round of "Oorahs" and, with tears in his eyes and a smile from ear to ear, the chaplain shook my hand and simply said, "Wow!" My family had thumbs up and beaming smiles, too. The recruits had to get on their buses and return to NTC San Diego and the chaplain led me to the loading area and I was able to shake hands and thank these young recruits for joining our navy. It made me realize that there were many watching and listening to all of us. Our country had been deeply divided for many years and most Americans were tired and looking for something positive to signal a new era when we could get moving upward and onward. I sensed more than ever that our group of returning POWs would be called upon to remind others of how great this nation truly is.

────────── ★ ──────────

In late April we heard that the President Nixon was planning a state dinner in honor of all the returned POWs. Each POW would be allowed to invite one guest. Some, who were not married, were inviting their moms. Of course, this started a most unusual series of calls from my mother who thought I would be inviting her. I told her on at least three occasions that Laura was the only one I would have by my side for this event. When the time came in May to fly back east, we had found a beautiful formal dress for Laura to wear and my first mess dress uniform with miniature medals was all set. The event was well planned and before the dinner there was a day-and-a-half of formal briefings and receptions for both the POWs and their wives. When the night came for the gala, we were taken on Greyhound buses from the Washington Hilton to the White House where a huge tent had been constructed on the south lawn with several covered tunnels from the White House to what was the rear of the tent. It was already starting to rain.

Before the dinner, President and Mrs. Nixon opened up the entire White House to their guests. Bob Hope had assembled an all-star cast to do one more USO show, just for us. There was a long list of Hollywood stars and entertainers including Tony Bennett, Sammy Davis Jr., John Wayne, Jimmy Stewart who was also a major general in the U.S. Air Force Reserve, and many others like Irving Berlin who had composed "God Bless America." The third floor Lincoln bedroom was one of the rooms I wanted to see, so up the grand stairs we went and past the second floor to the private living quarters on the third floor. When we were returning to the first floor the dinner bell was being sounded and there was a small gathering at the foot of the stairs. A gentleman in a black tuxedo had backed into Laura; he suddenly turned around and apologized — it was actor Ricardo Montalban, who proceeded to tell me, "My sincere apologies, sir, and my congratulations to you for having the most beautiful woman here tonight." His smile was as warm and genuine as any Hollywood type can give, but the warmth of his hand, the interest he then took in us, and his reaction to my wife telling him that I had been captured in Laos, revealed that he understood a lot more than most people about the POW situation; he was there because he wanted to be there to honor us.

It was a special night in so many ways. President Nixon proclaimed every lady being escorted by a POW a "First Lady for the Night," and he was constantly getting up and going around the huge tent to shake as many hands as he could. There were no crowds of press, and only ABC news drew the lot to videotape the night's entertainment. Although the Bob Hope show was broadcast live on ABC that night, the tape has never been available for either public sale or viewing. It still is considered the largest official state dinner ever held at the White House and I shall never forget how Irving Berlin, near the end of the entertainment after dinner, came onto the stage with Tony Bennett and Sammy Davis Jr. to lead us in singing "God Bless America." When the complete song was sung, Sammy Davis took the microphone almost out of the president's hand and said, "Excuse me, Mr. President and Mr. Berlin, but with a group like this we have to sing the chorus again." And so we all sang the chorus verse again. And to hear Bob and Dolores Hope sing 'Thanks for the Memories" with Les Brown and his Band of Renown was the most mellow, well-harmonized song I think I have ever heard sung. On the way back to the hotel, both Laura and I agreed that we would probably never again have a dinner or gala as special in our lives. It was truly a night to remember.

The next day many of the local news stations hot on the trail of the next breaking part of the Watergate investigations lambasted President Nixon for trying to use the former POWs to prop up his administration. There was not one mention of the political division the night of our dinner; instead, there were many references to what made America so great. And there were numerous references by many different POWs of appreciation for what this President and his team had done to see we all came home again. Not even the *Washington Post* or *Philadelphia Inquirer* mentioned anything about the difficult decisions that the President had made to ensure all Americans known to be held captive in Indochina were released and American forces were removed from South Vietnam. I recall someone older and wiser than me said, "Where you sit determines what you see." And for the small band of LULUs, we had been in the vice grips of the negotiations and had been, from the start to the finish of all the POW releases, the number one sticking point. The president's assessment of the Communist's willingness to promise one thing and do something entirely different was proven again and again throughout our last sixty days of captivity. Our country and our leaders' steadfast unwillingness to take anything on faith and to not permit any slow or small undoing of any part of the agreement was so important, especially after the service and sacrifice of the B-52 crews. It was Operation Linebacker II and all those aircrews who flew in the B-52s, and all the other tankers, jammers, and various types of support planes that brought the war home to the North Vietnamese capital city and their senior leadership.

Laura had to return to San Diego for several work and student obligations and she wanted me to have time to go back to my home town in Pennsylvania to visit with my family and the many friends who had known me all my life. I took the train from Union Station to Philadelphia and enjoyed every mile of the views and the people from the windows in my car. I first stayed with my father and his new wife in their house in Abington, just north of the Philadelphia County line. Then I spent a few days with my mom in Upper Moreland near Willow Grove and Hatboro. Given my mom's role as the Mid-Atlantic regional director for the League of Families, she had lots of contacts and a parade had been planned to take me down the Old York Road through Hatboro and then east along Byberry Road to Fulmar Heights where I had grown from a small child. I was amazed at how many people were along the road in the two communities. I also was amazed at how the towns had all grown while I was away. There was a picnic where the local congressman presented me with a watch in appreciation for my service to our country. It was all beyond any expectation that I had before coming east.

Before I left for the West Coast I wanted to go see Sam the Barber, who had given me my first haircut and many more in the years that followed. He was over retirement age, but kept the shop going with his crew. When I came in Sam rushed to the back wall and pulled a rope that dropped a banner covering the whole wall. The banner was yellow with big navy blue letters that said, "Welcome Home Jimmy!" There were no empty seats in his barber shop, and it had been expanded from four chairs to eight chairs. He asked me what it was like to be a hero and to be seen on national television. I was honest and told him, "I don't feel like a hero. I did my job to the best of my ability and served in the midst of some truly great Americans who were heroes in more ways than one. They really inspired me and still do. They were and are the real heroes of Hanoi." He smiled, padded my shoulder, and said, "That's the Jimmy I always knew."

After my return to San Diego, I was entitled to some convalescent leave. Ford Motor Company had made available to every returning POW a new Ford LTD for one year. After we had picked the color and features, we were amazed to have the local dealer call us in less than a week to say our car was ready to be picked up. Another offer to all of us was from the Holiday Inns of America for a free stay for one week at any Holiday Inn in the United States. Laura and I both agreed that we had to get reservations in mid-town Manhattan, just south of the Lincoln Center. We would tell no one and make it like a second honeymoon that would be longer than one night. We would get tickets for events being held at Lincoln Center. There was an award-winning set design and superb cast performing *Cat on a Hot Tin Roof*. The leading ballet stars at that time were doing special performances of their favorite dances, and there was some new Italian star performing at the Metropolitan Opera. So when we arrived, we had the car parked for the week in the Holiday Inn garage, dropped our luggage off in our room, and took a cab to Lincoln Center.

I had never seen so many people milling about at Lincoln Center. Apparently some tickets were just going on sale and it was indeed crowded. Laura saw the ballet, and we secured tickets for that evening's performance. The next night was the play, and we got good orchestra seats for that. Then we stood in line for the opera. I had never been to an opera, but Laura had been to several in San Diego and had taken a college music course on opera. When we finally got to the window, we saw the sign that stated all performances for *La Boheme* were sold out. Since the opening was two nights away, I still asked if they had a waiting list in case of cancellations.

Our ticket agent was a typical middle-aged New Yorker, slightly bald, and very fast talking. He looked at me in amazement and asked me if I was had been away a while and had not heard that this was "the first performance in America of the greatest tenor in the world." I blushed and said that I had been away a while, and I was hoping I could take my wife to one opera while we were in town. Laura very gently moved in front of me and told the man I had been a POW in Hanoi for over three years and had never heard of Luciano Pavarotti. The man did a double-take and said in a very firm voice, "Don't move! I think we got a cancellation just a few minutes ago." Then in a loud and obnoxious tone, he shouted to the whole ticket window area, "Who just got that cancellation for the opening night? I got a POW here and he needs those two tickets." Everyone just stopped, phones were dropped down, and I think everyone in the ticket office was looking at Laura and me. I turned as red as my hair. Then a small woman in the back waving two tickets in her hand said," Right here! I got 'em right here."

I reached through the little window to shake her hand. And then when I saw the price was one hundred seventy-five dollars each, I almost fainted, because that was a lot of money back in 1973. Laura saw me hesitate and nudged me before I could say anything. My brand new Master Card came out of my wallet and into the window. The man behind the ticket counter started the payment process that took a little longer back then. Other agents then started coming over and sticking their hands through the small opening to shake my hand.

"Good to have you home, sir."

"God Bless you, son."

"You're looking good, kid."

When we turned away with our tickets in hand, I marveled at how New Yorkers could surprise you like this. New York was truly an amazing city and this was turning out to be an amazing visit.

Our time in Manhattan also took us to Radio City Music hall and a Rockettes show, the Guggenheim Museum designed by Frank Lloyd Wright, the Metropolitan Art Museum, and Saint Patrick's Cathedral. Each morning and evening the Holiday Inn provided our meals and it was really a five-star restaurant.

Laura knew that I felt I would be able to enjoy the opera more if we bought at the Met bookstore the full libretto (published text) to read, so the day before the performance I tried to read through at least fifty pages. Thank goodness they had a summary section with the main plot and characters explained. Night came and I dressed in my best suit and tie. When we arrived, even I was surprised to see how close the second row, center section of the mezzanine was to the stage and our two seats were right on the dividing line of the theater's center line. Many were in dinner jackets and some in more standard tuxedos. New York really knows how to dress for these types of events.

About ten minutes before the start of the show, the audience in the orchestra section started standing up and clapping. "What's this?" I asked Laura. As we both peered over the railing of the first row, we saw a beautiful red-haired woman in a spectacular formal red dress walking down the center aisle; it was Beverly Sills. My favorite Sills' quotation was and still is, "Art is the signature of civilizations."

After the overture was played to perfection the curtain rose to the largest set and stage I had ever seen. As the first act continued, it was clear a new singer was soon going to take the stage and when Luciano Pavarotti walked on stage, the crowd applauded him so wildly that the orchestra had to stop. It took five minutes to start the show again, and when he began to sing, I thought I could feel the notes. They sounded so pure and so mellow. When he finished, the audience went nuts with a standing ovation that lasted longer than I can remember. The gentleman in the tux behind me was yelling "Bravo" and "Ole!" like it was bullfight or football game in Europe. The atmosphere was simply electric and exciting. This was an entirely new experience for both Laura and me.

The music, the dancing, the costumes, the set design, and all the lighting and other effects were so well done I thought it to be the culmination of all the arts in one performance—I was hooked. Laura told me afterward that it was the best opera she had heard and that San Diego Opera was just getting started. Little did I know at that time what a high standard the Metropolitan Opera set for all the world or how famous Pavarotti would become.

When we finished our week of honeymooning in Manhattan (mainly thanks to Ford, the Holiday Inns of American, and a very special ticket agent at the Met), we headed north to Croton-on-Hudson, New York, to visit with our friends, the Reynolds, and then south to Pennsylvania to visit my mom and attend a large family Fourth of July barbecue with my dad and his wife, Jane, and his new family. It was a very nice affair. My uncle Herman was there with my cousins Dotty and Ted Roschens. Uncle Herman worked for the Bank of Philadelphia and advised me to put any extra pay or funds into gold. It reminded me of that line in the film "The Graduate," only in that film the hot new market was supposedly plastics. I was glad to see my relatives and I think they were glad to see me. It finally closed the book for me on recovery and my mind started turning more to the navy and what I was going to do with my career.

Before we left for the West Coast my dad had a small ceremony at his office in Horsham, Pennsylvania to recognize my "return with honor and my service for God and Country." My dad was active in the Masonic Lodge and had a lot of construction friends. They had helped him renovate an old flag pole and install it in a base outside his office, but a bronze plaque for it took a little longer and would not be unveiled after a year of order processing and making the cast. When they unveiled it, I realized right away that at the time of order there had been no news and so my status was not known when it was made. My dad's oldest employee and a foreman for many years now, George Garey, was standing right next to me. He had known me since I was about five years old. He looked at it and wondered how I liked it. The inscription read in part: "In loving memory of LT William M. Bedinger and LTJG Henry J. Bedinger who gave their lives for God and Country." I told him with as straight as face as possible, "George, I think the reports of my demise are premature." I was also impressed with how many people came from the Lodge to pay their respects and wish us well. It was like many things I had come to appreciate with my journey to freedom: we Americans truly do care about our country and our countrymen.

Before leaving for the East Coast I had told the navy detailer that I didn't think my country or the navy owed me anything. I wanted to get involved and get busy. One of the positions the detailer was considering was a special project for the test improvement of base operations at NAS Miramar. There were too many people reporting to the CO of the base, so they wanted to reorganize so that all the non-appropriated managers (golf course, stables, officers club, chief's club, "acey deucy" club, consolidated package store, and special services managers) would report to one military officer who was now a navy commander with lots of experience. When Laura and I returned to San Diego, I called my detailer and told him that the job at Miramar sounded like it needed to be done right and might give me the kind of experience that would prove useful in a graduate program for a master's in business administration. The course had been set.

Since we had a Ford LTD and the Porsche, Laura let me drive the Porsche. She didn't mind shifting, but never liked to stop on a hill. I grew up driving stick-shift vehicles in my dad's business, so it felt very natural to me. With the Ford's automatic shift, Laura could drive more comfortably and have real air conditioning, too. The Porsche 914 had no factory air cooling system and in San Diego back then, I'm not sure one really needed A/C for more than two or three weeks in a year. When I drove behind the building I noticed another Porsche 914 in the front row of the parking lot. It was in a special space reserved for CDR Brannon. I was to learn in about five minutes that he was my new boss and was excited to have another 914 driver to talk with. His car was a beta model with a much larger Porsche 911 engine in it. He had special suspension on the rear axle that supported the bigger engine and his Porsche could literally fly. Ours was just fine for us, and we got a lot better gas mileage than he did. Of course, I never mentioned gas mileage to the commander. Within several days I was set and doing several things to prepare a plan for consolidating the personnel administrative offices for all the non-appropriated funded activities on the base.

I was back in the real navy. The years away had not diminished any of my enthusiasm or desire to learn more and I began to realize that my years in the Hanoi Hilton were a learning experience, too. The old naval aviation adage of *"Illegitimi Non Carborundum"* (don't let the bastards grind you down) remained with me and so would the memories of those explosive December nights when the B-52s came to ensure we would come home. In the end, fifteen B-52s were hit over Hanoi with a total of seven hundred twenty-nine sorties flown. That's about a two-percent loss rate, and lower than loss rates in any war before then. The North Vietnamese had fired more than one thousand two hundred forty-two SAMs in less than two weeks.[40]

---

40 McCarthy and Allison, *Linebacker II*, 173.

———————— ★ ————————

After I spent a few days getting used to the normal life, I began to think about what really helped me to survive captivity. I was asked to speak to several youth groups and also to a navy class going though survival training. They all asked similar questions about what things helped to prepare me the most. The superb navy training was a factor, but what came before all that? I quickly came to the conclusion that there were three legs that kept things level for me, just as a tripod keeps my camera level.

These three fundamental faiths were faith in God, faith in my country, and faith in my family and friends.

Faith in God was instilled into me from my earliest years. I served as an altar boy in church and went to Saint Peter's School in New York State. I was fond of singing hymns and after trying out for the Glee Club twice and failing, I finally made it on my third try as a junior and got to travel with the Glee Club to Florida. When I began officer training, I joined the Naval Aviation Command's choir that sang as a call to worship, "Rise Up, Oh Men of God." This was a Saint Peter's school song that served as our alma mater. It reinforced every week where I had come from and who I was to serve. I can still sing every verse of this hymn and my shower knows it, too.

Faith in my country was a strong core of everything I grew up with. I can remember to this day my father's reaction to President Harry Truman firing General Douglas MacArthur. My dad had perforated ear drums and was not allowed to serve in the armed services during World War II, so he responded to calls from the U.S. Department of Forest Services when he and his young wife, my mom, moved from New Jersey to just north of Minot, North Dakota. He would say to me, "That's where our country needed me, Jimmy." He hired any military man who asked for a job because one could always count on a marine or sailor to be "squared away and do a good job."

And in the end, when most had given up all hope that anyone missing in Laos would be returned, President Richard Nixon set a course that would ensure our return. We learned shortly after our return that the entire schedule of American POWs was delayed from February 7-12, 1973, because the North Vietnamese delayed adding a list of ten names (the LULUs) to the listing of "all American POWs held in Hanoi." With Dr. Henry Kissinger and the team in Paris, it was just not one issue, but several times they had to work overtime and late hours to keep our release on schedule within the sixty-day limit specified in the Paris treaty signed on January 28, 1973. And I shall never forget the service and sacrifices of all the B-52 crews and others who flew over Hanoi to bring us home. That is one more reason that I stand a little straighter when they play the National Anthem.

Faith in family and friends was bolstered when we learned of the POW bracelet program and other actions of the National League of Families. The idea of family grew year after year in Hanoi when I saw what our leaders were doing to resist the enemy and to protect us in any way they could. It may seem exaggerated now, but those POWs who did their best to follow their SROs and resist the enemy became a part of my family. I'm amazed to find people today who never knew I came back and want to return my bracelet they wore for ten or twenty years and then removed for safe keeping. I thank these people and ask them "to keep it as a reminder that our armed services still serve in hardship and hazard far from home and their loved ones. Keep them in your prayers so they may come home safely someday soon."

Faith in my family was no small thing. Yes, the Bedinger clan from Daniel on may be growing smaller by the years, but I remember and thank God that I was with men like ADM James Stockdale, Gen Robie Risner, and COL Ted Guy, and so many others who put themselves in harm's way by serving as our senior ranking officers. I never stop thinking of the times that MAJ Walt Stischer was beaten and CDR John McCain was taken away and restricted in a small, hot cell in handcuffs and leg irons day and night for two weeks just because he warned Ernie and me about the surprise inspection party coming our way. That warning gave Ernie and me time to eat notes meant for other POWs and saved Ernie and me from torture. And Ernie Brace was the perfect cellmate and a real friend. I only wish he was alive today so he could see how I have remembered him. I know he was proud of all of us who kept the faith, resisted our nation's enemies, and survived to come home and to do more for this great land we love.

Yes, three faiths that keep the tripod of my life level are as meaningful and needed today as when I fell behind the fight.

Operation Homecoming was a complete success. The planning and execution by the Air Force Military Airlift Command (MAC) was superb and to this day, many refer to the return of the POWs as MAC's "finest hour." There were six hundred prisoners (five hundred ninety-one Americans and nine foreign nationals) returned to U.S. custody—three hundred twenty-five U.S. Air Force, one hundred thirty-eight U.S. Navy, seventy-seven U.S. Army, twenty-six U.S. Marines, and twenty-five civilians.

But the number "one" exists in but one cell of a matrix that describes these components with the country they were captured in. The number one only existed in the "navy, captured in Laos," and that was me. This is my story of how I was freed from Laos: my freedom was secured because our county persevered to bring us home in honor and would not take on faith, or any other condition, our release. God bless all who helped to make that happen and God Bless America!

EPILOGUE

There were many assignments and benchmarks on my way to retirement. All cannot be neatly summarized here. Some may not seem important to others, but these are most of the important achievements and waypoints I passed in the rest of my career. I would finally retire from active duty in the fall of 1989 as a U.S. Navy Commander. I was blessed on many occasions and have far too many people to thank for helping to preserve and to achieve more. Here are some of those points.

Military Services Department, NAS Miramar:

As special projects officer I helped to design the consolidated personnel office that handled hirings, separations, and all administrative functions for the non-appropriated funded activities now known as Moral, Recreation, and Welfare.

San Diego State University, Master's in Business Administration:

Completed the MBA program in less than two years and was elected to the National Honor Society—Beta Gamma Sigma. I also wrote my MBA thesis titled *Prisoner-of-War Organization in Hanoi.*

VF-114 NAS Miramar:

Requalified in the F-14 Tomcat and flew missions both in Western Pacific (WESTPAC) from the *USS Kitty Hawk* and in the Mediterranean from the *USS America*. Achieved the Centurion Patch for 100 carrier landings on the *Kitty Hawk*.

Military Financial Systems Office (MFS),
Naval Military Personnel Command (NMPC-72):

Ran statistical analyses that negated navy audit conclusions on the relationship between end-strength and total military personnel appropriations. Selected and served as inaugural aide to President Reagan's family in 1981 for then for Dr. and Mrs. Loyal Davis, parents of Nancy Reagan. .

Weapons Procurement Navy POM Coordinator and Program Management
Proposal Coordinator, Deputy CNO for Air Warfare (OP-050):

Helped launch a new navy cost accounting and program request system to show reasons in clear, concise way for changes in unit cost for major naval aviation acquisition programs.

Strategic Plans and Program Resources Analysis Agency (SPRAA),
Office of the Joint Staff:

Executive Assistant to the Director for more than two years and then led cost team to load current data into the forces planning program model being developed at Institute for Defense Analyses(IDA) and ran model for the Joint Chiefs of Staff.

Comptroller, Naval Training Center (NTC) San Diego:

Managed major budget activity and accounting for four component commands. In two years, I succeeded in lowering operating expenses while through-put in both service schools command and recruit training Command was increasing.

───────────── ★ ─────────────

While at the naval training command I was asked to give several major speeches about my POW experience. I spoke to the combined recruiting command one year before Christmas on how we tried to celebrate this season in the Hanoi Hilton and received a standing ovation from the 2,000-plus recruits and instructors. I worked to improve my public speaking skills with Toastmasters International in San Diego and entered international speech contests. I won area and division contests and placed second in a TI District Five contest.

I retired from Navy in 1989 with more than 24 years of active duty service and was awarded the Navy's Meritorious Service Medal at the end of my career. During my naval service, my wife, Laura, gave birth to two sons who became interested in computers with the first-ever IBM PC. Today they are employed in the information services industry sector.

After retirement, I worked on a short term project at a state-chartered credit union. Then I was a general manager at a commercial laundry service. From there I accepted a position as the assistant controller for a micro-processing manufacturing company with Department of Defense and commercial contracts. In 1992 I began working for the United Services of America (USA) Federal Credit Union. First, I was the internal auditor, then vice president for finance and accounting, and then director for military affairs. During that time, I joined several organizations that supported our local military and their families, such as the San Diego Council Navy League, the San Diego Armed Services YMCA, the San Diego Chamber of Commerce Military Affairs Committee, the San Diego Military Advisory Council, the Warrior Foundation/Freedom Station, and several others doing great things for our service men and women and their families. USA Federal Credit Union was merged into the Navy Federal Credit Union in 2009 and I served as a membership outreach manager until retiring in 2015.

Later I joined the newly-formed San Diego Military Advisory Council Foundation and served for the first three years as its treasurer. In April of 2018 I was recognized for my ongoing support of military active duty and their families with being awarded the Rear Admiral Bruce Boland, USN, Lifetime Achievement Award.

All in all I served more than twenty-four years of active duty in the U.S. Navy and more than twenty-three years with credit unions whose primary field of membership was the armed services.

I have more to be thankful for than I can possibly write here. Humbly and sincerely, I say again: Thanks for the memories and all the help with those prayers and good wishes along the way.

May God Bless You and May God Bless America. [GBU & GBA]

APPENDIX A

MILITARY AND CIVILIAN PERSONNEL REFERENCED

(Ranks are at the date of Capture for the POWs or at first reference)

The LULUs: Legendary Union of Laotian Unfortunates

Bedinger	LTJG Henry James Bedinger, USN
Brace	Ernest "Ernie" Brace, American Civilian; former USMC captain
Butcher	Lt1 Jack M. Butcher, USAF
Gotner	Maj Norbert "Norm" A. Gotner, USAF
Leonard	Capt Edward "J.R." Leonard Jr., USAF
Long	Lt1 Stephen G. Long, USAF
Mattix	Samuel Allen Mattix, U.S. Missionary
Oppel	Lloyd D. Oppel, Canadian Missionary
Riess	Capt Charles F. "Chuck" Riess, USAF
Stischer	Maj Walter M. Stischer, USAF

1983 Reunion of the original four LULUs.
From left to right: CAPT Steve Long, Ernie Brace (civilian), LtCol Walt Stischer, and LT Henry J. Bedinger

Other Military & Civilian Personnel

Alberson	CDR William Alberson, USN
Allison	Col John V. Allison, USAF
Alvarez	LTJG Everett Alvarez Jr., USN
Anton	CW2 Francis G. Anton, US Army
Archer	Capt Bruce R. Archer Jr., USMC

Baird	Specialist William A. Baird, US Army
Bean	Col James E. Bean, USAF
Bedinger	Margery Bedinger, Head Librarian, U.S. Military Academy
Carey	LTJG David J. Carey, USN
Chenoweth	SGT Robert P. Chenoweth, US Army
Christian	LT Michael D. Christian, USN
Creed	LTJG Barton S. Creed III, USN
Denton	CDR Jeremiah Denton, USN
Deuter	Richard C. Deuter, USN
DiBernado	Capt James V. DiBernado, USMC
Deuter	LTJG Richard "Dick" C. Deuter, USN
Drummond	Capt David I. Drummond, USAF
Elliott	MAJ Artice "Art" W. Elliott, US Army
Enright	LTJG Mick Enright, USN
Flynn	Col John P. Flynn, USAF
Franklin	CAPT Billy D. Franklin, USN
Gaddis	Col C. Norman "Norm" Gaddis, USAF
Gillespie	CDR Charles "Chuck" Gillespie Jr., USN
Guy	Col Theodore W. Guy, USAF

Hall   CDR Haley Hall, USN

Harnavee   Sgt Chai Charn "Chip"Harnavee, Thai Special Forces

Hegdahl   Seaman Douglas B. Hegdahl, USN

Henry   PFC Nathan B. Henry, US Army

James   CDR Charlie N. James Jr., USN

Kirk   LtCol Thomas H. Kirk, USAF

Kavanaugh   SGT Abel Kavanaugh, USMC

Kissinger   Secretary of State Henry Kissinger, Ph.D.

Lawrence   CDR William P. Lawrence, USN

Ligon   Col Vernon P. Ligon Jr., USAF

Jenkins   CAPT Harry T. Jenkins Jr., USN

Johnson   LtCol Samuel R. Johnson, USAF

Kavanaugh   SGT Abel L. Kavanaugh, USMC

Kientzler   LCDR Phil Kientzler, USN

Kushner   Capt Floyd H. "Hal" Kushner, US Army (physician)

Matheny   LTJG David Matheny, USN

McCain   CDR John Sidney McCain III, USN

McCarthy   Gen James P. McCarthy, USAF

McClain   LT Donald McClain, USN

Miller   Lt Col Edison Miller, USMC

Montague   Capt Paul J. Montague, USMC

Moore   CDR Ernest M. "Mel" Moore, USN

Nguyen   Capt Dat Q. "Max" Nguyen, South Vietnamese Air Force

Resweber   CAPT Owen Resweber, USN

Riate   Cpl Alfonso R. Riate, USMC

Risner   Lt Col James Robinson "Robbie" Risner, USAF

Rutledge   CAPT Howard "Howie" E. Rutledge, USN

Schweitzer   CDR Robert J. Schweitzer, USN

Souder   LCDR James B. Souder, USN

Stockdale   CDR James Bond Stockdale, USN

Stortz   Lt Col. Ronald E. Storz, USAF

Stratton   LCDR Richard A. Stratton, USN

Telford   Intelligence Officer Earl H. Telford Jr., USAF

Thompson   Wayne Thompson, U.S. Air Force Historian

Triebel   LCDR Theodore W. Triebel, USN

Wheeler   LT Herb Wheeler, USN

Wickham   BG John A. Wickham, US Army

Wilbur   CAPT Walter E. "Gene" Wilber, USN

Winn   Col David W. Winn, USAF

Woodward   MG Gilbert H. Woodward, US Army

APPENDIX B

ACRONYMS & MILITARY RANKS

AAFES   Army/Air Force Exchange Store

ACM   Air Combat Maneuver

AFB   Air Force Base

ARM   Anti-radiation Missile, also called a Wild Weasel

AVROC   Aviation Reserve Officer Candidate

BARCAP   Barrier Combat Air Patrol

BCO   Base Commanding Officer

BG, B Gen, Brig Gen   Brigadier General

BUFF   Big Ugly Fat Fellow, nickname for B-52 Stratofortress aircraft

CAG   Carrier Air Group Commander

CACO   Casualty Assistance and Claims Officer

Capt, CAPT, CPT   Captain

CDR   Commander

COG   Commander, Air Group

Col, COL   Colonel

CSA   Confederate States of America

DFC   Distinguished Flying Cross; also "Distinguished Frantic Communicator"

DRV   Democratic Republic of Vietnam

FAC   Forward Air Controller

IFR   Instrument Flight Rule

IP   Initial Point

JRO   Junior Ranking Officer

KIA   Killed in Action

LCDR   Lieutenant Commander

1LT, 1st Lt, LT1   First Lieutenant

2LT, 2nd Lt, LT2   Second Lieutenant

LTC, Lt Col, LtCol   Lieutenant Colonel

LTJG   Lieutenant Junior Grade

LULU   Legendary Union of Laotian Unfortunates

MARCAD   Marine Aviator Cadet

MCAS   Marine Corps Air Station

MG   Major General

MIA   Missing in Action

NACC	Naval Aviation Crew Cadet
NAS	Naval Air Station
NASA	National Aeronautical & Space Administration
NFO	Naval Flight Officer
NTC	Naval Training Center
NVA	North Vietnamese Army
NVN	North Vietnamese
OIC	Office in Charge
ORI	Operational Readiness Inspection
PAO	Public Affairs Officer
POW	Prisoner of War
PRV	Provisional Revolutionary Government of the Republic of South Vietnam
RADM	Rear Admiral
RHIP	Rank Has Its Privileges
RIO	Radar Intercept Officer
ROTC	Reserve Officer Training Corps
SAC	Strategic Air Command
SAM	Surface to Air Missile
SERE	Survival, Evasion, Resistance & Escape

SRO	Senior Ranking Officer
STOL	Short Take-Off and Landing (aircraft)
SVA	South Vietnamese Army
Thud	F-105 Thunderchief aircraft
UCMJ	Uniform Code of Military Justice
USA	U.S. Army
USAF	U.S. Air Force
USMC	U.S. Marine Corps
USN	U.S. Navy
VADM	Vice Admiral
Wild Weasel	Anti-radiation Missile (ARM)
WWII	World War II
XO	Commanding Officer

SELECTED BIBLIOGRAPHY

A Treasury of the World's Best Loved Poems. New York: Crown Publishers, 1980.

Alvarez, Everett, Jr., and Anthony S. Pitch. *Chained Eagle.* New York: Dell Publishers, 1989.

Anton, Frank, with Tommy Denton. *Why Didn't You Get Me Out?* Satellite Beach, FL: Anton Publishing, 1997.

Bedinger Family History. www.bedinger.org, 2016.

Bedinger, Henry James. *Prisoner-of-War Organization in Hanoi.* MBA Thesis at San Diego State University, San Diego CA, 1976.

Brace, Ernest C. *A Code to Keep.* New York: St. Martin's Press, 1988.

Clarke, Marjorie A. *Captive on the Ho Chi Minh Trail.* Chicago: Moody Press, 1974.

Dandridge, Danske. *George Michael Bedinger: A Kentucky Pioneer.* Charlottesville, VA: Michie Company Printers, 1909.

Davis, Vernon E. *The Long Road Home: U.S. Policy and Planning in Southeast Asia.* Washington DC, Historical Office OSD, 2000.

Dengler, Dieter. *Escape from Laos.* San Rafael, CA: Presidio Press, 1979.

Denton, Jeremiah A., Jr., with Ed Brandt. *When Hell Was in Session.* Mobile, AL: Traditional Press, 1982.

Fischer, David Hackett. *Washington's Crossing.* New York: Oxford University Press, 2004.

Grant, Zalin. *Survivors.* New York: Norton, 1975.

Grubb, Evelyn, and Carol Jose. *You Are Not Forgotten.* St. Petersburg, FL: Vandamere, 2008.

Hubell, John G. *P.O.W.: A Definitive History of the American Prisoner-of-War in Vietnam 1964-1973.* New York: Reader's Digest Press, 1976.

Kiley, Frederick, and Stuart I. Rochester. *Honor Bound: American Prisoners of War in Southeast Asia, 1963-1973.* Annapolis, MD: Naval Institute Press, 1999.

Lawrence, William P., and Rosario Rausa. *Tennessee Patriot.* Annapolis, MD: Naval Institute Press, 2006.

Levin, Alexandra Lee. *This Awful War: General Edwin Gray Lee, C.S.A. and His Family.* New York: Vantage Press, 1987.

McCain, John, with Mark Salter. *Faith of My Fathers.* New York: Random House, 1999.

McCarthy, James R., and Robert B. Allison. *Linebacker II: A View From the Rock.* Washington DC: Office of the USAF History, 1985.

McGrath, John M. *Prisoner of War; Six Years in Hanoi.* Annapolis, MD: Naval Institute Press, 1975.

Morocca, John. *Rain of Fire: Air War 1969- 1973.* Boston, MA; Boston Publishing Co., 1985.

Risner, Robinson. *The Passing of the Night: My Seven Years as a Prisoner of the North Vietnamese.* New York: Random House, 1973.

Rowan, Steven A. *They Wouldn't Let Us Die: The Prisoners of War Tell Their Story.* Middle Village, NY: Jonathan David Publishers, 1973.

Stockdale, Jim, and Sybil. *In Love and War: The Story of a Family's Ordeal and Sacrifice During the Vietnam Years.* New York: Harper Row, 1984.

Tilford, Earl H. *Setup: The U.S. Air Force and North Vietnam, 1966-1973.* Maxwell Air Force Base, AL: Air University Press, 1991.

Thompson, Wayne. *To Hanoi and Back: The U.S. Air Force and North Vietnam, 1966-1973.* Washington D.C.: Smithsonian Press, 2002.

Townley, Alvin. *Defiant: The POWs Who Endured Vietnam's Most Infamous Prison, The Women Who Fought for Them, and The One Who Never Returned.* New York: St. Martin's Press, 2014.

Zaloga, Steven J. *Red SAM: The SA-2 Guideline Anti-Aircraft Missile.* Oxford, U.K.: Osprey Publishing, 2007.

INDEX

M

MAC (Military Airlift Command), 298

Maggot, 96, 100, 102–3, 106, 109, 111, 137, 145, 204–5, 223, 231, 233–36, 240, 247–48

malaria, 31, 193, 232, 262

Manila, 29, 35

Matheny, LTJG David, 306

Mattix, Sam 224, 227, 229, 232-34, 241, 251, 254, 262-63, 303 -304

McCain, John 91, 93, 95–96, 114, 103, 107–10, 114, 270, 275–76, 282

McCarthy, Gen James P., 221, 224–25, 227, 295, 306

McClain, LT Donald , 306

MIA, 92, 136, 243, 260

Michael, George, 6–8, 13

Michigan, 180–82

MIGs, 41–42, 225

Military Airlift Command (MAC), 298

Miller, 99, 145–46, 188

Miller Lt Col Edison, 307

Moore, CDR Ernest, 17, 105, 307

N

NASA, 101, 158

NAS Miramar, 22, 267–69, 273, 294, 299

Naval Base Yokosuka, 42–43

naval flight officer (NFO), 53, 311

New York, 4, 8–9, 17–19, 28, 76, 79, 92, 96, 127, 134, 292–93

New York City, 7–9, 157, 211, 223, 281

NFL, 91, 94

NFO (naval flight officer), 53, 311

Nixon Plan, 158–59, 174, 180

Northern Virginia, 13–14

North Vietnam, 58, 60, 63, 73, 76, 153–54, 159–60, 163, 173, 175, 180, 202–3, 207–8, 225–26, 283

North Vietnamese Army, 102, 178, 207

North Vietnamese forces, 226, 230, 263

NVA, 133, 149, 224, 244

O

operational readiness inspection (ORI), 23–24, 311

Operation Homecoming, 252, 260, 270, 298

Oppel, Lloyd, 232, 240–41, 263

orders, 33, 35, 37, 58, 64, 67, 91, 116, 135, 147, 168, 181, 192, 231, 242

ORI (operational readiness inspection), 23–24, 311

P

Pathet Lao, 243, 250, 260–61

Paul Doumer Bridge, 219, 221, 248

Peace Committee, 1, 111, 184–88, 193, 195–96, 203–4, 206, 218, 228, 236, 282

Philadelphia, 5, 7, 20, 118, 256, 269, 289, 293

Philippines, 35, 39, 45–46, 251, 253, 263–64, 274

Pickett's Charge, 15–16, 32

Porsche, 238–39, 256, 277, 295

POW cells, 179, 217

POWs

new, 101, 118, 146, 157, 208, 229, 232, 236

returned, 257, 264, 275, 282, 287

returning, 254, 258, 263, 265–66, 281, 286, 290

President Nixon, 99, 157, 207, 212–13, 222, 243, 287–88

Puking, 38, 69, 104, 239–40, 258

Puking Dogs, 21–23, 26, 43–44, 103, 238–39, 258

R

RA-5C, 46–47

radar intercept officer. *See* RIO

rank, date of, 135, 253

rash, 62, 74–75, 80, 82, 116, 181